To my wife, Diane,
and my children, Robert and David

Contents

List of figures and cases

Figures

Cases

Acknowledgements

My interest in the management of Advanced Manufacturing Technology (AMT) began in 1983 following the publication of the government sponsored report *New Opportunities in Manufacturing: The Management of Technology*. This emphasized the importance of the management context of an area I had always considered to be of concern primarily to engineers and computer specialists. A number of colleagues in the Management Centre at Staffordshire Polytechnic shared this concern and the Manpower Services Commission (MSC – now called the Training Agency) funded a project into appropriate forms of management development for AMT. This project was one of a number funded by the MSC at the time dealing with the management of technology. A report of its conclusions, which contains a number of case studies complementary to the ones included in this book, is available from the Training Agency (Harrison (ed.) (1987)). This report is based on contributions from a dozen or so colleagues from a variety of institutions and reflects the breadth of necessary input to AMT management.

This present book extends the MSC project report and is motivated by a realization of the need to disseminate AMT ideas to a wider audience. Full acknowledgement is therefore given to the underlying contributions of past and present colleagues and MSC staff. The other main contribution comes from managers of companies and those attending part-time courses at the Polytechnic. Their inputs have, sometimes unwittingly, set in motion lines of thought which, together with published literature, have provided a basis for the text and case studies of this book. However, if colleagues and students see themselves directly characterized in the cases, then their imaginations are at least partially at work!

Fortunately, the translation of my execrable handwriting has not been necessary as technology has intervened in the form of a wordprocessing package. Thanks are also due to colleagues for their support of a pre-occupied part-time writer and to staff at Pitman for their support of an apprentice author. My wife, Diane, and children, Robert and David, have long grown accustomed to the portable computer, piles of notes and references, and to a member of the household who periodically absents himself, physically or mentally, when an idea has occurred and must be committed to storage media of one form or another.

List of abbreviations

(Note: the chapter quoted may not include the only references to a given abbreviation)

AC	Adaptive Control	C(i)	Cash Flow at time i (in DCF)
ACI	Automatic Component Insertion	CAD	Computer Aided Design
ACWP	Actual Cost of Work Performed	CADCAM	Computer Aided Design; Computer Aided Manufacture
AGV	Automated Guided Vehicle	CAM	Computer Aided Manufacture
AMT	Advanced Manufacturing Technology	CAPM	Capital Asset Pricing Model
AoA	Activity on Arrow (Network Diagram)	CAPM	Computer Aided Production Management
AoN	Activity on Node (Network Diagram)	CAPP	Computer Aided Process Planning
APICS	American Production and Inventory Control Society	CIB	Computer Integrated Business
APT	Automatically Programmed Tools	CIM	Computer Integrated Manufacturing
BAC	Budget at Completion	CNC	Computer Numerically Controlled
BCG	Boston Consulting Group	CPA	Critical Path Analysis
BCWP	Budgeted Cost of Work Performed	CPI	Cost Performance Index
		CUSUM	Cumulative Sum
BCWS	Budgeted Cost of Work Scheduled	DCF	Discounted Cash Flow
		DNC	Direct (or Distributed) Numerical Control
BOM	Bill of Materials		
BPICS	British Production and Inventory Control Society	EF	Earliest Finish (in Network Diagram)
		EOQ	Economic Order Quantity

ES	Earliest Start (in Network Diagram)	PAC	Production Activity Control
ETCP	Estimated Total Cost for Project	PERT	Program Evaluation and Review Technique
FMC	Flexible Manufacturing Cell	PIMS	Profit Impact on Market Strategy
FMS	Flexible Manufacturing System	PLC	Product Life Cycle
FV	Future Value (in DCF)	PV	Present Value (in DCF)
GERT	Graphical Evaluation and Review Technique	r	Interest Rate (in DCF)
		RADR	Risk Adjusted Discount Rate (in DCF)
GT	Group Technology	RCCP	Rough Cut Capacity Planning
IRR	Internal Rate of Return (in DCF)	ROCE	Return on Capital Employed
JIT	Just-in-Time		
LF	Latest Finish (in Network Diagram)	RoI	Return on Investment
		SID	Strategic Investment Decision
LS	Latest Start (in Network Diagram)	SPC	Statistical Process Control
MAP	Manufacturing Automation Protocol	SPI	Schedule Performance Index
MLC	Market Life Cycle		
MPS	Master Production Schedule	SQC	Statistical Quality Control
MRP	Materials Requirements Planning	SSC	Statistical Stock Control
MRP II	Manufacturing Resources Planning	SSM	Soft Systems Methodology
n	Number of periods (in DCF)	TOP	Technical and Office Protocols
		TQC	Total Quality Control
NC	Numerical Control	TQM	Total Quality Management
NPV	Net Present Value (in DCF)	WBS	Work Breakdown Structure
OPT	Optimized Production Technology	ZD	Zero Defects

Introduction

This book was written as an introduction to the management of Advanced Manufacturing Technology (AMT) for current and future managers and technologists. It describes the range of technologies usually included under the banner of AMT. Some of these involve machines and computer systems. Others derive their strength from ideas and organizing principles. It shows that AMT implementation must be carefully managed, in particular in relationship to company strategic planning and financial appraisal.

Undergraduate and postgraduate business and management students will find here a critical introduction to how the more general ideas contained in their courses can be applied to a specific area of concern, developing a competitive edge in a manufacturing company through the use of recently developed ideas and technology.

Similarly, students of engineering, computing and technology management will find a challenge to mechanistic preconceptions regarding the role of advanced technology in manufacturing. The book does not assume any specific prior knowledge of business and management, but is most suitable for use either in the context of a secondary course taken after a basic introduction to managerial ideas, or as a companion to standard texts which contain more detailed information on financial, marketing and general management ideas and techniques.

Students taking courses in the social sciences often find that the management of technology, say from a sociological, psychological or economic perspective, figures prominently in their work. Though this book makes no attempt to analyse AMT formally in such contexts, its content and case studies provide ample opportunities for such analysis. This is of particular value to students who are considering an eventual career in human resource management within manufacturing companies.

Finally, managers within manufacturing companies, whether taking award-bearing courses leading to a Diploma in Management Studies or a Masters degree in Business Administration, or requiring general reading, will find here a genuine attempt to integrate managerial and technological ideas. The result is both a challenge to the notion of 'automate or liquidate' and also a suggestion that after applying the fashionable techniques of Just-in-Time (JIT) and Total Quality Management (TQM) the judicious use of AMT and computer based integration may well provide that extra competitive edge. An important point to note here is that such ideas are of importance not only to specialist manufacturing staff, but to managers of all functions. The introductory nature of the text and the control of jargon and acronyms (though these cannot be eliminated entirely) are intended to remove barriers to a wide appreciation of AMT by staff of all functions, such as personnel and finance, who have an important role to play in the improvement of manufacturing capability.

What is Advanced Manufacturing Technology?

The principal concepts dealt with in this book refer to a company manufacturing items, where a consistent output and possible wide variety of items must be allied to a competitive cost structure. The output must be consistent in that it is fit for use by the customer and available when needed. The capability of performing this task depends in part on engineering and computing expertise, but also on the organization of the manufacturing company as a whole, in other words on management.

The phrase which has been chosen to summarize this mixture is Advanced Manufacturing Technology (AMT). Definitions can pose a problem in this area. The characterization of AMT used here is borrowed from the government-sponsored report *New Opportunities in Manufacturing: The Management of Technology* (ACARD (1983)). This report used an intentionally loose definition:

AMT was regarded as any new technique which, when adopted, is likely to require a change not only in manufacturing practice, but also in management systems and the manufacturer's approach to the design and production engineering of the product.

Such a definition will not please everyone, indeed it is by no means sure that it is a definition. It might well have been improved by some mention of outcomes in terms of customers and manufacturing competitiveness. Yet its strength is its concentration on AMT as a change process.

A particular shortcoming in the definition might be thought to be its omission of any mention of computers and microprocessors. This is intentional in that although the use of microprocessor-based technology is highly pervasive and of critical importance in many of the new techniques, it is not by definition the root of AMT. It is far too easy to move from Integrated Manufacturing to Computer Integrated Manufacturing (CIM). Appropriate integration may be possible without computers. However, a key to AMT is effective operational decision-making and control. This requires data feedback from many sources, and high variety control situations require large quantities of data (or an appropriate use of simplified summary statistics in place of the crude and often misleading traditional information sources). Thus computers are inevitable for many AMT situations in terms of data flows for automated equipment, the development of product and commercial databases, and as the basis of management decision support systems.

The ACARD definition of AMT also refers to '...any new technique...' and for the uninitiated this can lead to confusion between technology and machinery. A very straightforward characterization of technology is as the sum of knowledge which supports practical actions. In an industrial situation this may require the use of machines and their 'built-in information' but may also refer to the application of new ideas on how a given situation may be managed.

The other word which often causes confusion in defining AMT is 'advanced'. Does this mean 'new to a given situation' as in the first use of a standard computer-controlled machine by a very traditional company, or does it mean 'new to everyone'? In the former case some of the problems of implementing radically new technology are present, but the company can avail itself of the mature experience of others. Yet if a technology is new to everyone, the pioneering companies might well have to be creative in adapting it to make it work at all. In practice most of the literature on this subject seems to refer to technologies which are thought to be past the pioneer stage, but which still require considerable learning on the part of the user organization. Cynics might say that some of the more ambitious integrative technologies such as Computer Integrated Manufacturing (CIM), despite years of description, are still definitely at the pioneer stage of application.

Having concentrated on the words 'advanced' and 'technology' we might ask if 'manufacturing' has any surprises. A dictionary will indicate that 'manu' signifies 'by hand' (as in 'manual') but the word 'manufacture' has long been associated with making articles by labour or machinery.

In Operations Management, the methodology of manufacturing operations is often contrasted with that of service operations, where the latter is obviously meant in a more general sense than 'after-sales service'. Many companies would argue that they market a product/service package where the physical object sold is only part of the attempt to meet the customer's needs. Other components of the package might be consultancy, training, finance, as well as a continuing commitment to repair and even update the physical object. AMT must not be seen as separate from the delivery of the service components of this package. In particular, if we include design technology in AMT, the effective tailoring of a standard product to a customer's particular needs becomes a service facilitated by AMT.

Thus AMT is the use of a potentially wide variety of techniques, some based on new machine technologies, whose implementation represents a real challenge to company staff and whose objective is to provide an increase in long-term profitability through some mixture of improved customer service and cost reduction.

Summary of contents − the key ideas

So far we have examined a definition of AMT and in particular we have noted that AMT requires a mixture of machine and human innovations. Shortly we shall describe in general terms why AMT is of such importance to manufacturing industry. In Chapter 2 we move on to a description of the machine and computer-based aspects of AMT. This includes a description of Computer-Aided Design and Manufacturing (CADCAM), as well as a consideration of general methodologies such as Group Technology. Much detail is included on the costs and benefits of such systems, in particular with reference to CAD and Flexible Manufacturing Systems (FMS). A dominant theme by the close of Chapter 2 is systems' integration, moving from CADCAM to CIM (Computer Integrated Manufacturing) and hence to speculate that CIB (Computer Integrated Business) is the real end point if this path is to be pursued. An example is given of a company pursuing CIB and gaining a real competitive edge.

Chapter 3 is concerned with the human resource development aspects of AMT. Mechanistic metaphors of work in a manufacturing unit are contrasted with a more entrepreneurial approach in keeping with current demands. Current social changes are described along with new ideas in management development. New ideas, such as the 'learning organization', are put forward and it is shown that established ideas, such as Soft Systems Methodology, have particular application to the design of CIM.

In Chapter 4 we move on to consider Production Management Systems. These are a crucial AMT systems component in linking technical and commercial aspects of a business at a day-to-day operational level. We contrast the general methodologies of scientific stock control, Manufacturing Resources Planning (MRP II), Just-in-Time (JIT) and Optimized Production Technology (OPT). In particular we emphasize the radical nature of the latter and the fundamental rethinking of approaches to organizational structure and performance measurement which are entailed by more recently developed methodologies.

Complementary to a consideration of Production Management Systems is a discussion of the management of Quality, an area which is currently very fashionable in British industry but not necessarily well-linked to AMT. Chapter 5 is a survey of key issues in the general context of TQM (Total Quality Management). The most obvious link between AMT and TQM is the use of Automated Testing Equipment as part of FMS. It is also well known that JIT will fail unless process control exists to maintain consistent quality at all stages of production. The value of Taguchi-style linking of design and conformance aspects of quality management are becoming increasingly appreciated. However, TQM and AMT are linked in more fundamental ways through their economic rationale and through their approach to developing human resources.

If Chapters 1 to 5 have been concerned with introducing key themes, Chapters 6 to 10 concentrate on a top down view of AMT planning through corporate objectives and performance measurement (Chapter 6), market strategy (Chapter 7), manufacturing strategy (Chapter 8) and the financial appraisal of AMT (Chapter 10). The arguments in Chapter 10 are quite technical and require an introduction to financial appraisal methods, built around Discounted Cash Flow, as contained in Chapter 9.

Chapters 6 and 7 in particular stand back from any narrow focus on AMT as an engineering issue. It should always be remembered that AMT may be a valid means to achieving defined ends but we must be very sure what the desired ends are in corporate, market and financial terms. Chapter 7 concludes with a description of how an eighteenth-century entrepreneur, Josiah Wedgwood, combined marketing flair with good manufacturing practice.

Chapter 8, which deals with manufacturing strategy, has an obvious central place in any treatment of AMT. The essence of modern approaches to manufacturing strategy is to build on corporate and market needs, but also to see manufacturing as making a positive contribution in the provision of new opportunities.

In Chapter 10 we take a managerial view of AMT appraisal as one form of strategic investment decision. Thus emphasis moves away from Discounted Cash Flow (DCF) and engineer/accountant confrontation to a consideration of the organizational processes of AMT appraisal. Chapter 10 is also the first to include the major case studies which feature in the later parts of the book. These cases are mostly based on real company experiences but include invented data and dramatic episodes.

Case 1 takes the form of a series of imagined extracts from minutes of a company's planning meetings. It illustrates how a bureaucratic approach lacking leadership may simply obstruct innovation. Case 2 refers to the appraisal of a CAD system in a small company. It is the most technically difficult of the cases and requires extensive calculations, preferably based on a spreadsheet, for its analysis. Most important however is the judgment required in the interpretation of the results. It is suggested that it be attempted, along with its companion, Case 5, on a group basis with extensive tutorial support over a period of time.

Chapter 10 ends with Case 3 which is technically less demanding than Case 2, but requires considerable care and judgment in the interpretation of the results. It is based on a company which has attempted MRP II implementation, a system's change which was justified at least partly on financial grounds similar to the ones presented in Case 3. It should be noted that Rockwood is to all intents and purposes precisely the kind of company for which MRP II was designed.

Chapters 11 to 14 are about AMT implementation. Human resource issues are dealt with in Chapters 11 and 12 while project management is the subject of Chapters 13 and 14. Chapter 11 starts with a consideration of the human barriers to technological change and moves on to management development issues relevant to the overcoming of these barriers. The basic issues of shop-floor job design, wage payment systems, safety, the role of trade unions and training are briefly introduced in Chapter 12.

Two major exercises occur towards the end of Chapter 12. The first is a ficticious proposal for an MRP II training programme, based on a real proposal and highly plausible. Uncovering the basic assumptions underlying this proposal should be an easy task for the reader, though drawing up an alternative proposal (if required) is somewhat more demanding. Chapter 12 also includes Case 4, the first involving the 'Linton Group' and their management development guru. This case leads the reader to a consideration of integrated rather than piecemeal management development.

Chapter 13 includes an introduction to network project planning methods in the context of a discussion of a range of general issues in project management. As in all such areas, management techniques must not be separated from a general understanding of their use in context. This theme is continued in Chapter 14 which shows some ways of monitoring project costs.

Chapter 14 also includes Case 5 which continues the story of UMC (see Case 2). The situation described here in a low-key fashion (the narrator is once again our management development guru) is potentially very dangerous for the future of the company. It is based on a real and as yet unresolved company situation.

Chapter 15 consists entirely of case studies, five in all. The first two of these, Cases 6 and 7, are based on real AMT implementation situations and are concerned with team management and control during actual systems introduction. They are written from the point of view of the visiting management guru once again. The remaining three cases in Chapter 15 are based on speculation about the organization of manufacturing and design in factories of the future. Case 8 concentrates on design and customer service. Case 9 introduces a new company, Eurman, and new characters along with a new concept in materials management, MRP III! This invention is less a serious suggestion than a device for discussing some issues in large-scale systems implementation in an electronic environment. Case 10 is also based on Eurman and is concerned with career development in the factory of the future. Cases 8 to 10 should be looked on as devices for starting a debate within groups of managers and engineers on the management of AMT-based factories in the future.

1 Machines and management

Since the beginning of the industrial revolution there has been a continuing attempt to improve manufacturing. Three senses of 'improvement' are of obvious importance:

- meeting the needs of customers
- increasing volumes of output
- reducing costs

Words like 'mechanization' and 'automation' carry the sense of augmenting and even totally replacing human power and skills with machines. The most obvious example this century is the development of fixed automation where a sequence of processing and assembly operations is fixed by the highly specialized equipment used. Such a production line might still be based on manual operations at individual workstations, or might replace these with machines designed to carry out simple and repetitive tasks with great speed and reliability.

Programmable automation allows for the possibility of changing the sequence of operations to vary the output in some desired way. Though one might immediately think of computers in this context, the principles are far older; they are seen, for example, in the use of the Jacquard loom in the early nineteenth century. In this context one assumes that sets of identical items are being produced together in batches, and therefore an important difference from fixed automation is the need for periods of time when equipment must be physically altered for the output to change from one type of item to another. This is usually called set-up time.

Flexible automation is the attempt to extend programmable automation to a system which combines the best of fixed and programmable automation, that is, flexibility of output with high volumes and low unit costs. A key target is the reduction of set-up times, hopefully to almost nil, when it becomes economic to produce very small batches of items.

Automation has in the past been characterized as a social evil, the manned production line reducing work to a sub-human repetition of trivial tasks. Yet this ongoing development from fixed to flexible automation has a great number of advantages. The most obvious is the cost of manufacturing an item. Groover (1987), which includes a very clear description of the technical aspects of automation, estimates that the cost of making a car engine block by conventional techniques would be 100 times that achieved by using automated mass production.

It may also be argued that highly automated factories are safer and that by reducing the manual work done they require less overtime working on the part of employees. An obvious corollary is the fact that they require less employees performing manual tasks. This will be partly offset by increases in the demand for employees with a great variety of skills in engineering and management.

A point that should be noted above is that the cost advantage of automation is measured in orders of magnitude rather than as a few percent at the margin. This is a theme to which we return on a number of occasions in this book. For example, the Just-in-Time techniques described later aim to reduce manufacturing lead-times and stock levels by similar orders of magnitude to the cost improvements mentioned above. Computer-based design and business systems have real impact if products can be designed in a fraction of the time previously taken and if this advantage can then be converted into an improved service to the customer. This last point in particular should be noted. Some limited manufacturing changes with the objective of reducing costs or, say, improving machine reliability may be seen as exclusively engineering issues, but changes which are meant to affect the basic relationship with the customer necessarily require an integration of technical and business systems.

The concepts of manufacturing improvement found in this book relate most easily to batch manufacturing. It might be remembered that manufacturing also takes place in contexts requiring extensive work on individual large products (e.g. in civil engineering). Even then such products will be more economically made if standard components can be used, and the manufacture of these will be in batches. However, the overall organization of work will be on an individual project basis and will be more similar to the AMT implementation projects described below. Many of the products used in everyday life, for example petrol, some basic foods and household materials, are made in a continuous process at highly automated plants. Such manufacture avoids the problems of variety which are central to flexible automation, though requiring highly specialist skills in order to maintain the necessary high quality allied to low costs and an avoidance of excessive storage.

This book is about management, specifically management in the context of manufacturing companies and the opportunities offered to them by Advanced Manufacturing Technology. It is not a book about machines and 'systems' in the narrow sense used by computer specialists. It is also not about the management of AMT implementation if this is interpreted as being in any way separated from the management of other changes in a manufacturing company. Indeed, if one accepts the ACARD definition of AMT (see page xxi) there is little desirable change in a manufacturing company which is not AMT related. Above all, this book is about the ways in which AMT can provide an opportunity for companies to meet their objectives. In the current worldwide manufacturing environment the main objective for many companies is short-term survival. For all companies the long-term objective is survival.

So often, when the word 'technology' occurs, a mechanistic technological quick fix is foreseen. If a manufacturing company's unit costs are too high and it is suffering disputes with its workforce, automation, preferably the workerless factory operating 24 hours a day, seems a golden opportunity. For a company with long lead-times for meeting order deadlines and developing new products CADCAM and CIM seem the answer. If a company's stocks and work-in-progress are far too high, why not introduce the computerized disciplines of MRP II? In particular, senior management may feel that once they have identified a problem and signed the large cheques for replacement equipment, or even for radically new systems, then operational management should produce the promised benefits in record time.

What is required is a matching of technology with human knowledge and skills at all levels in the organization. If this can be achieved, then order of magnitude changes in key operating parameters may be within an organization's grasp. Schonberger (1986), describing changes in a small number of mainly American companies in the mid-1980s, reports inventory down to a quarter of previous levels, scrap levels down to a tiny proportion of anything previously achieved, machine set-up times down from hours to minutes – a catalogue of real achievement based on all-round systems' improvement.

It is all too easy to forget that, to take a popular example, 'computer' in CAPM (Computer-Aided Production Management) is a means to an end, i.e. 'management'. In the early 1980s I ran a course on the opportunities offered by CAPM for a group of engineering staff from one factory of a major manufacturing company. As part of this course, one session was included on basic market awareness, the assumption being that if you want to know how to plan production it might be useful to know something about the source of demand – the customers. My colleague who ran this session made absolutely no progress as his simple questions about the needs and buying habits of the customers (major retailers and institutions) were met with blank indifference. Marketing was someone else's problem: it was functionally and geographically separate.

Not long afterwards, as part of major structural changes in the company, several million pounds were spent on basic training to raise the awareness of all managers in this company on a range of issues. Any manager you now approach will know the company's current objectives, will know which market niche the products he/she is working on are intended for and will display a good knowledge of how his/her current role is meant to contribute to meeting objectives. This company uses AMT and Total Quality Management intensively but always allied to the development of human resources. After years of crisis, re-organization and lack of profitability, the company is now profitable, although it must continue policies of radical adaptation as its highly competitive markets change.

A survey of the literature may leave the impression that AMT is only relevant to engineering batch manufacturing where concepts such as Flexible Manufacturing Systems have been developed and implemented. This may reflect the skills and imagination of engineers in these industries but the ideas in AMT are of very wide application, as long as care is taken in matching them to differing situations and strategies. AMT is relevant to a wide range of industries, an example being the manufacture of medical equipment where UK suppliers are facing levels of overseas competition which, though not unprecedented, must be met by firm action.

Medical equipment in the UK is a billion-pound market but a 1989 Design Council report comments, 'as in so many other areas of British manufacturing, high quality and technically superior foreign products are threatening the UK position'. Thus an industry which employs around 20,000 people in this country is under threat but is responding by designing state-of-the-art, often computer-aided, products. Unfortunately it has to live down a failure to exploit fully past brilliant inventions, such as body scanning equipment. The exploitation of inventions requires the mixture of engineering and business disciplines which is central to this book.

The key management decisions concerning AMT are the choice of technology (ignoring the faint possibility that nothing is relevant), when to start, whether to proceed in a revolutionary or evolutionary manner, how to develop human resources, in which order to implement technologies, and how to change simultaneously all other aspects of the company to make the most of AMT opportunities.

Much of the following relates to the formulation of appropriate corporate and manufacturing strategies to provide a suitable context in which manufacturing decisions can be made. A recurring theme is the financial appraisal of AMT (often ominously referred to as financial 'justification', as if AMT were an end in itself rather than a means to an end). In this context it might be useful to replace 'cost/benefit analysis' with 'cost/opportunity analysis' as we frequently emphasize that AMT provides no automatic benefits. All manufacturing systems fail without good management, that is, good management of all functions and not just production.

Above all we emphasize that AMT implementation is a continuing process of development. All designed systems have life cycles. They are implemented, hopefully reach a profitable maturity, and then decline (or sometimes obstruct) as new systems arrive to take their place. Yet, the environment continually changes and new opportunities present themselves, as do new competitive pressures. A developmentally static system may have a very short maturity, as will a product in a competitive market. Many companies aim for a process of continual, planned change with occasional more revolutionary episodes as technology demands.

This process of change is simply represented in Fig. 1.1. Changes independent of a plan may at times be necessary, though hopefully they are reactions rather than crises. Planned change may be evolutionary or revolutionary. It is fashionable, in the context of reported Japanese practice and the Just-in-Time methodology, to prefer evolutionary change (though JIT and TQM require a revolution in attitudes). However, some physical systems require major upheavals when implemented and similarly the necessary attitudinal changes which accompany AMT implementation may resemble revolutions in thinking.

| | Scale of current change | |
	Small	Large
Independent	Reaction	Crisis
Within plan	Evolution	Revolution

Figure 1.1 Management of change: basic classification

Fig. 1.2 shows a number of engineering changes which match our classification of systems' change. Two things are evident from this diagram. The first is that the existence of an engineering plan is not the same as having a corporate plan, a topic returned to frequently in following chapters. The second point is the frequent use of abbreviations and acronyms in AMT. This book uses around 70 of these, summarized in the early pages. An early resolve to eliminate them when writing the book was soon abandoned. Most of the acronyms used are widely understood and there seems little alternative but to live with them, always noting the barrier they present in communicating ideas to the uninitiated.

Scale of current change

	Small	Large
Independent	Machine replacement	Automation experiment
Within engineering strategy plan	CNC	FMS CADCAM
Within corporate plan	JIT/TQM	CIM

Figure 1.2 Management of change: typical AMT process innovations

A few further acronyms occur in Fig. 1.3 which shows how the major ideas in production management systems thinking reflect our

Scale of current change

	Small	Large
Independent	SSC	MRP
Within corporate plan	JIT/TQM	MRP II/OPT

Figure 1.3 Management of change: typical production management systems innovations

classification. Of particular importance is Fig. 1.4, which anticipates an analysis of the barriers to change contained in Chapter 11. These four figures reflect the basic building blocks of the book, i.e. a matching of machine automation, computer-based operational control systems and the development of human resources, all in the context of corporate and functional strategies and competitive market environments.

The only way in which most manufacturing companies (neglecting those with special competitive advantages) will still exist at the start of the next millenium is not through size or current profitability, but the ability to adapt as the worldwide manufacturing scene evolves.

Potential managerial barrier:	Type of change			
	Small		Large	
	Independent (reaction)	Within plan (evolution)	Independent (crisis)	Within plan (revolution)
Lack of future view	Ad hoc development with poor preparation	Plans continually changing due to environmental turbulence	Changes too large for effective implementation	Wrong long-term business plan
Lack of technical strategy	Lack of systems' compatibility	Plans continually changing due to technical developments	Alternative technologies not evaluated	Wrong long-term technical plan
Poor integration	Develop incompatible systems		Achieve technical but not business integration	
Technical illiteracy of senior managers	Little effect	Commercial opportunities of new technologies not grasped	Technological fix for commercial problem	Expensive and commercial inappropriate system implementation
Lack of business knowledge by technicians	Little effect	Technical opportunities seized but problems of implementation and achievement of business objectives		

Figure 1.4 Management of change: some potential effects of managerial barriers

Future trends in UK manufacturing

A particularly valuable source of projections of future manufacturing strategies is the Manufacturing Futures Surveys as reported in Ferdows, Miller, Nakane and Vollmann (1989). This involves surveys of 1,500 large manufacturers in Western Europe, North America and Japan in 1983, 1984 and 1985.

To concentrate only on the 1985 survey, the most highly rated concern in all three regions was manufacturing to quality standards, followed by issues which varied with the chosen geographical region, except for a common concern for new product introduction. Ageing plant and equipment ranked only eleventh as a European concern, and process technology came twelfth in North America compared with fourth in Japan. Cost and productivity issues were given higher rankings in the West compared with Japan. Unfortunately it is not possible to determine from these figures whether a 'concern' is something being done badly which must be improved or alternatively something being done well and providing an ongoing source of competitiveness.

More concrete are the action plans which companies have for the future. In Europe the consistently highly rated plan was reported as 'direct labour motivation' followed by a variety of plans including, as in America, an intention to develop integrated manufacturing information systems. This shows a concern for the improvement of the manufacturing infrastructure. In Japan the top 1985 action plans were developing Flexible Manufacturing Systems, automating jobs and developing new processes for new products. The production and inventory control systems for which Japan is famous have moved to fourth place. The authors of the report speculate that Japanese companies pursue a consistent strategy starting with the achievement of high quality, followed by delivery reliability, the reduction of production costs and finally the increase of production flexibility. On this evidence, Japanese companies, while maintaining a concern for quality standards, are in the later stages of this strategy. Progress in the years since 1985 has shown the strength of this strategy. In this context one is not quite sure how to judge the current UK concern with Total Quality Management.

A more detailed survey by New and Myers (1987) refers specifically to UK manufacturing operations in the period 1975 to 1985 and covers 240 manufacturing plants in a wide variety of industries. A point emphasized strongly in the report is the apparent misapplication of management effort in many companies through an over-emphasis on the control of direct labour. The breakdown of categories of cost was the same in 1985 as 1975, that is, bought-in materials and components accounted for, on average, 52 per cent of factory cost while direct labour was 18 per cent and overheads 30 per cent. Yet, an emphasis on the use of work study applied to the labour force remains when it is obvious that attempts to improve purchasing effectiveness might be more appropriate. Possibly this has led to the growth in interest in 'Supplier JIT' (see Chapter 4), a most unfortunate choice if divorced from a general application of the JIT methodology.

This survey does report some good news in terms of reduced manufacturing lead-times and investment in new technology. Yet UK industry's notoriously poor delivery record, lack of focus on high performance products and apparent inability to profitably implement advanced process technology were reported as worrying factors.

One should, however, be most careful in interpreting business surveys from even the most recent past. The current climate of opinion in manufacturing management worldwide is that action must be taken to improve manufacturing effectiveness and the above reported findings are widely known. A leading article in the British Institute of Management's Journal in September 1988 (Caulkin (1988)) reports on the achievements of six UK manufacturing plants (only one of which is Japanese-owned). Some of the six are highly automated, while they all appear to consistently use the ideas relating to quality and materials flow management discussed elsewhere in this book. The article abounds with performance statistics, such as:

● manufacturing leadtime cut from 55 to 12 days
● inventory turns up to 34 per annum
● productivity up 50%
● direct labour productivity up 125%
● cost of quality halved
● scrap reduced by a factor of 4
● manufacturing leadtime a third the industry average while product variety four times the industry average.

The very powerful point made here is that while the traditional manufacturing wisdom is that cost, quality and flexibility (however measured) are conflicting aims which necessitate a trade-off, the modern state-of-the-art manufacturer aims for excellence in all three. The BIM report emphasizes that this requires a coherent strategy, great attention to quality and a transformation in the attitudes of all people in a company. It may require complex process technology and production management systems, or may be based on a common-sense approach to the basics of plant layout and other techniques which are often now collectively referred to as 'in-plant JIT' if accompanied by determined attempts to reduce inventory.

One comment made in the BIM report and frequently heard elsewhere is that a good strategy is to rationalize manufacturing operations as if pursuing some advanced technological strategy such as Computer Integrated Manufacturing, but to stop before actually bringing in the computers. In other words, the greatest benefits are in the human and simple systems rationalizations which are essential before implementing complex automated systems. There is a great deal of sense in this approach but it sounds ominously like settling for 'second-best' in comparison with the Japanese strategy of simplification before automation. One might wonder whether there is such a thing as second place in the future manufacturing race.

The Institution of Production Engineers (1985) have attempted to look into the future of UK manufacturing by means of Delphi Surveys. The predictions for the UK in 1994–5 mention the wider diffusion of technologies discussed in Chapter 2 below, but in many cases predict earlier adoption in the USA and Japan. Such a steady and conservative approach may not be commercially successful.

Whilst in the above we have concentrated on worldwide competitive pressures, one can hardly forget the changes which will take place in European markets in 1992 and the social changes likely to occur in the 1990s. Here we are not referring only to the expectations of consumers and workers, but to demographic changes which will have a profound effect on the availability of human resources.

The most striking change in the UK will be the decrease in the numbers of schoolleavers and graduates entering the workforce. For example, the Office of Population Censuses and Surveys (OPCS) predicts the number of 18-year olds in Great Britain to fall from around 900,000 in 1985 to 800,000 in 1990 and 620,000 in 1995, while recovering to 700,000 before 2000. Youth unemployment is expected to vanish and the demand for trainees and for skilled labour to greatly increase. Thus the age structure of the workforce will change dramatically. Also in this context we should note the continuing move towards employment in the service sector, where other demographic changes such as the increased number of very elderly will increase the need for employees.

Thus, in the future, manufacturing industry must not expect a ready supply of direct labour and will have to work very hard to attract, train and retain the skilled employees on which so much will depend. The comparison with the highly educated Japanese workforce could not be more stark and points to the need for UK manufacturing companies to find decisive strategies based on developing both technology and people if they are to survive in future world markets. Dramatic improvement in a few enlightened companies is too little and too late.

2 Advanced Manufacturing Technology

Introduction

In this chapter we will first of all describe a number of new individual technologies which are generally included under Advanced Manufacturing Technology (AMT) and then move on to describe the ways in which these are integrated to form technical, operational and commercial systems. Several key questions should be asked during this description:

- Does the technology provide a new way of serving customers' needs or does it reduce the costs of maintaining the current service?
- How fundamentally does the technology affect the way in which a company manages its business? In particular what are the implications for the information flows throughout a company?
- Can the technology be introduced in a gradual or evolutionary manner or does it require dramatic change to the company or some of its sub-systems?
- How expensive and risky is the adoption of the technology?

In practice, AMT covers a fairly limited range of individual technologies which facilitate the following activities:

- The transforming of materials through the physical operations of cutting, mixing, printing, fabrication and assembly.
- The movement of materials by means of conveyors, robots, guided vehicles, and so forth.
- The examination and inspection of materials through the use of automated testing equipment.
- The storage of materials and their fast retrieval.

- Product design in terms of shape and properties such as strength and weight.
- Determining how a product should be manufactured, for example through simulation of the action of cutting tools when programming Computer Numerical Control (CNC) equipment.
- Production management systems which schedule products and control the level of inventories.

The power of AMT is further evident when these individual technologies are linked together. Such linkages may be obviously physical, as when several CNC machines, robots and items of testing equipment are put together to form a Flexible Manufacturing Cell (FMC). This leads us to reappraise what exactly we mean by 'a machine' and shows the value of using a systems terminology to describe such situations. Unfortunately, much traditional factory terminology, such as in cost accounting, is based on the idea that a machine is a separate unit whose performance can be individually monitored in a meaningful way.

More fundamental are the changes which take place when systems are linked by the flow of information. This does not mean that AMT is necessarily computerized. The Just-in-Time methodology applied within a sub-system aims to simplify information flows so that computers are not required in that sub-system, although as we argue later a computerized planning framework will usually be needed. However, in practice microprocessors permeate AMT applications through their use in controlling individual pieces of equipment, their co-ordination of the action of such equipment to form systems, the use of electronic databases to hold product and manufacturing information, and the total management of the design and manufacturing process.

Computer Aided Design (CAD)

(The term CAD is used to cover two quite different approaches to the use of computers in draughting and design) (The first and rather limited use is when a video screen and specialist keyboard are used to mimic the set of tasks traditionally carried out by a draughtsman, that is to produce a two-dimensional representation of an object to be made in the future.)

(Such 2-D draughting systems may be all that are required in some professions where the required output is in the form of plans from which, for example, a building may be constructed. It should be remembered that a great deal of experience is needed in producing and interpreting such drawings as a number of conventions are used in the representation of complex 3-D objects by 2-D means.) X

Similarly, (companies which engage in design and factory-based manufacture may feel that 2-D draughting systems provide a simple first step in computerizing a drawing office.(This may be so, but it should be remembered that a 2-D system does not provide a suitable database for the outputs of the design function to be directly linked to manufacturing.) This requires a 3-D geometric modelling system whereby a designer produces a mathematical description or model of the required object. (A 3-D model may be used as the basis of screen images of an object,)but, (more important, the information in the model forms the basis for an analysis of the properties of the object and for determining how it will be physically made.)

(Three-dimensional models are either wire-frame or solid, the latter being the more recent development and of most value,)although not surprisingly the most expensive in computer usage. A 3-D solid model is constructed either by using standard shapes or by the modification of other models.(Some CAD systems have features which allow for colour representations of the designed object on a graphics screen, and also for animation which allows the mechanisms of an object to be seen in motion.)

Three-dimensional solid models are of particular value when an engineering analysis of the designed object's properties is to be undertaken. This might involve analysis of its mass properties (volume, surface area, weight, centre of gravity, etc.) or of its engineering properties such as strength, heat transfer or deflection under load. A particularly useful tool here is finite element analysis. Here the 3-D solid model of a complex component is analysed by splitting it into smaller, standard finite elements. The analysis of these elements, although underpinned by some sophisticated mathematics, may be computerized to produce a practical design analysis system. Finite element analysis is a good example of the way in which a computer-based system may provide a real design advantage provided an investment has been made in a basic information system to support such analysis (see Hawkes (1988) for a simple introduction).

The costs and benefits of CAD systems have been frequently summarized in the literature. Typical categories of cost include the following.

Initial costs

- Hardware (processor, terminals, plotters, data storage, communications equipment including links to existing computers)
- Software (including the costs of software customization and of licences)
- Installation (including building alterations, air conditioning, clean power supply, security (e.g. fire-proof safe)
- External consultancy and employment costs of the internal project team
- Database development
- Operator training and systems familiarization for other staff
- Disruption costs during implementation (in particular overtime working and loss of revenue due to delays and customer dissatisfaction)

Recurring costs

- Maintenance contracts, insurance and running costs of the system
- Consumables (in particular for plotters)
- Continuing software development and updating
- Continuing training for existing and new staff
- Systems operation and management costs
- Extra employee costs due to higher salaries or overtime working.

Some indication of the relative magnitude of the above costs may be obtained from trade literature, a typical example being the following from the *Industrial Computing Sourcebook* (1989):

Workstations – 93 different products listed, ranging in price from £2,000 to £191,000.

3-D CAD systems – 47 different products listed, ranging in price from £300 (software for use on a PC) to £100,000 (complete systems).

Finite element analysis software – 42 different products listed, ranging in price from £177 to £800 per month rental or £30,000.

Plotters – 13 different products listed, ranging in price from £2,300 to £120,000.

Consultants' daily fees can be anywhere between £120 and £700 and training can cost anywhere between £75 and £200 per delegate per day.

The above does not include suppliers whose prices are 'on application' and possibly tailored to the customer. This data shows the vast range in products on offer and prices charged, thus emphasizing the need for a thorough investigation of needs before a purchase is made.

The benefits of CAD are even harder to quantify, but the following (based on the comprehensive Primrose, Creamer and Leonard (1985)) provide a guide.

Productivity:

- Savings in the drawing office (reduce number of draughtsmen and other staff, avoid sub-contracting of design and artwork, take on sub-contracting)

Lead-time and inventory management:

- Reduce delivery times (reduce design and documentation time, improve drawing quality, thus reducing delays due to mistakes in production, reduce incorrect ordering of components)
- Increase sales (faster and better presented quotations, reliable delivery dates, faster product introduction, better company image)
- Reduce stock levels (reduce production lead time, standardize components used)

Quality of design:

● Design products which are too complex to be designed manually (e.g. in advanced electronics)
● Reduce production costs (easier manufacture and assembly, reduce scrap, improve materials flow, larger batches due to component standardization, better designs to reduce production and material costs)

Information flows:

● Improve cost control (better estimating and quoting)
● CADCAM link (avoid manual NC part programming, use CAD data in company-wide systems)

It will readily be seen that many of these potential benefits depend not only on actions taken within the design office but also elsewhere in the company. Thus CAD may be able to facilitate the operation of an improved quotation service but such improvement is most certainly not automatic. It depends both on the effectiveness of the marketing function and on the relationship between marketing and sales. Similarly, many of the CAD benefits relate to production, even if a full CADCAM link is not in operation.

Senker (1985) reports on a survey in the early 1980s when the growth in the sales of minicomputer-based turnkey CAD systems was beginning. In this survey the majority of managers who had to justify such expenditure attempted to do so on labour savings in the drawing office and many readily admitted that such justification was totally spurious. They simply did not have sufficient data to produce reliable forecasts of benefits. In particular Senker quotes four major sources of error in the estimation of benefits:

● underestimating the time needed for effective implementation
● overestimating the achievable utilization rate
● underestimating the need to make adjustments to the system once in operation
● underestimating the human relations problems of change, including formal union agreements on new working practices.

Such delays and problems may refer exclusively to the drawing office. Thus the implementation of a CAD system may be a disaster even within this narrow focus. Similarly, such delays may refer to other functions and the process of integration. Surely no further emphasis is required on the need for a strategic and integrated approach to such investments.

Computer-based production equipment

Though a great deal of technology (based on machines and on sophisticated working practices) is involved in high volume assembly line systems, our interest in manufacture begins with programmable automation, that is, the use of numerically controlled (NC) machine tools.

Numerical control (NC) is defined as 'the automatic control of a process performed by a device that makes use of numerical data usually introduced as the operation is in progress' (definitions are based on those of the Machine Tool Industry Research Association). The earliest NC machine tools were developed in the 1950s. Modern equipment uses computer numerical control (CNC) whereby the control unit in the machine uses microprocessor technology to store and execute a programme which controls the work done. This covers almost all engineering machining processes (drilling, milling, turning, grinding and so forth) and has obvious applications to operations in other areas of manufacturing (control of plastic injection moulding machines, printing presses, etc.).

The advantages of CNC systems are seen mainly in situations requiring change, that is, when small batches are required (set-up time at the beginning of a batch is significant) or when items within different batches are slightly different (such changes being made, and checked for validity, through modifications to the programme rather than during manufacture). Such systems also come into their own in the manufacture and testing of complex items requiring many machining operations and high levels of consistent quality.

Direct (or more recently distributed) numerical control (DNC) describes the situation whereby a central computer directs the operation of a number of machine tools. DNC is defined as 'a system connecting a set of NC machines to a common memory for part-program or machine-program storage with provision for on- demand distribution of data to the machines'. In a typical modern application complete programs are stored centrally and downloaded to individual machine controllers as required.

This is an important step towards the integration of the activities of various machines. However, in order to obtain improvements in the actual operating characteristics of a given machine (other than improving the proportion of time it runs by reducing set-up times) some form of adaptive control (AC) is required. AC is a 'control system which adjusts the response from conditions detected during the work'. Typically, several process variables are continually measured and adjustments made to the machine's settings in order to maximize productivity and also to increase the life of the cutting tools used.

It should be evident from the above that a combination of CNC and AC along with a variety of ancillary systems which feed materials and tools to a machine allow for the possibility of unmanned machining. This is further facilitated by developments in industrial robotics.

Industrial robots are programmable machines designed to move objects around and perform certain tasks which would ordinarily be done by humans. They are of particular value in dangerous work environments or as part of a repetitive work cycle. Typical robot applications are materials handling, processing (such as welding and painting) and assembly. The comparative strengths of human operators and robots are explored in Towill (1985), as well as the costs and advantages of introducing robots into the manufacturing system. The following points are of particular interest. Robots are necessarily parts of more complex engineering systems and their support equipment may cost many times more than the robot itself. Thus, a considerable amount of thought and planning is necessary before the introduction of robots, as the inherent flexibility of these machines gives them a wide range of potential uses and potential benefits. Of particular importance is the need to plan carefully the interface between robots and human operators and select the most appropriate set of tasks for each to perform.

Other forms of automated materials handling are also available, including the recent development of automated guided vehicles (AGVs). Similarly, automated storage and retrieval systems are increasingly becoming the norm in manufacturing. It is obvious that a total systems approach must be taken in designing the layout of these various items of plant if the resulting workplace is to operate effectively. Increasingly the benefits of individual items of plant are their contribution to the operation of the total manufacturing system.

Finally, some mention should be made here of the use of automated inspection and testing equipment. The modern approach to quality management (see Chapter 5) emphasizes the importance of process control. This may be greatly facilitated by the use of sensor and measuring equipment to gather data from a continuing process allied to computer analysis of such data and feedback in terms of automatic corrective action or the signalling to operators and management of the existence, or gradual development, of problems which require manual intervention. This in no way detracts from the motivational importance of statistical process control (SPC) and the cause and effect analysis tools so central to current thinking in quality management. The use of automated testing equipment should be complementary to such activity.

Group Technology (GT)

It is useful at this point to provide a break in the catalogue of useful equipment to mention a 'technology' which is based on ideas rather than machines.

One of the major problems in batch manufacturing is coping with the inherent variety in the range of items produced. Mass production reduces variety by aiming at a narrow range of standard products and parts. Jobbing must accept variety as a fact of life and handle it through the employment of human skills and management ability. The managers of a batch production facility may feel they must produce a vast range of items while also aiming for the economies of automated production.

Group Technology (GT) is a fundamental organizing principle whereby parts produced are systematically ordered into a small number of families of similar items. This may lead to an actual reduction in variety if a number of designs are seen to be redundant, being only minor variations on other designs. Even when considerable variety remains, GT provides a methodology for its classification and management through improvements in, for example, machine layout in manufacturing.

There are two basic ways in which manufactured items may be similar. They may have similar design attributes (typically size and shape) or they may have similar manufacturing attributes (they have been or may be made in similar sequences of processing stages).

This latter point is particularly relevant to machine layout. A traditional layout may group similar machines (say lathes) together and thus require extensive movements of batches of materials back and forth between groups of machines. This is not only wasteful but might promote a tendency towards larger batch sizes (and certainly against batch splitting for transportation) which is totally against modern ideas in JIT and OPT (see Chapter 4). If flexible automation is aiming for batches of one, it is counter-productive for such batches to be continually in transit round the shop floor. GT allows the redesign of layouts so that families of parts may be completely manufactured within a small group of machines, usually termed a cell. So important is this idea that such cells may be termed 'GT cells', with a possible confusion between the general methodology of GT and one of its outcomes.

It should be obvious from this description that the classification process is crucial. A faulty classification may not only result in the needless duplication of equipment but also still require excessive materials movement and stock. A number of systems are available for parts classification and coding and these have considerable benefits for the effective management of the design process and the design-manufacture interface as well as machine layout.

If we turn to the organization of a given GT cell care must now be taken in managing the flow of materials. An effective cell might perform as a small mass production unit, depending on the variety evident within a family of parts. Materials handling may be manual or automated, the most highly automated forms being within flexible manufacturing cells.

Flexible Manufacturing Systems (FMS)

A Flexible Manufacturing System (FMS) is defined as 'an automated manufacturing system which is capable, with a minimum of manual intervention, of manufacturing any of a family of components'. An FMS will usually be designed to manufacture in medium volumes and variety and incorporate the means to schedule and route production within the system and produce reports on its own operation. A small FMS may be termed a flexible manufacturing cell (FMC). Allowing for some doubt as to when a given system actually is an FMS, Bessant and Haywood (1986) estimate the worldwide population of FMS to have been around 500 in 1985 (compared with 100 in 1982) and to have been just over twenty in the UK in 1985.

Flexible Manufacturing Systems bring together the technologies of flexible automation, GT, CNC or DNC machine tools, automated and robotic handling and automatic testing. In an FMS a number of machine tools and items of handling and testing equipment are integrated by computer control to process simultaneously a variety of parts. The major advantage of this arrangement is that once a batch of items is within the system a considerable amount of work is carried out on items in the batch with little time lost for machine set-ups and manual intervention. Details and examples are included in Greenwood (1988) including projections of future developments and the place of FMS within CIM (see below).

A dedicated FMS is used to produce a limited variety of parts and thus may use more specialist equipment. A random-order FMS uses general purpose equipment and can accommodate greater variations in parts produced, although it requires more sophisticated computer control. Thus FMS may be seen to bridge the gap between high volume (low variety) production and the use of stand-alone CNC machines producing small batches of highly individual product. FMS should be more flexible than the former but more productive and economic than the latter.

It should not be thought that FMS eliminates the need for human beings. Loading and unloading of materials at the boundary of the system may be necessary, along with tool changes, general maintenance and systems management. However, it is not difficult to see forms of automation which reduce manual intervention, in particular materials handling and tool changing. Even the most casual inspection of state-of-the-art FMS reveals an apparent lack of people, except perhaps visitors and prospective customers being shown round the facility. This can be most misleading as a great deal of effort is required in planning the system, product and manufacturing design, scheduling operations and troubleshooting. However, the basic philosophy is one of professional, central planning rather than the hands-on factory floor orientated management style we discuss elsewhere.

The financial appraisal of FMS is a most difficult area and the literature which attempts to discuss this in detail all too often becomes lost in issues of stock valuation, productivity increases and the nature of intangible benefits. Indeed, surveys show a general disappointment felt by companies at the low levels of financial return generated by FMS. One basic problem is that the implementation of an FMS may be judged as a single revolutionary change, which should be financially self-supporting, rather than as a stage in an evolutionary process. FMS introduction is an example of a change whose scale is awkward to classify. It is too large to be justified as a small system with mainly local improvements (e.g. labour saving, increased productivity, etc.) but seems to fall short of a major company restructuring when financial analysis would be carried out relating to all functions and projected changes to the company's financial reports.

The recommendation in this book is that an analysis for a business unit is inevitable. This is clearly seen if one attempts to analyse systematically the benefits of FMS. Typically these include the following:

- Reduction in inventory (only likely to arise if the production control system in the business as a whole is improved).
- Increased throughput/productivity (as FMS does not in itself entail reductions in machining times, this can only come from better planning and control of the flow of work allied to reduced set-up times).
- Unmanned operation (e.g., in third-shift working) (which has obvious implications for a company's relationship with its

workforce and also requires care in the provision of round-the-clock support services such as maintenance).

● Improved flexibility (the potential for technical flexibility does not easily translate into the actuality of business flexibility which itself is only one part of a pattern which may be managed to improve profits).

However, the point that must not be missed is the scale of the improvement which is sought by the introduction of flexible automation. In one engineering company a particular component, when originally machined manually, required 200 hours of machining time and spent around nine months in the machine shop. The introduction of a machining centre reduced machining time to 80 hours, and an FMS has the capability of reducing it to fourteen hours. The reduction of a manufacturing lead-time from nine months to fourteen hours can dramatically affect a business, provided this really is achieved with not too adverse an effect on costs. If savings in machine time are merely lost in other delays in the system (for example administration and order processing), the effective lead-time continues to be measured in months and all the engineering systems effort has been wasted. The interim survey results shown in Bessant and Haywood (1986) suggest that dramatic improvements in lead-time, stock turnover and machine utilization are quite possible.

It should also be remembered that improvements in productivity are of interest only if a market exists for the products and a reduction in delivery time to the customer will produce dividends only if delivery responsiveness wins orders. Thus we are brought back firmly to market and business objectives and our overall strategy for meeting them.

From CADCAM to CIM

Computer-aided manufacturing (CAM) refers to the use of computers in the management and control of manufacturing. As such it embraces many of the functions described in this chapter, but gains particular power when linked with CAD to facilitate the effective development and change of the products being made and the methods of production used.

The 3-D solid model described above in the section on CAD forms part of the engineering database on which CADCAM depends. CADCAM uses data on the properties of a required object to create the set of instructions needed for its production.

The use of numerically controlled machine tools requires that programmes are written describing the sequence of processing steps to be performed in making an object. Initially this was done manually by an NC part programmer and is as tedious as writing a computer programme in a low-level language. Gradually, higher level languages have been introduced, and computer-assisted part programming, using, for example, APT has become popular. APT (Automatically Programmed Tools) is a general-purpose language not limited to specific machine tools so an additional computer programme called a postprocessor is required to make the general instruction produced by APT suitable for a particular CNC machine.

The next logical step is for the tasks of the part programmer in defining the geometry of the required object and the tool path required for its manufacture to be automated using the information inherent in a 3-D solid model. The part programmer may work on the 3-D solid model using the facilities of the CADCAM system to produce a part programme. This is a form of partial automation as a number of decisions need to be made by the programmer in this process. Totally computer automated part programming is the obvious eventual goal, which in turn brings us to the subject of process planning.

Computer-aided process planning (CAPP) is the ultimate link between computer based design and manufacture but is particularly hard to implement because many of the traditional skills of process planning (i.e. determining the sequence of operations to be performed and the operating characteristics of the machines used) require considerable judgment and experience. One way to automate this process is to use retrieval CAPP whereby standard process plans are stored and used again for families of parts with similar characteristics (see Group Technology above). A more ambitious approach is generative CAPP where a computer system mimics the logical procedures used by a human process planner. Generative CAPP requires the use of expert systems, including a knowledge base derived from an analysis of the work of highly competent process planners.

So far we have concentrated on the technical system's links between CAD and CAM. Business systems such as MRP II also require the input of engineering and manufacturing data to facilitate not only the planning of material flows but also the production of quotations for prospective customers, and to act as links to accounting and control systems. Once again the product databases resulting from 3-D solid modelling are of great value in facilitating integration.

Thus CADCAM brings together design (of the product and its method of manufacture) and actual manufacturing into a coherent system which necessarily includes at least the engineering aspects of a company's business systems. It is a point of debate where CADCAM ends and Computer Integrated Manufacture (CIM) begins. CIM includes the engineering functions of CADCAM and also the operational and information processing functions of the manufacturing unit as a whole.

The word 'integration' has a particular meaning in management literature and contrasts with 'differentiation' (specialization, division of labour). The latter aims to improve efficiency and productivity and encourage the development of narrow but important skills. It has long been recognized that integrating these specialist activities is a key managerial role and that information systems (along with training, appropriate organizational structures and culture, etc.) are a crucial part of integration strategies.

Integration may be seen at many levels. Much of this book is concerned with strategic integration (ensuring consistency between business, market, human resource development, financial and manufacturing strategies) and the integrating concepts which are so important a part of the modern management philosophies of materials flow and quality management. This chapter has moved steadily towards a description of technical integration in terms of production techniques. A vast literature exists on the integration of information processing systems which in turn opens up new possibilities for the design of organizational structures (in simple terms, jobs and their inter-relationships change).

CIM is usually described as the culmination of a historical process leading from mechanization (replacing human labour by machine) through point automation (individual CNC machines) and islands

of automation (FMS) to the computer-based integration of a total
manufacturing system. This still falls short of what some writers term
Computer Integrated Business (CIB) (see Browne, Harhen and
Shivnan (1988)). The example given at the end of this chapter is a
situation better described as CIB than CIM in an engineering sense,
that is, there is full integration between commercial and engineering
computer systems. Thus we are using the term CIM as describing
integration within the four walls of a factory. CIB is essentially
corporate and includes functions which deal with the outside
environment such as sales, marketing and purchasing. Though this
distinction between CIM and CIB is used here for convenience it is
by no means standard. The relationship between these various forms
of systems integration is illustrated in Fig. 2.1.

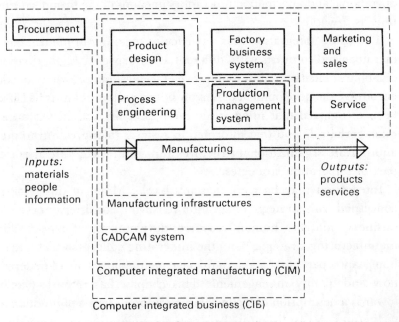

Figure 2.1 Systems integration

Though the above discussion emphasizes the managerial aspects
of CIM, much of the literature is concerned with the narrower issue
of the interface between computer systems and the software problems
which have in the past proved a major barrier to computer systems
integration. In simple terms, the historic development of CAD, CAM

and office systems has followed a number of individual paths and the need exists in CIM and CIB for data to be transferable between individual computer systems. This entails the development of protocols, sets of mutually agreed rules for exchanging information between computer systems of very different origin. Examples are MAP (Manufacturing Automation Protocol) and TOP (Technical and Office Protocols). The narrower problems of software standards within CADCAM are summarized in Bowman and Bowman (1987), but the main source of information in the rapidly changing area of the technical aspects of integration must be current journals and the trade press.

One very real danger in the CIM/CIB approach is the temptation to think that total integration of everything with everything else is an immediate goal. Whilst recognizing the need to ensure that the potential exists for future integration, a set of priorities for integration must be arrived at depending on current corporate, market and manufacturing strategies. Meyer and Ferdows (1989) report on a major international survey (see similar work in Chapter 1) which shows that the priorities of companies in Europe, the US and Japan in 1984 were quite different. Whereas European companies emphasized forms of integration which supported top-down planning and the management of demand, Japanese and US companies seemed more interested in controlling the flow of materials at shop-floor level. At that particular time, however, the most favoured form of integration in all three regions was quality control. It is argued that the revealed priorities are in turn linked to current competitive criteria and hence will change over time.

Whilst the goals of CIM are admirable, such wholescale integration brings with it problems of complexity. Indeed a piece of practical advice often quoted for CIM systems designers is 'simplify, then integrate, then computerize', functions which are all too often attempted in the reverse order.

The long-term goal of all this activity is often termed the factory of the future. A typical characterization might be a small number of interconnected and highly versatile machines with no 'point-of-production' human involvement, working round the clock to manufacture small batches directly for customer orders with greatly reduced manufacturing and design lead-times. All aspects of the process, including machine performance and product quality, will be continually monitored and corrective action automatically taken as even the possibility of future faults or malfunctions are revealed. It seems to be taken by many as an act of faith that such an arrangement is actually feasible, meets business objectives and is economical compared with less automated systems. In particular, if it proves feasible for a given situation it may not be economic or flexible in response to changing needs.

Such a goal is very definitely CIM orientated. An even more ambitious objective is to paint the picture of totally automated business, i.e. CIB replacing the professional and managerial staff of a business as well as manufacturing staff. A more reasonable picture is that CIB emphasizes the support of human decision-making and control by computer-based information systems while automating routine procedures such as order-processing and despatch. This is perfectly feasible with current technology and consistent with business strategies in many cases.

The implementation of CIM, however, presents a number of very real problems as explored with the aid of a case study in Ebers and Lieb (1989). This paper argues that CIM is a technical solution to an organizational problem and that for such comprehensive automation to be achieved, even assuming it to be desirable, both administrative and technical innovations must proceed at a balanced rate. That is, the way in which the company carries out its business must change.

One problem in CIM implementation which is emphasized by Ebers and Lieb is that as a company searches for economies while automating, it reduces organizational slack (spare capacity) and thus removes the system's buffering which previously absorbed uncertainty. In other words, the increased systems' coupling which is the objective of CIM reduces the total system's ability to cope in the face of environmental turbulence and data inaccuracy. There is a greater risk of inappropriate data being used as less human filtering takes place. Unfortunately we may not be able to assess in advance which slack resources are redundant and which are necessary for smooth operations.

It should also be remembered that one of the aims of management development is the creation of managerial slack to facilitate future innovation and development. This is illustrated in Fig. 2.2, a further demonstration of the need to develop people and systems simultaneously. In this figure we show how a positive circle of management development and effective operations allows managers more time to really manage, thus allowing buffering against operational problems as well as further time for development.

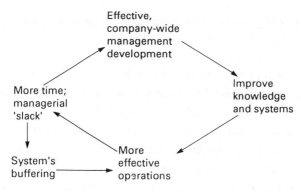

Figure 2.2 Management development and systems' buffering

The Ebers and Lieb case also describes a number of more basic problems, such as inter-functional conflict caused by flaws in the database and leading to that most damaging problem in a supposedly integrated information system, several incompatible databases being used concurrently. The problem here seems to have been not one of discipline but a failure to secure real agreement on what measures and data were right for controlling this business. There is often a naive assumption in business that all problems of data definition and measurement may be overcome by referring to traditional techniques of cost accounting and industrial engineering. Yet approaches such as OPT (see Chapter 4) argue that this is simply not the case. Computer systems designers may wish to stand back frcm this controversy by designing databases which hold only 'facts' and by allowing the user to construct from these whatever statistics are thought necessary to support decision making. Yet it is doubtful that one could arrive at a universal definition of 'useful, objective organizational facts' and certainly problematic to say whether or not all managers have the skills necessary to invent their own formal information systems.

Yet many managers are most competent in developing their own informal information systems, both in terms of facts collected and the use which is made of them. Is the integration of such systems either feasible or desirable, or is this yet another manifestation of the mechanistic metaphor of organizational life that industry is finding such difficulty in escaping from?

Computer Integrated Business — a non-engineering case study

Though much of this chapter has had a strong engineering bias, it should be remembered that the systems described here are applicable in a far wider range of industries. We now describe a system used by a garment manufacturer and retailer which is as close to CIB as most advanced engineering applications.

This company sells its products worldwide through 70 agents who transmit orders through a communications network to a central order-processing system which also updates the agents' file of information on products and prices. In addition, a pilot scheme is in operation whereby point-of-sale information is gathered from shops and directly fed to the order- processing system in order to improve forecasting.

Each year the company manufactures around 50 million garments in 3,000 designs and 200 colours. Added to the range of sizes required this poses formidable design and manufacturing control problems. Yet it is precisely this need for variety which can be exploited by using CIB to gain a competitive advantage. A CAD system is used for design, the production of templates for a full range of sizes and the calculation of the best way to lay the templates on fabric to minimize waste. Designs are then automatically downloaded to machines. Garments are only manufactured in response to orders. The link between production and despatch is also fully automated down to the putting of individualized labels and prices (in one of 60 currencies) onto the garments, packaging goods according to destination and loading onto vehicles. Considerable use is made of bar-coding on garment labels and boxes to facilitate these processes.

The company believes it can get new goods into shops two months faster than its competitors and produce and supply re- orders within 15 days, whilst strictly controlling stock levels. In the fashion industry such a mixture of fast, reliable response and control on a global scale provides a formidable competitive edge. The key to this is computer-based integration of design, manufacture and business operations.

3 Human resource management

Introduction

A characterization, familiar to many people, of work in the 'machine age' is of boredom and mindless ritual. It is likely that work in earlier times was often similarly unfulfilling, but the Chaplinesque caricature of machine-paced work reducing the worker to robotic movements is deeply ingrained in our thinking. Similarly, a phrase regularly repeated in surveys on the nature of factory work is 'when I come here I leave my brain at home'. There is an obvious danger that AMT may be seen as a continuation of this situation, at least to the extent that factories in the future will require any human resources.

We have over the years accepted as inevitable a decisive split between people employed to perform tasks for which machines are not yet economically available and people who are expected to manage or provide technical expertise. The former 'factors of production' receive a wage in exchange for their time at work. The latter 'staff' are rewarded by careers, promotion, job satisfaction and a salary for the bearing of responsibility and provision of expert knowledge.

If this description seems emotively one-sided, it might also be noted that many staff, in particular junior management, may be paid far less than skilled workers of similar age, may be inadequately trained and expected to work long hours in exchange for the promise of long-term personal gains. The conscientious senior manager may similarly find that long hours performing duties which are onerous and fragmented deserves more security than that enjoyed by many at the sharp end of the commercial world.

There is a very long tradition of social scientists exploring the world of industrial work from a variety of standpoints. Some scientists are concerned with what is seen as the plight of workers caught in a relentless and uncaring system; some are fascinated by the sub-cultures which develop in such situations while others are concerned with the design and manipulation of social sub-systems in order to meet organizational objectives more effectively. In particular, the relationship between people and machines on the factory floor, and more recently in the office, has been studied endlessly.

Two quite different approaches are evident in the social science literature. One is essentially tactical in nature, accepting the underlying status quo of organizational life and seeking to improve the procedures whereby tasks are designed and individuals chosen and trained to perform them. The other approach is revolutionary in that it posits changes in the fundamental nature of work and social relationships in an organization. This may be from a concern for the individual, or in order to dramatically improve organizational performance through the use of technological opportunities and new thinking in the management of people.

Much early work, in particular the 'scientific management' of Taylor and his contemporaries, was concerned with tactical efficiency and also with fairness in defining a reasonable expectation for the amount of work which could be performed in a given time along with appropriate rewards. The tools of work measurement and methods study which were developed may be abused by both parties: by management to progressively increase efficiency for little extra reward, and by workers to establish the precedents of slack work-time estimates in order to manipulate the wage payment system. Many would, however, feel completely lost without the database of machine and worker information provided by such a methodology. The road which has been taken from scientific management and bureaucratic organization theory to the 'excellence' movement, intrapreneurship and a plethora of other ideas is well covered in a number of standard texts, for example Buchanan and Huczinski (1985) and Child (1984).

Of particular interest and value here is Morgan (1986), which contrasts a series of organizational metaphors and the effects these have on people working within those organizations. It will come as no surprise that the first metaphor is 'organizations as machines', which not only provides an excellent and clear description of Taylorism but also shows how organizations that use this crude form of 'scientific management' will have problems in adapting to changing circumstances. Morgan continues by describing organizations as organisms, brains, political systems and so forth. The latter, in particular, will provide food for thought for those CIM specialists who think in terms of integration of databases rather than in terms of 'information as power'.

In this book, although 'people' issues form a background to all the discussion, there are three chapters which provide an introduction to the relationship between AMT and human resources. This chapter is concerned with basic ideas and classifications, while Chapter 11 considers barriers to the development of AMT systems, i.e. why it seems so difficult in practice to introduce radically new systems. Chapter 11 also outlines some systems models of managerial change and development, while Chapter 12 is concerned with jobs, skills, training and safety as we move towards the 'factory of the future'. Thus it will be seen that we are here taking an essentially managerial viewpoint, in line with the objectives of the book, rather than tackling more general social issues. Also our approach is based on simple views of systems theories and some of the more recent popular movements in people management. For a more sophisticated view founded in current trends in organization theory the reader must use current journals and specialist texts.

Company objectives and the complexity of operations

As we shall demonstrate in Chapter 6, it is mechanistic and unreasonable to expect so complex a socio-technical system as a manufacturing unit to be completely specified in terms of its cause and effect relationships. The dream of some computer specialists of a machine-based intelligent program capable of running all aspects of such a system is more in tune with older, bureaucracy-based models of management than the more modern emphasis on the need for creative, entrepreneurial action on the part of all staff.

The following is a suggested set of general objectives for the management of a company looking to introduce or extend AMT.

- To design a physical/human/information manufacturing system which is capable of being managed to meet corporate objectives over a period of time in the context of a range of forecast environments.
- To manage the transition from existing to proposed systems in a cost-effective manner.

One should note the use of the word 'design' in the above. This is not intended in the narrow sense of product or process design but in the sense put forward by Simon (1981) of the design of a socio-technical artefact. Designing management systems, structures and procedures involves creativity, vision, logic and the making of choices between alternatives. Indeed ideas common to product design, such as the foolproofing of products, may usefully be imported to the design of management systems.

In Fig. 3.1 we illustrate some aspects of the management of technological change in a manufacturing context. This diagram

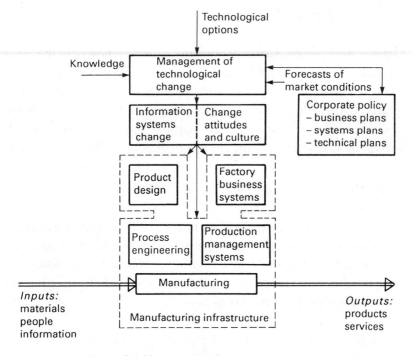

Figure 3.1 Management of technological change

contrasts the need to maintain performance of manufacturing and design sub-systems while continually improving the capability of all parts of the system. Thus the product design function is continually introducing changes into the manufacturing system through product improvement and introduction whilst itself being changed through developments in CAD. The range of issues in managing change was explored in a recent study involving a number of manufacturing companies (Harrison (1987)) and some results are summarized below.

Corporate strategy

Effective top management systems must be developed to make AMT-related choices, such as the timing of product and process change, whether to obtain new or proven technology, and how to make available all necessary resources, in particular the development of human resources and information systems.

Design and manufacturing

Many companies are earnestly pursuing plans to innovate in the areas of CAD, automation, MRP and so forth. The technical problems often seem to obliterate the systems and commercial implications of such changes. Most companies are well aware of the need to update technical staff and train operators but may approach this in a half-hearted manner, not realizing the extent of human change necessary.

Finance

There is an increasing realization that traditional capital appraisal and management accounting systems need to be re-examined in the light of their effectiveness in a highly automated environment. In particular, accounting systems have some difficulty in treating human and information resources as assets.

People

If we examine an organization in a traditional, functional manner the following themes are evident.

Operators: issues include the shortage of skilled labour, attitudes to technical change, problems of motivation and of creating a positive attitude to improving processes and products.

Technical support staff: where high levels of skill are needed, extensive training may be necessary (in particular with functions involving maintenance, programming, materials planning and so forth).

Manufacturing engineers and management: project management involves high levels of engineering and management ability, a point recently taken on board by those concerned with the undergraduate training of engineers.

First-level manufacturing management: companies vary greatly in their attitudes to the training of supervisory staff and their responsibilities. Such staff are crucial if, for example, JIT and TQM (Total Quality Management) are to be taken seriously.

Non-manufacturing middle management: these may vary greatly in terms of their knowledge and attitude to AMT. However, the contributions of personnel, marketing and financial staff may be decisive in enabling or blocking AMT developments.

Top management: their vision of the future, style and expectations may be as important as their knowledge and skills.

For the individual, technical change may be viewed as a threat or more positively as an opportunity to demonstrate ability.

The social environment

Changes within a company cannot be seen in isolation from the economic, technical and social environments within which the company operates. Changes in these environments, which must be viewed on a global scale, are of some concern to management.

The shortage of skilled staff has long been recognized as a potential problem for companies developing AMT. In a UK survey in the mid 1980s, 41 per cent of employers viewed lack of qualified staff as a major external constraint on product and process innovation. The problem extends from skilled labour to qualified engineers.

The population of 18-year olds in Great Britain will fall from around 850,000 in 1989 to around 620,000 in the mid 1990s. A recovery to 700,000 is expected early next century. Thus the Training Agency reports that in the 1990s youth unemployment will shrink to virtually zero while the demand for skilled staff will greatly increase. The main priority will therefore be the retraining of the existing workforce.

Another major structural change in the composition of the workforce will be a higher proportion of older workers, women (particularly returners to work) and members of ethnic minorities. Thus, imaginative approaches to training at national, industry and company level will be essential.

Within the workforce attitudes to the required flexibility of work patterns and conditions of service are gradually changing. We may still be far away from the more radical approaches to work patterns, such as holding a portfolio of part-time jobs or widespread working from a home base, but many organizations will undoubtedly have to be more imaginative and flexible in the future in the way they treat their human resources.

In the last few years, considerable attention has been focused on Japanese approaches to employee management, both in Japan and in Japanese-managed factories in the UK. A useful general survey of the Japanese approach to technological innovation and management development is Goodridge and Twiss (1986). This includes discussion of the effects of the Japanese tradition of life-long employment (training of existing workers is not inhibited by the fear of them leaving), the emphasis placed on consensus decision making and the very high proportion of graduates within the workforce of manufacturing industry. A further point is the relative freedom with which employees move between departments during their careers in their chosen company, with the result that inter-functional conflict is reduced and a high proportion of top management have a technical background. This situation is of obvious value in facilitating technological process and product development.

Thus the Japanese do not owe their position to low wages, the deployment of vast amounts of technology and an oriental culture. As Parnaby points out (Parnaby (1987)) they are well paid and use similar levels of technology to the best Western companies, though this technology is often deployed with far greater care within a coherent total philosophy of manufacturing practice.

Specific manufacturing philosophies such as Just-in-Time production were originally associated with Japanese companies and often thought to be unworkable elsewhere due to particular characteristics of Japanese culture and industrial structure. This appears not to be the case, as experienced by companies in this country with and without Japanese management. So, it seems that ideas on the management of people can be imported and adapted to UK manufacturing.

New ideas in management development

Technology is not the only sphere in manufacturing where dramatic changes have been taking place. As we described above and will return to in the next two Chapters, a considerable rethinking of ways in which manufacturing may be managed is taking place. This is seen particularly in the use of unifying concepts such as Just-in-Time and Total Quality Management. Both of these are more than sets of techniques. They show different ways in which the role of manufacturing manager may be performed.

Such total approaches must in turn be seen in the context of new ideas regarding the practice of management and of ways in which managers may be trained, educated and developed.

At a very basic level one must challenge whether management is a series of roles undertaken by a variety of individuals in combination with other professional tasks, or whether the term 'manager' describes a job. Taking management to involve responsibility for resources, in particular human resources, it seems evident that a number of jobs are at least partly managerial. In the context of implementing and managing AMT systems, engineering and technical staff will have responsibilities which by any definition are 'managerial'. Yet traditionally many engineers have considered themselves apart from management, the latter being seen as a senior group of staff who run the business.

In the context of the engineer as a manager, one might note the following characterization of the engineering profession (from Beuret and Webb (1983)):

> 'There can be few occupations which are as complex and demanding as engineering. The manipulation of technical data to produce desired results from imperfect information under multiple uncertainty and pressure of time owes as much to art as to science.'

First of all we might wonder if the engineer produces results only by the manipulation of technical data. The implementation of product and process design must surely be part of engineering and inevitably involves inter-personal and other skills usually described as 'managerial'. This point is fully recognized in current thinking on the design of courses of study leading to engineering qualifications.

A second point emerges if we make minor changes to the above quotation as follows:

> There can be few occupations which are as complex and demanding as management. The meeting of organizational objectives through decision making and control based on imperfect information under multiple uncertainty and pressure of time owes as much to art as to science.

This is not to say that engineering is management, though some might wish to characterize management as social engineering at the organizational level. Each profession involves the development of appropriate skills and ways of looking at the world. They do, however, seem to share a pre-occupation with producing practical results in complex settings.

Unfortunately, a mechanistic carrying-over of engineering ideas into management can lead to systems which are inappropriate in many situations. The basic concepts of bureaucracy, developed from a desire to legitimize the idea of authority in an institutional setting, provide a way of looking at organizations which is most valuable in highlighting chains of command and the need to define carefully the responsibilities of individuals. If adopted as a universal model it may lead to rigidity of thought in responding to the challenges thrown up by a rapidly changing environment. This is not because ideas of authority and responsibility suddenly become obsolete in such situations but because they should be seen in the context of less hierarchical structures such as those based on project teams and groups of professional workers.

In particular, much modern, popular managerial writing emphasizes a different set of priorities for effective management. The ideas presented in Peters and Waterman (1982) started what might be called the 'excellence' movement of which a recent offering is Peters (1987), interestingly titled *Thriving on Chaos*. This latest book lists 45 prescriptions centring on a company's relationship with its customers, its pursuit of rapid innovation and its development of people (in particular leadership) and simple and effective management systems.

This emphasis on enterprising behaviour, entrepreneurialism and even on 'intrapreneurialism' (i.e. the entrepreneur working within an established firm) provides a set of guidelines for all professional workers in an organization, a group which should eventually include all workers. Typical characteristics of entrepreneurs are usually taken to include drive, energy, selfconfidence, persistence, working towards long-term objectives, a tolerance for uncertainty, competitiveness, self-motivation and self-control. It is interesting to speculate what proportion of manufacturing companies genuinely support such individuals or even understand the implications for the firm of entrepreneurial behaviour.

Accompanying these changing ideas there are emerging in the UK guidelines for the development of managerial skills through the listing of the competencies required by managers to perform various functions effectively. These include on the one hand data analysis skills which will be familiar to those with a technical education. On the other hand, skills relating to the management of people and of taking initiatives in an organizational setting are equally important to a wide cross-section of staff.

The learning organization

A valuable concept which has recently come out of the literature associated with the excellence movement is that of the 'learning organization'. This concept is central to 'dynamic manufacturing' (see Hayes, Wheelwright and Clark (1988)) and is well explored in a UK context in Pedler, Boydell and Burgoyne (1989). We follow the latter reference by defining the learning company as 'an organization which facilitates the learning of all its members and continuously transforms itself'. It should be emphasized that a company which spends heavily on training does not automatically satisfy this definition. The learning company is also concerned with individuals' self-development and the diffusion of learning in order to adapt to the current environment. This may include the extension of the learning culture to customers and suppliers. In particular, a human resource development strategy becomes central to corporate policy and results in a continuous process of organizational change initiated from within. This is elegantly expressed by a reported quotation from the head of a major manufacturing company – 'our business is learning and we sell the by-products of that learning . . .'

In Morgan (1986), when dealing with the metaphor 'organizations as brains', we find the concept of double-loop learning as shown in Fig. 3.2. Morgan argues that 'single-loop learning' is typical of highly computerized bureaucracies. Double-loop learning, which systematically challenges current policies, seems hard to achieve in such organizations. Individuals in such organizations may well appear inefficient, unhelpful and even deviant if they spend time on such behaviour. Furthermore, the organizational performance measurement and reward systems are likely to be linked to existing goals. Questioning the goals therefore seems counterproductive. Particular problems are likely to arise as plans, budgets and targets are perceived to be increasingly inappropriate as market environments change. Does an organization encourage responsible experimentation to cope with a changing environment and learn for the future, or is the individual constrained by a variety of procedures and social norms of behaviour simply to continue using existing ways in attempts to meet pre-set goals? If, in the latter case, failure occurs 'it wasn't my

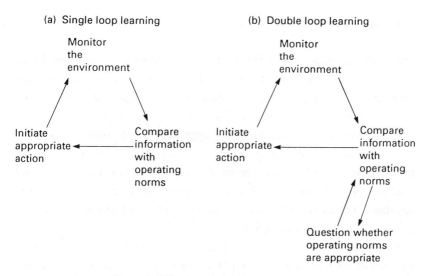

Figure 3.2 Single and double loop learning

fault. I was going by the book!'.

A number of themes comes from the research carried out by Pedler, Boydell and Burgoyne mentioned above. The following questions illustrate points of particular relevance to the management of AMT:

(i) Can we create 'opportunity structures' which help people develop whilst ensuring that 'hard systems implementation' also takes place?

(ii) Can the total process of strategy formulation, investment and implementation be viewed as a learning process?

(iii) Can managerial control systems be developed which promote learning rather than view training, like failure, as a cost rather than an investment?

(iv) Can we develop information systems which support individuals in exploring and questioning current operations and processes?

(v) Can we create a climate wherein information and experience is readily diffused within the organization and with relevant environmental systems?

(vi) Can we create a culture which encourages experimentation and the systematic learning from both success and failure?

The soft systems approach

While the emphasis above has been on ideas which are currently being explored in management generally, as well as AMT specific management, a number of techniques for analysing and modelling organizational systems are available.

One prominent and challenging approach was originally described in Checkland (1981) and is usually referred to as soft systems methodology (SSM). This term was coined to contrast with more traditional systems analysis approaches (familiar to many from engineering and computing literature), the latter being referred to as the hard systems approach.

Fundamental to SSM is the concept of a human activity system. Models of such systems are dependent on the 'Weltanschauung' (or implicit 'world-view') of the modeller. Thus many conceptual models are possible for the same system. Systems and their models may be viewed hierarchically. Systems are named by root definitions and it is suggested that the constituent parts of such definitions may be arrived at through consideration of the following list (helpfully referenced by a mnemonic):

C   Client or beneficiary of the system's action
A   Agents who carry out the system's activities
T   Transformation – the process carried out by the system
W   Weltanschauung of the analyst
O   Owner of the system
E   Environment of the system

This simple description does little justice to a methodology of considerable flexibility and subtlety. Of particular interest for modelling AMT systems in an organizational context, is the ability of SSM to reflect different points of view about the operation of a socio-technical manufacturing system.

An interesting attempt has been made to marry SSM to a standard technique for modelling Computer Integrated Manufacturing systems developed in the USA in the late 1970s. Wang and Smith (1988) show the similarities between the two approaches and argue that the sophistication of SSM complements the computer graphics of the CIM modelling technique, thus allowing effective development and communication of systems models.

These modelling approaches are mentioned not because of their extensive use or proven value in AMT systems design but to show how human and machine systems present differing challenges to their designers. Such challenges may be met by the use of well thought out methodologies. However, the choice of methodology must be given serious attention if mechanistic organizational structures are to be avoided and Computer Integrated Business is to be both entrepreneurial and efficient.

Conclusion

The notion of the learning organization is at the core of the ideas explored in this chapter. We speculate that in the learning organization everyone will be a manager with responsibility for money, people or projects. The manager's life will be a continual process of learning and self- development. It would not be unreasonable to expect that 20 to 30 per cent of the intelligent manager's time be devoted to improvement of him/herself and their immediate colleagues, and that a major source of learning be the questioning of existing standards and practice allied to controlled experimentation with alternative ways of doing things.

If we note the speed of technological change, which also necessitates continual updating by concerned professionals, we begin to see why the principal assets of a company could be regarded as its people and the learning embodied in its systems.

4 Production management systems

Introduction

The impetus for introducing AMT may be obvious to all concerned, for example, new advanced machinery may make possible the manufacture of radically new products, or existing products may be produced at far less cost. More subtle reasons for AMT innovation, but ones which are equally important, are related to the issues dealt with in this and the next chapter. These are about the relationship between AMT and the management of material flow and quality. These issues are crucial in managing the factory of the future.

In this chapter we outline key current issues in an area variously referred to as 'Production Planning and Control', 'Computer Aided Production Management' (CAPM) or 'Production Management Systems'. It concerns the set of decisions involved in planning and controlling the flow of materials from the purchase of components and raw materials, through the scheduling of work inside a factory (or with sub-contractors) to the distribution of goods to customers. We are not referring here to the physical problems of materials handling or routing, but to the control of stock levels, meeting customer deadlines, the avoidance of shortages, the effective use of resources through planning and scheduling, and the planning of new systems. In particular, CIM may be seen as the integration of physical manufacturing and planning systems, and Manufacturing Resource Planning (see below) is often referred to as a component system of AMT.

The topics dealt with here are covered by a vast and growing literature. Indeed, several professional institutions in the UK are concerned with developing the skills of their members in performing production planning-related functions. In particular, the British Production and Inventory Control Society (BPICS), the UK offshoot of the American equivalent (APICS), provides a system of training related to this area. APICS itself was highly influential in the early development of Material Requirements Planning (MRP) and its evolution into integrated business management systems and thus may claim to be amongst the earliest developers of AMT systems. More detailed accounts of the techniques involved may be found in Buffa and Sarin (1987) and in Browne, Harhen and Shivnan (1988).

Objectives of production management systems

The basic objective of production management systems is often stated as meeting required customer service levels at minimum cost. This begs the question of what do we mean by service level and leaves open some crucial issues in cost measurement. It also ignores systems development and learning, i.e. the long term perspective in systems improvement. A traditional view would be based on the following set of propositions.

(i) The prime objective is to ensure a reliable and competitive delivery service level to the customer.
(ii) This must be achieved whilst holding minimum possible stock levels due to the high costs of holding stock.
(iii) As the above objectives appear to be in direct conflict, some way of trading-off service and stock-holding cost must be found.
(iv) Upon analysis a whole range of other related costs are uncovered which must be included in our system.

A more radical view, popularized in the writings of the OPT specialists (see in particular Goldratt and Fox (1986)) is to reject the normal concept of cost as misleading and to characterize systems objectives as follows.

(i) The real, ultimate measures of performance (i.e. making money) are:

● net profit

- return on investment
- maintaining a sufficient flow of cash to survive

(ii) These may be directly linked to managerial and engineering decisions through a consideration of:

- throughput (actual revenue from sales)
- inventory
- operating expense

The linkages between these various things are quite complex, but intelligible and persuasive and their use will be further considered below and in Chapter 6.

What is particularly important to note is that some very fundamental issues exist here in the characterization of production management systems and these issues must not be ignored if one is to assess properly the potential benefits of AMT. We now illustrate this by considering several different approaches which differ dramatically in their prescriptions for managerial action.

Scientific Stock Control (SSC)

The approach which we characterize as 'scientific' stock control can be traced back to the invention of the 'EOQ' formula in the 1920s. Its main development, usually under the umbrella of Operational Research (OR), took place in the 1960s. It is based on a systems disaggregation approach which concentrates on individual points in a system where stock is held and attempts to arrive at policies for minimizing costs at such points while maintaining a required service level.

Thus, in the simpler formulations, each item and stock-holding point is considered independently. The key decisions are the determining of the timing of input orders and specifying the amounts which should be ordered. These may well be adjusted if management feels it necessary, say, to increase orders to safeguard supply or to take advantage of manufacturing economies of scale.

Thus the key concept is the de-coupling of input and output at a stock-holding point. The usual analogy is with the suspension system of a car which provides a smooth ride to passengers despite uneven road surfaces. The output from stock may be variable and fluctuating but the input can be controlled and economical, at least in theory. The problem is that such decoupling may also be achieved simply by holding excessive stock, an approach which may make life easy for lower levels of management but not for the organization as a whole. The cost of holding stock depends on the industry concerned but figures of around 25 to 40 per cent of stock value per annum show a very real opportunity for cost reduction. Indeed, as stock is an asset, its reduction impacts on a company's return on investment in two ways – an increase in profits (through cost reduction) and a reduction in assets required and hence in the need for working capital.

Associated with this approach are a number of simple techniques such as the use of Pareto Analysis for establishing priorities and the construction of stock/time diagrams. The latter are most valuable in demonstrating inefficiencies in stock-holding practice, and an example is included in Fig. 4.1.

The success of this method is particularly dependent on the reliability

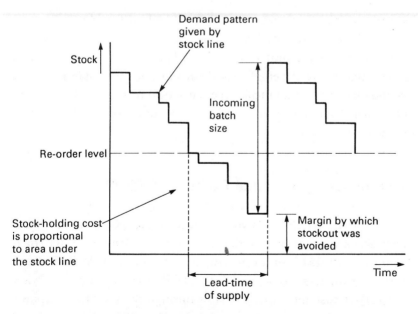

Figure 4.1 Scientific stock control: stock/time diagram

of demand and lead-time forecasting systems. Much effort has been expended in the last 30 years in the development of statistical forecasting systems. These are based on the extrapolation of demand patterns uncovered by often highly sophisticated analysis. Unfortunately, demand for items (which may be original demand from end-users or the usage of components by a production unit further down the chain) is an intrinsically complex phenomenon, often involving the anticipation of future needs as much as actual usage. Thus, future demand patterns may be radically different from those shown by the data. However, all the systems discussed in this chapter require demand forecasts to some greater or lesser extent and the objective statistical approach has the great advantage of quantifying the variability of demand, thus providing essential information on the underlying uncertainties in assessing future materials flow.

More controversial are attempts to forecast lead-times, an issue on which the approaches discussed in this chapter differ dramatically. Similarly, the approach to costs in SSC seems pedestrian, even assuming costs can be meaningfully measured. The tendency is to see costs as variables to be measured rather than reduced, in sharp contrast to the Just-in-Time approach. This is particularly true of manufacturing set-up costs. Such costs, if high, will lead to large batch sizes and increased stock levels, thus increasing cost in a number of ways. Just-in-Time practitioners have led the way in showing how good engineering practice, based on old and new manufacturing technology, may dramatically reduce set-up times and set-up costs. This turns out to have value far beyond a simple cost saving in stock holding.

Manufacturing Resource Planning (MRP II)

The acronym 'MRP' has two related meanings. General interest in the basic formulation of Material Requirements Planning (MRP) dates from the early 1970s and was strongly influenced by APICS and by software suppliers. At its simplest, MRP aims to maintain a valid schedule of customer delivery dates through the use of a computer-based planning and control system. It differs from Scientific Stock

Control by considering within-company demands as dependent on the demand for finished goods, which is rather obvious in principle but surprisingly difficult to organize in practice. Thus the approach is one of centralized planning, requiring comprehensive databases covering a variety of entities.

An outline form of MRP, often called a Type I installation, is shown in Fig. 4.2, though it should be emphasized that even such simple formulations of MRP require far more dataflows to work. The key features are listed below:

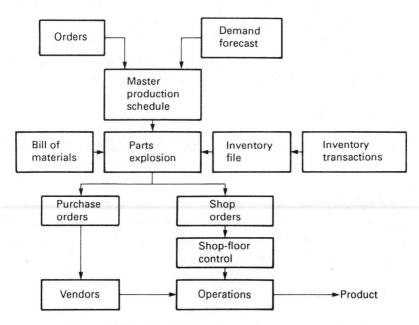

Figure 4.2 Material requirements planning: type I open loop

Master Production Schedule (MPS)

This provides an interface between sales/marketing activities and production. It is a time-phased set of customer requirements, that is, a list of dates at which particular amounts of differing product must be shipped to customers. If customers order products with a required supply lead-time less than the manufacturing lead-time then some finished stock will be required. This is provided for in the system by including some make-for-stock orders in the MPS, though these should obviously be carefully controlled.

Bill of Materials (BOM)

This database provides information on the materials required to make particular finished goods in terms of amounts and lead-times. Data is usually arranged in hierarchical form. That is, a given product is divided first into major sub-assemblies (noting the time needed for bringing these together to form the final product). Each sub-assembly is then itself broken down, and so on until one arrives at bought-in components whose supply lead-times are noted. It is generally recognized that MRP is of most use when complex products requiring many levels in their BOMs are being manufactured.

Inventory file

The repository of information on the amount and location of all components and finished goods in the factory. This database has to be far more accurate than is normal in most pre-MRP systems. MRP essentially depends on knowing where everything is at all times and thus entails very high levels of discipline in data recording, an activity which can be made far more effective by the hardware and communications parts of AMT systems.

Parts explosion

This is sometimes confusingly referred to as MRP. It is the stage in the process where the requirements listed in the MPS are broken down, using the BOM, into time-phased requirements at all levels of sub-assembly. These are compared with existing stocks and thus the need to manufacture and buy in parts is determined, once again with an emphasis on timing.

Production Activity Control (PAC)

This controls the release of work onto the shop floor and its subsequent flow, with a particular emphasis on the loading of facilities.

Procurement

Similar to PAC but dealing with outside suppliers. This can easily become a major problem area if long and erratic supply lead-times exist.

A particularly important issue here is the frequency with which the MPS is changed and the implications of such changes being fed through the system. In theory MRP seems eminently suited for handling such alterations to plans but in practice care must be taken not to make the whole system unstable. This usually involves a freeze on replanning orders in the near future.

However, MRP in the simple form outlined here will almost certainly prove ineffective for a number of reasons, of which the following tend to recur with great regularity. The first is the lack of feedback in the system to cater for delays, excessive scrap, and so forth, in supply and production. Similarly Bills of Materials are likely to be continually changing as products and production methods are improved. This situation necessitates the development of a system of engineering change control.

The next obvious point is that there is more to marketing than simply taking customer orders! The system must allow for new initiatives in the market place, promotions, reserving capacity for priority customers and so forth. If the MPS is to act as an effective interface between marketing and production, it must reflect commercial realities as well as manufacturing logic.

Finally, this simple approach in effect assumes the factory has infinite capacity, that is, customer needs in terms of amount and timing are simply recorded and fed into the system. In practice customers will negotiate on delivery dates and expect these to be kept to. To support such planning the manufacturer needs to know the impact of his/her plans on available production resources. This is surprisingly difficult to achieve and a number of ways of allowing for limited capacity have been developed. The simplest is to apply a basic check on the aggregate volume of goods flowing through the factory prior to changing the MPS, i.e. the company knows how many items (allowing for differing product lines) it can make in a year and assumes short-term fluctuations and problems can be handled by over-time working, small adjustments in delivery dates, re-scheduling, sub-contracting, and so forth. This approach is typical of pre-MRP operations, although it still plays an important role with MRP.

A more systematic check is provided by Rough Cut Capacity Planning (RCCP) where the MPS is analysed using accurate data on resource capacities. This still falls short of detailed capacity planning which takes place through simulating schedules of shop loadings. Though desirable in theory, this latter approach has proved to be problematic if carried out far in advance of events, as the results may well be sensitive to the inevitable changes to the MPS and to fluctuations in supply lead-times and production rates. RCCP possibly provides the most pragmatic approach to capacity planning for all but very expert and experienced MRP users.

The diagram in Fig. 4.3 illustrates an MRP system with the above refinements, giving what is usually called a 'closed loop' or a Type II system.

More recently MRP systems have been expanded to become complete planning and control mechanisms giving rise to the new term 'Manufacturing Resource Planning' (MRP II), a Type III system in the confusing classification normally used. MRP II is conceived as a wide-ranging, closed loop business control system, designed to carry out detailed planning and monitoring of plans. This is done by integrating all the related business and transaction aspects of manufacturing, including MRP, capacity planning, inventory control, product costing, shop floor control, finance, marketing, engineering and human resource management.

MRP II is a 'top down' system which depends heavily on a valid MPS, efficient data feedback and highly disciplined staff. In a recent report on a workshop comparing production control methodologies (Waterlow and Richards (1988)), the assumptions underlying MRP II and the organizational implications of its use are listed in some detail, including the following questionable assumptions (in addition to points above):

● lead times at all stages of manufacture and supply can be specified and preferably the aggregate lead time is less than the required

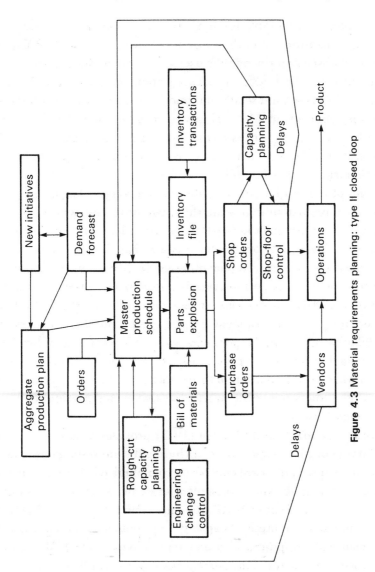

Figure 4.3 Material requirements planning: type II closed loop

product delivery lead time;

● organizational structures are capable of adapting to a centralization of materials management and all relevant functional managers will use the MRP II system as the central business planning and control system.

The first of these points will be the focus of some debate below. The second has considerable implications for education and training in an organization. At the simplest level, all staff must be comprehensively trained in the use of the system. Such training may not, however, affect basic attitudes regarding the planning and control of materials flow, and senior and middle management may find that the discipline of an MRP II system conflicts with their habitual freedom of action. An extensive literature exists, pointing to the potential problems which exist with the human parts of this rather mechanistic approach.

One of the originators of MRP, Oliver Wight, has developed a classification system indicating the range of success which has been achieved by companies in MRP implementation. The top class is 'A' where a Type III or similar system has been achieved, top management runs the company through the MPS, inventory is under control and delivery performance is considered excellent. Around 10 per cent of MRP installations are thought to be successful at this level. A warning note is sounded by the larger number of class 'C' installations (roughly 50 per cent) where a Type I system produces marginal benefits; or even the class 'D' installations (roughly 10 per cent) where a combination of inaccurate records, wrong attitudes or even non-functioning systems suggests that even recurring costs may outweigh benefits.

Brown, Harhen and Shivnan (1988) provides a useful summary of surveys of MRP experiences, including the interesting observation that many installations are only partly computerized. Thus, in a survey published in 1986, and consistent with earlier studies, it was found that only 61 per cent of MRP users had computerized the MPS, 42 per cent had computerized capacity requirements planning, and 52 per cent had computerized production activity control. While even a glance at the pages of the current trade press will show determined attempts by computer systems vendors to change this situation by offering ever improved variations on MRP/JIT/OPT, it is interesting to speculate on whether partial computerization might provide at least a short-term stable system. However, any attempt to move towards CIM or CIB must be based on comprehensive databases or materials related information will not be widely available to support decision making throughout an organization.

Surveys which relate to MRP failure usually point to problems with the interface between the computer system and the organization. An obvious cause of difficulties is lack of data integrity and the improvement of data accuracy may easily become an obsession hiding more fundamental organizational problems. MRP may be looked on as a solution to organizational problems, that is, MRP II will remove functional boundaries, improve materials flow performance, free management time and so forth. It will by itself do none of these things. It is a too! to be used to achieve objectives and if staff at all levels are not clear on what they are required to achieve or how to meet their objectives, the computer system, assuming its data is accurate, will at best report on the company's bad performance.

The Just-in-Time approach (JIT)

It is difficult to believe that the JIT approach is of comparatively recent origin, such has been the interest it has generated amongst manufacturing managers. One reason has been the stunning successes reported by some companies in implementing JIT. Schonberger (1986) describes some of these, including order of magnitude improvements in lead-times and stock holding performance. Such changes have the potential to alter radically the competitive balance within particular industries.

Another reason for interest is the intellectual challenge presented by the approach. At first sight, particularly to engineers and managers brought up on scientific inventory control, the idea of eliminating stock entirely (except of course for work literally being processed) and of suppliers delivering parts just when they are required seems nonsense. How can one allow for the inevitable fluctuations, delays, breakdowns and so on in a supply and manufacture chain except through keeping some safety stock? Yet the ideas which accompany JIT (typically worker involvement in process improvement, product simplification, preventive maintenance, improved quality management) seem natural and hardly new. Indeed, the KANBAN card, identified initially in the West as almost synonymous with JIT, seems merely an imaginative alternative to existing stock control procedures.

A further set of reasons for interest in this approach in the context of this book refers to its relationship with AMT. JIT is an essentially evolutionary and gradual approach, whereas AMT implementation is often characterized as revolutionary. Also the literature on JIT often appears to set JIT up as anti-AMT, that is, much store is set by the improvement of existing facilities and engineering changes to existing machines rather than radical, computer-based innovations.

The understanding of JIT has been improved by some excellent literature and seminars on the subject in recent years. JIT evolved from the Japanese concern with production efficiency and the reduction of waste so necessary for a country attempting to build an effective manufacturing base whilst having to import much raw material. The original approach, and the KANBAN card, are credited to Toyota but recent surveys show an eclectic attitude within modern Japanese industry where JIT is seen merely as one aspect of a generally disciplined approach to manufacturing.

A typical characterization of JIT is as follows:

> JIT is a disciplined programme for improving overall productivity and waste. It provides for the cost-effective production and delivery of only the necessary quality parts, in the right quantity, at the right time and place, while using a minimum amount of facilities, equipment, materials and human resources. JIT is dependent upon the balance between the supplier's flexibility and the user's stability. It is accomplished through the application of specific techniques which require total employee involvement and teamwork.

This general approach is often given other names, e.g. stockless production (Hewlett-Packard) or continuous flow manufacturing (IBM). Its essence is a beguiling simplicity which may however mask a somewhat limited applicability.

JIT cannot be seen as separate from its implementation, indeed unlike some of the other methodologies presented in this chapter, it may be argued that JIT is a process for improvement rather than a final goal. This implementation programme must however proceed in a logical sequence. In particular 'supplier JIT' is only feasible after 'in-company JIT' has been achieved. This latter point is of some importance, as some companies have seized on JIT merely as a banner under which to insist on unrealistic supply flexibility. If a company's use of raw materials really is fluctuating, unpredictable and erratic, a supplier has an impossible task in providing JIT performance, except by maintaining stocks of finished goods in a warehouse adjacent to the user's factory! This is not a genuine implementation of JIT but an exercise of power by a customer in demanding favourable supply conditions whilst cutting his own raw material stocks. As Porter shows this is a naive view of competitive strategy which may easily rebound (see Chapter 7 and Porter (1985)).

The basic elements of JIT are waste elimination, Total Quality Control (TQC) and attention to the development of human resources. The first of these is often wrongly seen as merely cutting stock levels, but in fact waste may also occur as scrap, queues, set-up times, materials handling and movement or machine downtime. The linkage between JIT and TQC is so fundamental that they should be examined together when discussing the operational management of AMT.

The development of human resources is central to the Japanese approach to the extent that one frequent criticism of the use of JIT in the West is that it is based on Japanese 'culture' and therefore unworkable. Certainly the 'working culture' evident in the larger Japanese companies is somewhat different from that normal in the West. However, the logic of the JIT approach does not imply the importation of a Japanese working culture but the development of an appropriate mode of operation for achieving waste reduction and TQC. There is no reason to believe that employee problem solving, flexibility of working practices, imaginative engineering, good communications and so forth are intrinsically the product of an Eastern culture. Japanese companies have found ways of doing these things which are natural to them and Western companies must do likewise if they want to achieve the same results.

However, the logic of JIT may mean that it is only applicable in certain manufacturing situations and to explore this we must consider a typical implementation path in some detail. Following the prescription in Voss (1987) we divide implementation into several stages which must occur in the correct sequence.

Stage 1 JIT

This involves the systematic application of a series of concurrent changes designed to simplify and improve the manufacturing situation in preparation for the more dramatic techniques to be used. Typical activities are as follows.

Product simplification

The use of JIT requires a company to rationalize its product line by pruning products with little demand and simplifying the remainder in terms of their use of components and manufacturing methods.

Total Quality Control

As described in Chapter 5 the total quality system should be improved with an emphasis on process control.

Preventive maintenance

Equipment breakdowns and malfunctioning must be eliminated to the extent that problems which do occur are seen as very serious and given immediate attention. This will demand very high standards of engineering consistency.

Set-up time reduction

Voss (1987) records an instance of a 17-minute set-up on a major machine being reduced to 8 seconds at minimal cost and mainly through the efforts of shop-floor staff working on a systematic productivity improvement programme. Such improvements have value far beyond the saving in productive time on the machine.

Layout

A recurring theme in JIT literature is the use of Group Technology to identify families of products and components, followed by dramatic changes to plant layout, with the objective of reducing the distance material must travel to an absolute minimum, even if this involves the duplication of some facilities.

Small machines
The idea is that through the use of a number of small machines in place of one large machine, compact layout and product focusing are possible (see Chapter 8). It may also be easier on such machines to utilize in-house innovation skills to reduce set-up times and improve material and tool handling.

The need for these changes may seem mysterious at first but the techniques required are not new and should be familiar to engineers and manufacturing management. In particular the outlay in terms of capital expenditure is comparatively small and may even be recouped in terms of tactical benefits occurring during stage 1.

One item in this list, the use of small machines, is thought by some to be directly opposed to trends in AMT development. This is a natural result of the identification of AMT with large, integrated production facilities. As we argue repeatedly in this book, AMT involves the use of relevant technology whatever its physical size and integration and is based on computers and people.

Stage 2 JIT

Stage 1 has prepared the way for a number of radical changes which may be difficult to implement in isolation but together have the potential for dramatic improvements in operating performance.

Multi-functional workforce
The effective operation of JIT requires the re-allocation of workers from areas of low demand to areas of high demand on a regular basis. Similarly workers are expected to contribute to problem solving and systems fault recognition as a normal part of their working lives. Job grades, payment schemes and training must match these objectives fully.

Problem visibility
A fundamental tenet of JIT and TQC is that problems must not be hidden but should be highlighted in order that preventive action can be taken. This might involve the use of charts displaying all the key

features of an operational system and the acceptance that when a problem occurs the relevant operator has the authority to stop production and demand immediate expert assistance.)

Enforced improvement

This is the interesting idea that management continually reduces the assets needed for manufacturing and so creates problems which must be solved without increasing other assets. Typically, the assets reduced may be machines, labour, buffer stocks, space and so forth, though care must be taken with the sequence of reduction.

Pull scheduling

One objective of JIT is to achieve a continuous flow of material based on short lead-times, very small batch sizes and pull scheduling, the latter being the discipline that no manufacturing action takes place at any stage in a production process until an instruction to manufacture or move an item comes from the next stage down the line. It should now be obvious why the changes listed in stage 1 were necessary. This type of production control requires simple products, simple manufacturing methods, short lines, good communication, flexible workforce and no breakdowns!

JIT purchasing

Having made all the changes listed above, a manufacturer will have achieved a smooth flow of goods based on a narrow range of material requirements. It is now possible that a close relationship with a supplier could be managed to the mutual benefit of both parties.

Of the techniques listed above, the use of enforced problem solving may seem the most perverse, though it may be argued that it is a common enough technique applied by autocratic and distant managers to long-suffering production staff! The essence of the technique as part of JIT is that the way has been prepared for effective problem solving by rationalization of the manufacturing process, the problem solvers have been adequately trained and management are part of the problem-solving team.

Pull scheduling should be seen in contrast to push scheduling where orders for supply or manufacture are released according to a plan, as is typical with MRP. Logically MRP schedules may be seen as the result of customers' 'pulling', provided the manufacturing lead-time is less than that required by the customer for delivery. Though the mechanisms of pull scheduling are quite simple, the implications for its practical use are considerable, except in the most stable of manufacturing situations (i.e. repetitive manufacture of a simple product with high demand).

A clever analogy is found in Wheatley (1989) where JIT is compared to the design of a modern combat plane. The latter is inherently unstable, requiring continual corrective action for safe flight, but this very instability gives it an important edge in combat manoeuvrability. Scientific stock control uses buffer stocks to give stability to a manufacturing system. JIT removes such stocks and relies on continual adaptation to immediate market needs for survival.

Interestingly, JIT is usually characterized as an essentially 'human' control system, while the modern combat fighter relies on a mixture of computer and human control. Increasingly interest is being focused on the interface between JIT and MRP. OPT, as described in the next section, is also an interesting mixture of human and computer parts.

Optimized Production Technology (OPT)

This approach is of very recent origin, usually associated with E.M.Goldratt and popularized through his book *The Goal*, a novel based on a few months in the life of a production manager. OPT links together a number of useful ideas for improving material flow with a clear view of how such improvements affect a company's financial performance (see Goldratt and Cox (1986), Goldratt and Fox (1986) and Goldratt (1985)). A controversial aspect of OPT is the use of expensive software as part of the consultancy package offered by consultants trained in this approach. Details of the software are not generally available. In 1986 it was reported that Goldratt parted company with the major OPT consultancy and is now developing more general problem diagnosis and solving techniques.

We mentioned earlier the OPT approach to the setting of objectives through the use of the concepts of throughput, inventory and operating expense. OPT is particularly innovative and ambitious in its linking of business and production decision-making and control systems. At this level it provides an indicator of what might be achieved if one is willing to rethink such basic areas as cost accounting in conjunction with materials management. A similar questioning approach to the concept of cost and the measurement of financial performance is found in some recent approaches to quality assurance.

It appears that one may view OPT either as a set of ideas or as a computer-based finite capacity scheduling package. The latter may be seen as complementary to MRP. It differs, however, in deriving lead-times from schedules which are set with reference to due dates and priorities.

A key concept in this approach is the bottleneck, a resource constraint which directly affects throughput. OPT concentrates on maximizing the flow of materials through bottlenecks, schedules for other facilities being derived to support the bottleneck flows. Indeed, provided the bottlenecks are efficiently handled, other facilities may be approached on a JIT basis in order to keep non-essential inventory to a minimum. Some of the practical details of OPT are summarized in the 'Nine Rules of OPT' (see Goldratt (1985)), rules which are of value for the management of material flow in any context. These rules emphasize the importance of bottlenecks, the derivative nature of lead-times, and the need to be flexible in setting the sizes of process batches and transfer batches.

In total, OPT is a mixture of ideas and prescriptions, some of the latter being embodied in expensive software. The ideas are radical and challenging and may well illuminate any approach to production systems management. It is difficult to assess objectively whether companies who have adopted OPT in its totality have found it cost-effective as a technical solution or whether reported improvements have been due to managements' reassessments of the production control task.

Conclusions

The four fundamentally different approaches described above all have something to contribute to the management of the flow of materials in manufacturing. One may find circumstances which are ideally suited to a particular approach or circumstances where the use of a given method in total would be inappropriate. Of particular importance therefore, is the matching of circumstances to methodology or the integration of ideas from various sources.

Such integration should not, however, be determined only with the intention of managing material flows. As we describe in the next chapter, the management of quality is equally important, as is providing an appropriate interface between design and manufacturing.

In the past there has been a tendency to see production systems management as a narrow, technical area. Indeed, some of the more mathematical approaches give the impression that such management can be achieved by the selection of the right formulae or software. The strength of MRP, JIT and OPT is the way in which they address the need for human resource development, for integration with other systems, for changes in cost accounting practice and for a holistic view of materials management.

5 The management of quality

Introduction

As the briefest glance at recent literature on manufacturing management will show, the management of quality is a key issue. Quality management gurus, including Deming, Taguchi and Crosby, emphasize the central importance of their subject for Japanese and US companies. Yet most of the ideas presented are not new. Books on Statistical Process Control (SPC) rework simple techniques which have been known for many years. Even the sophisticated Taguchi method has upset some statisticians who argue that its approach is either well-known, wrong or both. The 'right first time' concept periodically recurs in the popular and serious literature. What is new is the thoroughness and determination with which these ideas are being propagated as central to the performance of companies, as opposed to quality control being seen as an irritating constraint on productivity. As with JIT, Total Quality Management (TQM) integrates separate ideas and techniques into a powerful methodology with real relevance to companies seriously seeking to improve their effectiveness.

At its simplest, TQM may be seen as the totality of quality- related techniques applied consistently to every aspect of company life. Its objective is to provide co-ordination and direction in the pursuit of effectiveness through looking at every quality-related set of issues. This does not only mean an obsession with product quality but with the quality of every aspect of organizational performance. Thus one stage of production must provide high quality output for the next; office staff must provide a quality service to line management, and so forth.

A more elegant characterization of TQM is provided in Cullen and

Hollingum (1987) who define the central objective of a total quality policy as 'the elimination of waste by the minimization of manufacturing variance'. Echoes of JIT are very strong here. TQM and JIT may be seen as complimentary evolutionary philosophies for manufacturing improvement. They do, however, have a differing focus and use some different techniques, which suggests that a joint TQM/JIT methodology is called for. The main problem in this case might be that what were essentially simple approaches with clear aims become confusing and difficult to use as company-wide crusades, and so lose the whole point of their implication.

Advanced Manufacturing Technology has an important role to play here also. Modern automatic testing equipment greatly facilitates process control and the routine collection of quality-related data. Alternative solutions to design and manufacturing problems may more easily be explored through CADCAM links. Similarly, the potential of AMT to provide a competitive edge may be wasted if attitudes to quality management and procedures are wrong in a company. Advances in the development of production management systems may be rendered completely ineffective if a comprehensive approach to quality management is not in place.

What is meant by quality?

The word 'quality' is often used in a very narrow sense in an industrial context. Whereas everyday usage of the word is vague, referring often to the customer's reaction to an unspecified range of product or service attributes, the specialist defines quality as conformance to a specification or to customer requirements. Thus, the cheapest, mass produced item is a quality product if its performance meets a specification which in turn reflects customers' requirements and reasonable expectations.

The main problem with this definition is its conflict with ordinary uses of the word and its failure to reflect quality issues for the product designer. Thus we will qualify the word, where its meaning is not obvious from the context, by referring to 'conformance quality' and 'design quality'. Conformance quality is the ability of a product or service to meet its specification or stated requirements, regardless of whether the specification is correct or the requirements correctly understood. Design quality refers to the totality of product or service attributes which affect the customer's assessment of its value and usefulness. Thus both design and conformance quality are important and are obviously inter-related.

It will be noted that the quality of a service is mentioned above as well as product quality. The argument here is based on the view that a customer buys a complete product-service package. The service elements in the package might include customer support, training, consultancy, after-sales service, and so on. Such service elements are capable of specification and their effectiveness must be monitored and controlled to the same extent as product characteristics. This is not a side issue as far as AMT is concerned. A typical service which a company may offer is that of prompt and accurate quotations, produced in response to customer enquiries. The production of quotations may be greatly facilitated by AMT systems and further enhanced if reliable delivery dates are produced by the production management system. Indeed, it may be argued that keeping to due dates for product delivery is a conformance quality issue, as delivery performance is a service element. However, this may prove a confusing way of referring to delivery performance unless 'quality thinking' totally permeates one's approach to management. Some argue that it should.

One definition of quality is 'fitness for use' though this may be misused by hard-pressed production managers. A typical example might be a batch of products which fails to meet some specified parameters, but is urgently required by a customer and is shipped on the basis that its performance will be adequate in this instance. This exemplifies the tension which is often seen to exist between quality control and productivity. The dangers of relaxing quality control in this way are very great. Simple logic demonstrates that either the specification was incorrect in such an instance, or the customer's requirement for the product was misunderstood, and hence the product fails to reflect customer needs. Once such practices are allowed, precedents are set for poor quality management. Overspecification of a product can be a very real problem if it leads to the deterioration of quality assurance systems.

This example illustrates one of the major problems for TQM – communication between those who interpret customers' needs (marketing, technical and design staff), those who design a product and its specification to meet those needs, those who design the manufacturing methods, and those responsible for actual manufacturing. The solution to this problem is partly the drawing up of good procedures for quality assurance, partly the discipline of staff in following such procedures, but largely the attitude of all staff towards quality and the solving of quality-related problems.

Design quality

The product designer is concerned with the totality of product features as seen by the customer, the manufacturability of the product and its cost. These concerns should always be equally present in the designer's mind.

Product features might typically include performance and attributes. The customer is also likely to be concerned with the reliability, durability and serviceability of the product. This is not to say that all products are excellent on all features. The product package also includes price. Similarly, the aesthetic aspects of the product will be of importance depending on context. In a fashion market this will include originality of the design. For most products the customer will arrive at a perception of total product quality which will relate to price. In some instances this relationship is quite complex, for example, the price of the product, along with company image and brand name, will help determine perceptions of its quality. Obviously such things must be seen in the context of competing products.

The product designer's task, therefore, is to provide a bridge between customer needs and expectations and a detailed manufacturing specification. This task may be seen as knowledge conversion and is illustrated in Fig. 5.1.

It might be useful at this stage to be clear about the use of some terms which are a potential source of confusion. Customer needs may be clearly set out, as when an engineering company uses the services

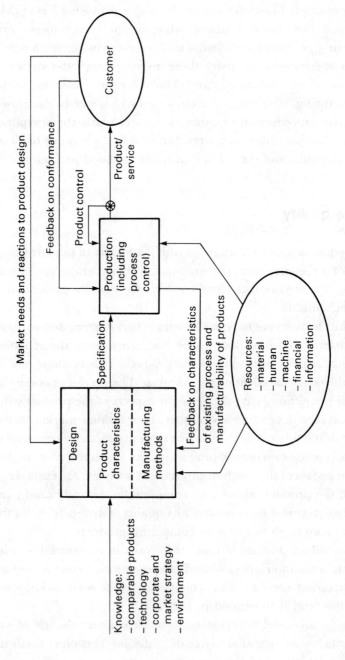

Figure 5.1 Quality: a systems view

of a specialist sub-contractor, or may be vague and negotiable. Both the design and the marketing functions have a role to play in moving from an assessment of customer needs to a statement of customer requirements. This may involve the actual customer or may be done on behalf of the future intended customers. Product and manufacturing specifications are quite different in that they involve exhaustive detail on what the product is, what it can do, the properties of its components and how it is to be made. Thus a given statement of customer requirements could give rise to a wide variety of specifications. Ultimately, though, most customers are concerned with their requirements being met. The specification is only of importance if parts of it are included in the requirements. The exception to this is the expert customer, usually an industrial manufacturer, who might state requirements in the form of a specification, thus eliminating the designer's role. Even then some manufacturing decisions are likely to remain.

These ideas are also summarized in Fig. 5.1 and though they are not usually spelled out in this way they help to clarify some potential confusions. This acceptance of non-conforming items as being fit for use shows that a gap has developed between a specification and the requirements of a particular customer. This may be inevitable when one specification is meant to serve many sets of requirements, but should also be seen as a symptom of a potentially damaging problem. Similarly, customers may agree to a requirement but then change their minds as their needs or the environment in which they are working change. Marketing, design and manufacturing staff must be aware of these problems and pay attention to developing and using the channels of communication between various functions and customers.

Accepting that some discrepancies between needs, stated requirements and specifications are likely to arise, we see that communication and problem-solving skills are of major importance. These are inherent in the modern approach to Total Quality Management which emphasizes training in problem diagnosis and solution, communication, the developing of appropriate procedures and above all else a positive attitude to ensuring that the customer receives a satisfactory product.

All this is in contrast to traditional approaches where wage payment schemes emphasized productivity and at best the paying of lip-service to the detail of a specification. Similarly, the breakdown of communication between the marketing, design and manufacturing functions is likely to lead to a lack of flexibility in responding to a changing customer and supplier environment.

Advanced Manufacturing Technology, in conjunction with appropriate managerial systems, has a key role to play in facilitating the achievement of quality-related goals. This is partly through the maintenance of consistent standards of manufacturing and partly through cost-effective flexibility and the CADCAM link.

Conformance quality

If we are satisfied that a specification is valid, the problem arises of ensuring that manufactured products actually meet the specification. The same argument applies to service aspects of a company's relationship with its customers. Some texts tend to define quality management as ensuring conformance to specification, though this is obviously too narrow. Some define it as ensuring conformance to requirements, but this approach needs further explication.

We would like to see actual products meet actual customer needs. This is most obviously achievable in a craft environment or a project form of manufacture where the customer maintains contact with the producer and can communicate his/her evolving needs and monitor progress. The best alternative is for products and services to conform to an agreed statement of requirements, though this requires the continuing validity of such a statement. The mechanisms for ensuring conformance to requirements are those concerned with drawing up specifications and those concerned with ensuring conformance to specifications. Thus, as we have emphasized above, two inter-related processes are involved in conforming to requirements unless a statement of requirements is sufficiently detailed to directly become a specification. This may be so in situations where a common-sense approach leads us to connect actions with results, but most industrial manufacture requires considerable technical engineering decision-making.

A company must in the long term meet customer needs. In the short term this may be characterized as meeting stated requirements, provided mechanisms exist for ensuring the continuing validity of such a statement. At a tactical, functional level most attention is likely to be paid to meeting a specification and once again mechanisms must exist for ensuring the continuing validity of the specification as the market, supply and technological environment change.

Feedback on quality performance.

In Fig. 5.1 we show some aspects of feedback. Indeed, to a large extent TQM may be characterized by the variety of feedback loops it contains. The most decisive indicator of poor quality is the refusal of customers to buy a product, either because actual products do not conform to expectations or because the product is not appealing. Similarly damaging is a high number of customer complaints, returned products or high levels of unexpected after-sales servicing. It is essential that such events are carefully monitored and classified so that appropriate corrective action can be taken.

The next level of feedback shown in Fig. 5.1 is product control, either by full inspection of all key properties of all products or by some form of acceptance sampling. This may provide information on manufacturing problems or may indicate poor design or poor control of material inputs. The latter problems should, however, be diagnosed by other means. Statistical Process Control (SPC) has the objective of ensuring that manufacturing processes remain under control. The most immediate form of control is the continuing vigilance of operators and production staff during manufacturing operations.

The control of the design process is more complex and indirect. The ultimate control may be customer satisfaction, but this involves a substantial time delay. However, the concept of bringing a large number of products to market and allowing customer choice to arbitrate between them has some attractions if it can be performed at reasonable cost. A step in this direction is provided by the speedy production of prototypes and simulations of the product. These various strategies may be facilitated by AMT. Indeed, any technological aid which enables a designer to obtain performance feedback at an early stage is likely to be of value. Finally, the experience of the designer and other product and process development staff should facilitate the production of a valid specification.

The overlapping nature of these feedback loops once again shows the need for good communications, procedures and training in providing effective Total Quality Management. It might also be noted that the need for performance feedback is not only related to products and materials, but also to tools, maintenance activity and other aspects of a manufacturing system. Feedback should also exist for management, and in particular the effectiveness of quality management procedures must be audited.

'Zero Defects' and 'Right First Time'

Two phrases which have been part of quality management for a number of years are 'Zero Defects' (ZD) and 'Right First Time'. ZD is usually applied to materials or products and indicates a performance standard which is intended to contrast with the concept of an acceptable quality level (i.e. an acceptable level of defects or of defectives) in product control. It may be applied to goods delivered to customers, to components received from suppliers, or to intermediate stages of production. There is no reason why it should not be applied to a service, provided performance can be reliably measured against appropriate standards.

The Right First Time concept indicates an approach to producing things whereby a mixture of engineering and training ensures that non-conformance does not occur. This obviously requires high levels of direct attention to production tasks, short time-scale feedback on the development of problems and possibly higher levels of investment to improve process capability.

ZD performance may be achieved by Right First Time manufacture or by extensive examination and selection of products and materials, though it should be remembered that inspection and selection is itself a process which is prone to error and requires control mechanisms. It is generally thought that Right First Time production is the preferable way to achieve ZD. It should be noted that ZD cannot be achieved by sampling inspection of the product as this inevitably involves risks of poor products not being in the sample taken. Sampling might, however, be useful in providing some check on the effectiveness of selection procedures.

Right First Time production requires high levels of material input quality. Indeed, if the process is sensitive to the specified properties of material input (which presumably should be the case) then ZD input is necessary. Thus, ZD and Right First Time ideas are not identical, but are closely related and exist well together in quality assurance systems.

The gurus of modern quality management

One unusual feature of the management of quality is the number of individuals whose names have become attached to particular philosophies and techniques – the gurus of quality management. This has come about partly because of the tendency for quality management to atrophy in many companies and require fresh impetus for the involvement of all staff in its aims. It might also be argued that the economic excuses for avoiding preventive action are similar to those in health management; defectives, like illness, are ignored in the hope they will simply go away! Thus, quality management has benefited from the injection of ideas from those with a clear and practical view of why quality management is important.

Quality gurus are usually American or Japanese, or, in the case of Deming, an American whose ideas have been embraced most readily in Japan. Deming was an early exponent of TQM and SPC ideas along with a third essential feature, the promotion of positive cooperation in a company rather than 'management by conflict'. Traditional bureaucratic quality systems, based on inspection, have a tendency to exacerbate the conflict inherent in attempts to trade-off quality against productivity. Whilst understanding that many quality assurance systems, in particular those satisfying Defence Industry requirements, include checks on product quality as a safeguard, such checks are inappropriate as the main driving force in the improvement of attitudes towards quality.

Philip Crosby is another US-based exponent of practical quality systems whose ideas have been found useful by many companies looking for a clear and forceful approach to quality management. In Crosby (1979), provocatively titled *Quality is Free*, he sets out his four 'absolutes of quality management'. The first three of them defines quality as conformance to requirements, argue in favour of prevention rather than inspection and set the standard as Zero Defects. The fourth is an idea which, although obvious on reflection, is particularly powerful but demanding to implement. This idea is that the measurement of quality is the price of non-conformance. The recommendation here is that considerable effort should be applied to measuring the opportunity cost of producing poor goods. This will involve measuring far more than the cost of scrap and rework in terms of labour and materials, and the obvious intention is that management faced with the real cost of poor quality will see an economic advantage in the installation of preventive systems. We return to this theme in the next section.

Genichi Taguchi presents an altogether more sophisticated approach, embracing design (off-the-line quality control) and manufacturing (on-the-line quality control) and challenging the validity of simple ideas, such as Zero Defects. He defines product quality as 'the loss imparted by the product to society from the time the product is shipped'. Thus the Taguchi philosophy is not only comprehensive but also ecologically sound. A potential problem with this approach is its highly mathematical nature which carries the danger that quality engineering will once again become the domain of a few experts applying arcane techniques and whose dictates all other staff must obey.

By way of contrast, there exists also a range of simple and practical techniques developed for use by staff in quality circles. These include a statistical approach to the occurrence of faults, using Pareto diagrams to determine priorities for action and the application of the Ishikawa diagram to explore the probable causes of quality problems. In fact, these techniques may be used in a range of systems improvement settings and are not restricted to solving the more obvious quality-related problems. They illustrate the profound idea, previously discussed under the JIT methodology, that all employees have a contribution to make in problem solving and systems improvement.

Economics of quality assurance

A classic view of the economics of quality assurance is shown in Fig. 5.2. This summarizes the widely-held view that an economically optimal quality system is arrived at by trading off investment costs in high performance production systems against the costs of scrap and rework. Although an economically optimal manufacturing system is a reasonable objective, it is doubtful if the concept of optimizing quality management as a separate system is valid, as we show below.

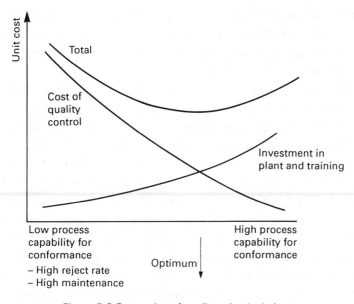

Figure 5.2 Economics of quality: classical view

Let us assume that a high level of quality is required by the customer, i.e. this discussion is not concerned with the dubious economics of shipping poor goods to customers and relying on them to return the goods if not satisfied! High quality output may be achieved by high levels of process capability with minimal rectification, selection and so forth, or by some lower level of capability combined with appropriate control systems. Fig. 5.2. is based on the idea that high levels of process capability entail high costs (investment in plant, training, maintenance and so on) which gradually decrease as capability decreases. Alternatively, low process capability must be compensated by high quality assurance costs which gradually decrease as capability increases. The assumption is that a middle region exists where the total cost is minimized.

The first problem with this argument is the crude handling of the cost concept. Assuming that our measure of economic performance is, say, average cost per year, then fixed costs and recurring costs are mixed together to produce such an average. It is highly unlikely that this will produce smooth cost functions, as the fixed costs of plant investment and of quality management systems will be dramatically different between large regions of process capability. For example, unless process capability is very high and reliable, an extensive quality assurance must be in place and the direct costs of scrap and rework may be comparatively small.

The last of Crosby's 'absolutes of quality management' provides us with an indication of another problem by drawing our attention to the price of non-conformance. This may be defined as the total of all costs of manufacturing and service that would not have been incurred had the product been built exactly Right First Time. Obviously, this will include the costs of scrap, rework, inspection and further testing. It also includes quality management costs as mentioned above. Perhaps most seriously of all it must include the cost of buffer stocks necessary to ensure a smooth flow of materials when quality is unreliable, and it must include the cost of excess capacity to cater for delays and rework.

The key issue here is whether the impact of such less obvious costs is adequately included in our trade-off. No doubt some standard cost of labour and machine time may be included but this will substantially underestimate the opportunity costs involved in allowing for poor quality. Indeed, if a JIT-based materials management system is in operation, the opportunity costs of poor quality may well exceed all the other costs in consideration here.

Thus Fig. 5.2 is missing an essential third dimension to indicate the probable impact of the opportunity cost of non-conformance on other parts of the manufacturing system. If we use OPT style terminology, such costs will be very high at bottlenecks as a loss of throughput is the result of non-conformance. At non-bottlenecks the cost is in extra stock and an inability to reduce the extra capacity. In a poorly managed environment where excessive stocks and capacity are the norm the opportunity cost of non-conformance is tactically very low (scrapped material and variable costs of rework, say) though the strategic cost, measured as the inability to improve materials flow, is high. Where the total system's cost of non-conformance is high, Fig. 5.3 may provide a more realistic picture of the total situation and here we see the necessity for high process capability to be reliably maintained. Whether this should actually involve a policy of Zero Defects is still open to question. Similarly, whether high process capability is maintained by advanced engineering of the process or

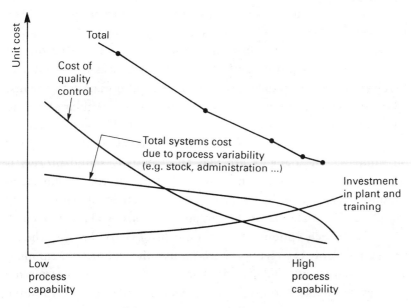

Figure 5.3 Economics of quality: modern view

by use of simple but well maintained processes, is a key decision for any manufacturing company.

It is of particular importance to note here the need to re-assess whether traditional costing systems are adequate in providing appropriate information for quality management (see examples and discussion in Cullen and Hollingum (1988)). This is a topic we return to in Chapter 6.

Statistical quality control

Quality assurance is one of the areas of management which traditionally has had a high technical input from statisticians in the development of appropriate sampling procedures. These may be based on measurements of key variables of materials and products or on attributes, usually summarized as a decision that a sampled item is or is not defective (or sometimes on a count of the number of defects).

Statistical Quality Control (SQC) involves two sets of procedures which are quite different in construction. Statistical Process Control (SPC) has as its objective the provision of a control system to maintain process performance through the use of samples of output. Typically, the output from a process is regularly sampled, measurements of key variables are taken, various statistics (such as mean and standard deviation) are calculated from the measurements and decisions on the maintenance of process performance are taken, usually to continue, to re-sample or to stop the process and make appropriate adjustments. Thus SPC is a dynamic control mechanism where regular sampling and immediate feedback of results are important. The statistical input is to make clear the balance of risks involved in making decisions based on samples. The dangers are that an essentially sound process is stopped or a process which is going out of control is allowed to continue, in each case due to the inevitable variability of items actually sampled. SPC makes clear the sampling options available to control these risks. Such options include pre-control charts for use when a process has newly been set up, charts for use when a process is running, and cumulative sum (CUSUM) charts, the latter being an example of a device intended to give advance warning that an unfavourable trend in sample results is developing.

The fact noted above that SPC usually involves charting, based on simple statistics, shows that its procedures were quite rightly in the past designed for manual use by operators and inspectors with relatively little training in statistics. This situation may be dramatically changed by the use of AMT though the potential for:

- the use of automatic test and measuring equipment
- the computer-based calculation of statistics of greater complexity if appropriate for decision making

- the automatic display of graphs showing dynamic features of the evolving performance of a process
- the maintenance of a comprehensive database of process statistics for long-term control

SPC is a key decision-making aid in quality management, whether traditional or JIT-style systems are in operation, and one which may be considerably enhanced by AMT. However, it should be remembered that maintaining control in the sense used in SPC does not ensure that tolerances are met. A process may be adjusted to produce at its best, but that may still not be sufficient, i.e. the process may lack capability. In this case, either a high level of defective output must be accepted as the norm or a selection process instituted for the output. In this case SPC has two important roles. One is to keep the process producing at its, admittedly inadequate, best in order to keep defectives to a minimum. The other role is as a control mechanism applied to the selection process itself as this is now critical to ensuring quality.

The other major branch of SQC is product control by acceptance sampling. Here a batch of materials or products is sampled and a decision is taken to accept or reject the batch (when the batch is then submitted to 100 per cent inspection and selection). This decision will be based on measurements of variables or on attributes and may involve re-sampling in marginal cases. Once again statistical theory provides a basis for the assessment of the risks of wrongly accepting or wrongly rejecting the batch. Use is normally made of the BS 6000 series of sampling plans when designing acceptance sampling procedures. Such procedures also provide a possibly delayed feedback on the general performance of preceding processes or on the performance of materials suppliers.

Quality assurance through BS 5750

The British Standard (BS) 5750 sets standards for quality assurance systems, embracing all the quality-related procedures in a company from supply to delivery. It is intended for use in companies of any size, which means it has wider applicability than the Defence Standards from which it evolved. In its 1987 form it has an international standard, ISO 9000, associated with it. The British Standards Institution argues that BS 5750 will set the standard for quality management for the majority of companies in the near future.

The standard is based on the idea that quality means fitness for purpose, a notion which embraces the ideas developed above. A company wishing to obtain BS 5750 certification must develop a Quality Manual which comprehensively states its procedures for quality management, its objectives and the responsibilities of staff involved. It is then subjected to an audit and must take care to maintain its quality systems. The scope of the systems depends on the company and may involve design, manufacture and final inspection.

It is expected that companies gaining BS 5750 will be making good use of SPC, of problem-solving techniques, planned maintenance and so forth. Indeed the standard is very demanding, particularly for the smaller firm, but its value in bringing together a wide range of quality management ideas and welding them into a set of procedures tailored for individual companies is very considerable, provided equal care is also taken in changing attitudes to quality management.

6 Corporate objectives and strategy

Introduction

It is tempting to dismiss any prolonged discussion on management systems' objectives by arguing that 'profitability' is the objective of any commercial venture. In this case each sub-system of a manufacturing company should act as a profit centre and each decision taken by management should be based on increasing future profitability. Investments in AMT should therefore be made with the intention of directly reducing costs or increasing revenue. This line of argument leaves open a number of issues which we explore below and point to ways in which a company's purpose might be better articulated for the benefit of management and a range of stakeholders.

What is meant by 'profitability'?

Companies are owned by their shareholders, who might reasonably expect management to make decisions which give them the best returns for their investment. Such returns take two basic forms (ignoring perks such as price reductions on products and services): dividends, and increases in the market value of the shares themselves, though the latter in turn reflect a market expectation of future dividends. Thus share prices show the market's current valuation of a company and management should in theory make investment decisions that 'maximize' the value of the company.

This statement focuses attention on a series of major problems, in particular the timing and uncertainty of future dividends and the flow of information to shareholders on the desirability of particular investments (particularly if seen as 'high tech').

Dividends are generated by a company's profitability which must be seen relative to the capital employed. Return on Investment (RoI), also known as Return on Capital Employed (ROCE), is generally regarded as providing an indication of the health of an enterprise in a given period of time. This leaves open the question of whether the market will value highly a company with current strong RoI but little expenditure on product and process development, or whether it will prefer a company with more modest current performance if the company can persuade investors that future potential for growth and profitability is enormous. In particular, how can a company persuade its investors that its plans are consistent with their objectives (without, of course, alerting its competitors to commercially sensitive details of these plans)? The techniques of investment appraisal detailed in Chapters 9 and 10 develop models which provide a quantified basis for analysis, which includes taking account of attitudes to risk and timing of cash flows for management and shareholders. Thus, ideas of profitability cannot be detached from other aspects of company performance.

This is a useful point at which to go back to first principles and ask if a more suitable fundamental objective for a company is to remain viable, i.e. to survive? Presumably viability must include satisfying the aspirations of shareholders to some degree at least and thus ideas such as maximizing profitability, value or RoI become sub-objectives. In particular, the 'viability' objective allows for the view that the firm should seek to provide a 'satisfactory' return for shareholders rather than attempt to maximize returns, the latter notion being problematic unless a complete mathematical model of a company and its environment is available (otherwise how does one know that an alternative set of actions would not lead to even greater profit?).

If viability seems a somewhat unhelpful operational measure of performance, one might note that a prime requirement is that viability must be continual – a company must not only be potentially profitable at some future point in time but must keep going until then, in terms of liquidity for example (i.e. be able to pay short-term debts). There is little point in developing a superb manufacturing system only for it to fail due to short-term liquidity problems (no doubt blamed on lack of faith and foresight by banks and other providers of capital). The result is even worse if a more pragmatic competitor then buys up your equipment at knock down prices and hires your expensively trained staff!

Environmental turbulence and uncertainty

The financial techniques mentioned above provide mathematical guidance in dealing with uncertain futures, if only to the extent that such risks can be quantified or even imagined. However, companies have competitors in their product markets, and may also experience severe competition when trying to obtain skilled labour, materials and state-of-art equipment. A crucial decision for a company is often whether to buy, say, current manufacturing or computing technology or to wait until such equipment has been tried out on competitors before buying new and improved versions. This is indeed a gamble, because a more innovative competitor can make a great success of his investment and gain time and market advantage to prevent the company ever regaining lost ground.

So, a major problem is forecasting all aspects of a future in which rapidly advancing technology plays a major part. The best that can be hoped is that the techniques available provide a way of structuring decision situations and of handling quantifiable factors so far as they exist. The result should be persuasive scenarios for the benefit of all parties whose confidence in the decision-making process is necessary.

Cause and effect

In Chapter 2 we examined a variety of systems' development situations. Imagine the simplest of these, say the replacement of a machine by a similar but cheaper to run alternative. If we make a number of assumptions regarding continuation of product demand, choice of discount rate and so forth, it is not unreasonable to link this specific investment decision with its impact on future profits (via reduction in cost) and hence on future RoI and viability.

Alternatively, consider the situation which arises if investment is proposed in developing a Flexible Manufacturing System, a Computer Aided Design facility or some essential but incomplete computer-based sub-system of a proposed Computer Integrated Manufacturing system. Professionals within the company may have no doubt as to the importance of the changes envisaged but to expect specific cause and effect linkages to be made to future cash flows is unreasonable. Perhaps most dangerous is the temptation to invent plausible connections based on whatever quantified factors are thought to be organizationally acceptable. Thus, computer systems have been bought on the basis of imagined savings in staff costs rather than improved availability of management information. This problem is explored in Chapters 10 and 14 where it is emphasized that realistic appraisal documentation is essential for project control, and for learning how to carry out more effective project appraisal in the future.

The series of diagrams shown in Fig. 6.1 illustrates the logic underlying this situation. Diagram A shows the simplest situation described above where investment leads directly to changes in profitability due to all other factors remaining constant. More usual is the situation reflected in Diagram B where a given investment is only one of a wide range of interacting factors affecting profitability. If the effects of these other factors can be forecasted (though no doubt with some residual uncertainty remaining), a comparison of the alternative scenarios 'invest' and 'not invest' should highlight specific changes in profitability and other performance measures attributable to the decision (though one must expect probabilities to be attached to outcomes).

Yet a company is rarely in the situation of making a single, isolated investment. More usually a range of process, product and infrastructure changes are made whose effects may best be articulated as intended changes in productivity, flexibility, cost structure and so forth. These intervening factors may then be linked with future RoI, allowing for uncertainty (Diagram C).

This is still a somewhat mechanistic approach – invest and results will automatically follow (with some riskiness related to the environment). It is surely more reasonable to invest in creating systems which may be managed to meet stated objectives.

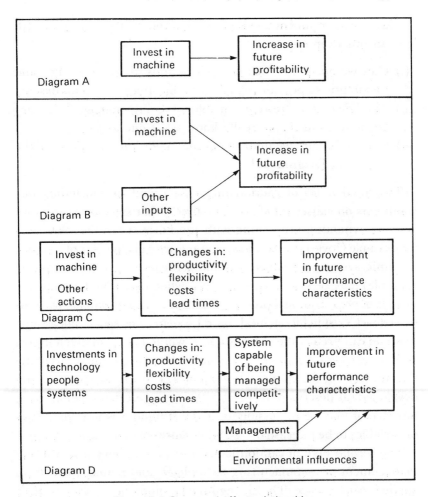

Figure 6.1 Cause and effect relationships

Consider the following hypothetical company objective (see p. 37):

> To design a (physical/human/information) manufacturing system which is capable of being managed to meet corporate objectives over a period of time in the context of a range of forecast environments.

The resulting causal pattern is given in Fig. 6.1, Diagram D, where 'management' should be interpreted as all relevant decision-makers rather than in any status related 'top management' sense.

This line of argument lays bare several important issues dealt with later in this chapter:

(i)   Can we adequately define such notions as 'productivity' and 'flexibility' to provide reliable sub-objectives in systems design?

(ii) The idea of a 'system capable of being managed' is very attractive, but do we really know what one looks like?

(iii) Can we be sure we understand the major linkages given by the arrows in Diagram D?

Two final notes of caution might be useful in concluding our comments on cause and effect. The first is that substantial work on systems dynamics, originating with Jay Forrester in the 1960s (see for example Coyle (1977)), shows that the actual behaviour of complex dynamic systems (of which a manufacturing company is a prime example) may be very surprising even when based on deterministic models of organizational procedures. That is, when complex patterns of feedback exist in hierarchical control systems, one should not assume that one can predict the outputs which will follow from given inputs without at least substantial experience in handling simulations of the system. Indeed, the mathematical models of chaotic systems recently developed (as described in Gleick (1987)) suggest that medium term forecasting may be impossible in many situations where the values of variables to be forecasted are highly sensitive to initial conditions.

The second note of caution is that our major concern is with the management of manufacturing technology, and management is an applied social science. The distinguished philosopher of science, Karl Popper, has commented that 'the characteristic problems of the social sciences arise only out of our wish to know the unintended consequences, and more especially the unwanted consequences which may arise if we do certain things' (Popper (1965)). Cause and effect relationships may be harder to determine than in the engineering disciplines also at work in developing new manufacturing systems.

The organizational context

Our discussion so far in this chapter has been intentionally unsophisticated in its placing of manufacturing process change in an organizational context. Such changes occur only as part of the on-going development of a company, development which in totality is reflected by the strategic management of the company.

Specialists in strategic management have developed a more comprehensive vocabulary for describing what we have so far simply referred to as objectives. The starting point is the notion of corporate values, enduring ideas that guide decisions within an organization over a long period of time. Typically one might point to the Rolls Royce emphasis on engineering excellence as part of a long-term company value system which affects all decision making in that company.

A company's values and purpose may be reflected in a 'mission statement', an example being that used publicly by ICL: 'ICL is an International Company dedicated to applying Information Technology to provide profitable, high value customer solutions for improved operational and management effectiveness.' Such a statement is of importance both in presenting the company to the outside world and also in providing general guidance for internal decision-makers. A mission statement will reflect long-term corporate strategy and will point to a company's long-term goals, which in turn might include, say, increasing its share in a specific market segment or developing new products to meet emerging market needs. Viability is assumed to be an over-riding goal. A high level of profitability relative to competitors might also be a long-term goal!

Only now can objectives be defined. These are precise, well-specified and quantifiable targets with stated times for their attainment. Typical might be stated growth rates, market shares and RoI to be achieved within a specific period of time. 'Maximize profitability' would be neither an objective nor a goal – it is simply not well-specified. Productivity, flexibility, human resource development, cost reduction, lead-time reduction and so forth may form the basis of objectives provided they can be precisely specified and adequately linked to long-term goals.

Strategic alternatives may now be developed to meet agreed goals and objectives. An obvious point is that alternative strategies and plans must embrace all functions in an organization, a point dealt with at length in Chapters 7 and 8. In particular, the pattern of objectives must be consistent with the organizational hierarchy which exists to meet them, that is, it must be possible to map objectives onto areas of responsibility using sub-objectives and operational action plans.

One problem area which is likely to figure prominently in the above, is the need to resolve potential conflicts between objectives, to make trade-offs and to ensure that the pursuit of a goal is not hindered by organizational in-fighting. For example, any organization has only limited resources which must be allocated to varying areas of need. An important part of this allocation process is the set of investment appraisal methods used. The grand designs of corporate planning may be defeated by 'accountant v. engineer' battles unless senior management can effectively promote an organizational culture which encourages co-operation.

A final point to remember is that organizations are not the only human activity systems under consideration here – individuals at all levels in a company have personal objectives which might not easily fit with each other or with the goals and objectives of the organization.

Manufacturing sub-objectives

Productivity

Productivity is generally taken to mean efficiency in industrial production and may be measured nationally to reflect economic health, or measured at factory or even machine level. In the latter cases it must not be confused with output measures. Productivity is a measure of how well a manufacturing system performs in terms of relating inputs to outputs.

As such it is an example of what in general business terms is called an efficiency measure. Four key types of index have been suggested for measuring the performance of firms (see for example Rowe, Mason and Dickel (1986)). These are:

(i) Efficiency – which relates outputs to the resource inputs consumed.
(ii) Effectiveness – which measures the extent to which an organization's goals and objectives have been achieved.
(iii) Equity – which measures the fairness with which an organization's activities have been conducted with respect to the legitimate expectations of differing groups of stakeholders.
(iv) Responsiveness – which measures the extent to which reasonable demands placed on the organization are satisfied.

Much work has been done by economists in charting productivity trends for various countries and sectors and in relating productivity at differing levels to input factors such as labour, rate of technological change and so forth. Such analysis is fraught with difficulty as evidenced by attempts, for example, to compare productivity in the car industry by quoting annual output per employee at plants in different countries without allowing for differences in automation of the plants and differences in vertical integration.

A classic problem is the confusion between machine utilization and productivity. It is all too easy to argue that an increase in utilization of an item of plant from, say, 80 per cent to 90 per cent is an increase in productivity, and hence will lead to greater output from the factory and therefore to greater profitability. Factory managers may even be monitored and rewarded on the levels of utilization of assets that they achieve. This in turn leads to the abberation of workers and machines busily producing items for stock in the hope that customer demand may occur.

For reasons such as the above, efficiency measures are often scorned by management theorists in favour of measures of effectiveness, ignoring the fact that, if carefully designed, efficiency and productivity measures can act as useful diagnostic aids and provide early warning that a plant may not be operating effectively. This was explored in Chapter 4 under the heading of OPT where it was emphasized that bottleneck resources should be managed efficiently.

However, it must always be remembered that, in terms of Fig. 6.1, investment in AMT may well improve some productivity index while not improving future effectiveness (Diagram C) nor the manageability of the system (Diagram D). Indeed, a system may be less manageable if investment has improved productivity whilst increasing costs, increasing lead-times or reducing flexibility (a measure related to responsiveness).

Flexibility

One gains the impression from current engineering literature that flexibility is desirable and fashionable. It is amusing to note how rarely management authors attempt to define it! An honourable exception is contained in Slack (1987) which attempts through a management survey and analysis of previous literature to classify some meanings of the word.

Central to this classification is a differentiation between range and response flexibility. The former relates to the range of things a system is capable of doing while the latter refers to the ease (in terms of time and cost) with which a system can be changed from doing one thing to another. These notions in turn may be related to changes in products, volumes of output, product mix and delivery. The various facilitating factors, i.e. sub-systems which may be flexible, are technology, labour, production planning procedures and so forth. An important point to note is that the managers in Slack's survey saw flexibility as a means to other ends rather than as an end in itself. A more comprehensive discussion of flexibility and adaptivity in the context of FMS is contained in Mandelbaum and Brill (1989), and Cox (1989) explores ways of measuring manufacturing flexibility.

So, although once again much care is required in definition, measures of flexibility have an important role to play in terms of Fig. 6.1 (Diagram D). Investments may clearly be seen to lead to improvements in some measure of flexibility, which then directly addresses the issue of the extent to which a system may be managed competitively.

Flexibility is also important in the strategic sense that as long-term forecasting may be particularly difficult, it is essential that major investment decisions taken now do not reduce the manageability of the company in the future, a point returned to in Chapter 8. A similar line of argument applies to the need to exercise care in defining cost and lead-time improvement measures, issues explored in later chapters. The importance of measuring the cost of non-conformance and of developing other quality-related measures was discussed in Chapter 5.

Management accounting

There has been a great deal of concern in recent years about the adequacy of traditional cost accounting in supporting decision making in integrated and automated environments. A general critique is contained in Johnson and Kaplan (1987), elegantly titled *Relevance Lost: The Rise and Fall of Management Accounting*. The worry is that traditional management accounting may be worse than useless in many situations. It may actually mislead and force managers to make poor decisions.

One positive point is that AMT has great potential for supporting any costing system through the direct gathering of information on resource usage, for example, the monitoring of the use of energy by each machine in a system. The major problem, however, seems not to be the accumulation of direct costs but the conventions involved in overhead allocation, depreciation and stock valuation. One approach, advocated in Ballew and Schlesinger (1989) is the adjustment of product costing systems to improve their relevance for decision-making in modern factories. Their approach seems somewhat complex and may be contrasted with the advice, typical of the 'excellence' movement, contained in Peters (1987) which states that control measurements should relate to a small number of crucially important variables and may be highly unusual, provided their implications have been thought through. Yet more radical is the OPT proposal (see Chapter 4) that the traditional costing system be abandoned entirely and replaced by a simple form of throughput accounting. There are reported instances of JIT based operations which adopt a similar approach.

A naïve view is that one index of success is possible in a manufacturing concern. Yet, even 'profitability' fails to achieve this. We have instead shown the need for a large number of inter-related performance measurements and inevitably this makes the task of management harder to comprehend, though hopefully easier to perform. In order to help the manager cope with this complexity, multiple criteria decision methods are available (for example see Buffa and Sarin (1987)) to help in arriving at trade-offs between conflicting sub-objectives.

7 Market strategy

The marketing function

A manufacturing company deals with many types of market, e.g. for labour, materials, equipment and so forth. In this chapter we will be concerned with the markets in which it exchanges products and services for the revenue essential for survival.

We begin with a consideration of the marketing function within a company and the managerial processes involved in exploring the needs of current and potential customers. This is an important topic for consideration, partly because of the ignorance which exists in many companies amongst manufacturing and technical staff of the contribution of their marketing colleagues. The marketing function is responsible for:

- identifying the requirements of those individuals in the environment that the company might reasonably expect to be customers in the future;
- forecasting the levels of demand which might be expected for particular products and services and the price, quality and delivery that the market will accept as attractive in the face of competition from other suppliers;
- co-ordinating the activities of the company to develop and improve products which should meet customer requirements;
- developing channels of information to customers which inform and persuade;
- ensuring actual delivery of the product and service when the customer requires it and to a level of quality which is satisfactory for meeting customers' evolving requirements;

- providing a service to ensure the product continues to meet requirements for an agreed period;
- monitoring customer satisfaction with the intention of maintaining the loyalty of the customer to the company's market offerings;
- monitoring the costs involved in this whole exercise to ensure that budgeted goals are attained.

The totality of the above may be summarized as the 'marketing process' and is illustrated in Fig. 7.1. Certain items in this figure, though of central concern to marketing staff, will not be explored here further. In particular, the exploration of the environment through various forms of market research (see for example Clifton, Nguyen and Nutt (1985)), the development of marketing mix strategies (the well known '4 Ps' of Product, Price, Promotion and Place, which could well be augmented by the 'S' of Service), and the practical

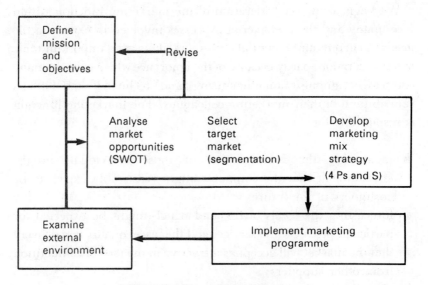

Figure 7.1 The marketing process

considerations of implementing a marketing programme are well covered in the many texts which exist describing this function. However, several related issues are of interest and are dealt with below, as they may be directly linked with the development of design and manufacturing strategies. These are the promotion of a marketing orientation within a company, the development of a competitive strategy, market segmentation, product positioning, life cycle models, the product portfolio approach and technological innovation.

Market orientation and competitive strategy

Marketing professionals rightly emphasize the importance not only of communication with the customer but also of communication within the company. If a company is to be customer-oriented rather than merely selling its existing product line, the marketing function has an important role to play in championing the customer's needs and requirements within the organization. This is often referred to as the need for a marketing orientation within a company – a corporate frame of mind which is very clear on the business the firm is in (its mission), what customer needs must be satisfied, where the company is heading in terms of developing the capability to satisfy those needs (this may include developments in processes, products, information systems etc.), and how the company must manage its internal and external activities to actually satisfy those customer needs while at the same time meeting its own objectives in terms of growth, profitability and ultimately survival. Such a mission statement must not be merely a collection of corporate platitudes but must surprise and motivate. In particular, it must set the company apart from its direct competitors in some important way.

Though many of the above activities are specific to marketing professionals and managers, it is obvious that there is a need for the development of marketing strategies which are intelligible to all staff in a company and which help to co-ordinate activities amongst individuals whose day-to-day concerns are quite disparate. As we shall argue, such a strategy is also essential for the development of manufacturing strategy, human resource development strategy and the specification of information systems.

Such strategies are particularly valuable in the face of market competition. Indeed they should be seen as essential components of a company's total 'competitive strategy'. A particular theme in current research in the area of corporate strategy is the development of such competitive strategies and the accompanying competitive tactics which may be employed to remain viable. Competition is present in many forms within an industry (see Porter (1985)). Obviously direct competition from similar products and services is likely unless some very favourable patents or copyrights exist. However, competition is also present in the markets which supply resources such as materials and labour. This may be to a company's advantage if supply exceeds demand, but if, for example, a number of manufacturers require scarce electronic components or new capital equipment then the suppliers of such goods are in a strong bargaining position. Also, existing patterns of competition within defined markets may be broken by new entrants to those markets and by the development of new products. Such innovations may be of technological origin or may be due to the inventiveness of competing companies in transferring existing technology to meet as yet unsatisfied or not recognized needs. Indeed invention may well be non-technological in designing a service or pattern of customer support which is particularly appreciated!

Porter lists three main ways in which companies may compete within an industry:

- overall cost leadership (based on the experience curve)
- product differentiation
- focus

Each of these is based on both marketing and manufacturing excellence and each requires well-developed and integrated marketing and manufacturing strategies (in the context of corporate planning, including also financial, human resource development and information strategies). For these strategies to be effectively developed, analytical tools such as the ones illustrated in this chapter are essential.

Market segmentation and product positioning

So far we have referred to 'markets' and 'products' as if we were quite sure that such concepts are unambiguous and intelligible. As we increase our knowledge of a particular market we will often find it consists less of a homogeneous set of identical customers and more of a grouping of roughly similar sub-markets. Such market segments may all purchase the same product if nothing else is available, but they could alternatively be profitable targets for a company with more refined market intelligence of the needs of a given segment and an ability to match such segments with more appropriate variations of the product.

An example might be the market for electrically powered hand tools, such as the electric drill, found not only in most homes but also in many work situations. It is obvious that the home owner with occasional aspirations to craftsmanship has radically different needs to the carpenter faced with a large estate of unfinished houses. Their needs differ in terms of the power of the drill, its reliability and the fittings which may be attached to convert it to other uses. A leading manufacturer of such tools might either develop an extensive product range to suit each market segment or develop a more limited range where each member of the range is suitable, possibly with minor adjustments, to meeting the requirements of consumers in several segments. A new or a smaller supplier to this market might select a limited number of market segments as his niche in the total market, and design products exclusively for them with a competitive emphasis on price, quality or product attributes as appropriate to the chosen segments. Creative suppliers will be continually looking for new market segments which might be satisfied by existing or modified products or for radically new ways of satisfying existing segments.

The process we are describing is essentially dynamic with changes frequently occurring in customers' expectations and suppliers' responses. The product and/or service being offered may thus be in a continual state of development and refinement. One useful concept in this context is that of the three levels of product:

- the *core product* is that which satisfies basic minimum requirements;
- the *formal product* is that more commonly found for sale and includes packaging, a brand name and so forth;
- the *augmented product* is the state-of-the-art offering including such additional features as are likely to attract the more adventurous buyer.

As will readily be observed from both consumer and industrial products and services, an augmented product may soon become standard while a core product may equally become unsatisfactory as customers' perceptions of their requirements, and even their actual needs, change over time.

The implications of these simple observations for design and manufacturing are profound. In particular, the need for the reduction of design lead-times, the development of more effective interfaces between design and manufacturing, and for greater flexibility in manufacturing have been felt by many companies.

Market segmentation and research is concerned with identifying customers and their basic product requirements. There is also an urgent need to know the actual basis on which buying decisions are made. In particular, a manufacturer must know which product attributes are essential, which are desirable, what quality and reliability levels must be met, what prices are competitive, what delivery lead-times are acceptable, what accompanying services are required (e.g. finance, maintenance, training, consultancy), and above all else such information must be seen in the light of current and possible future offerings from competitors.

Product positioning is a very useful concept in that it refers to the position of a particular product/service in a given market segment in comparison to competing products. The comparison is made through perceptions of customers' preferences measured on scales which reflect the basis on which buying decisions are made at the current time and forecasted into the future. Forecasts are also necessary of competitive actions along such scales, and indeed of events which might change the very basis of decision-making (for example, a radically new and superior product which will be bought by most customers even at high prices and with long delivery delays).

A useful device in carrying out product positioning is the construction of perceptual maps for a given segment of the market. Consumer research is used to list the factors which influence buyers' choices between competing products in the given market segment (it is important to note that such factors are likely to vary between segments). Some factors will reflect basic, mandatory or 'qualifying' features of the product/service, i.e. reflect criteria which must be satisfied for purchase to be even considered by the customer. What remains are the factors on which suppliers of the product actually compete. For a perceptual map to be constructed the crucial sub-set of such factors must be identified and the strength of customer preference measured. Typically, two measurable factors will then form the basis for a graph (a hypothetical example is given in Fig. 7.2 – real graphs require substantial investment in research resources, incorporate confidential information including attitudes and intentions of the company concerned, and are not readily available).

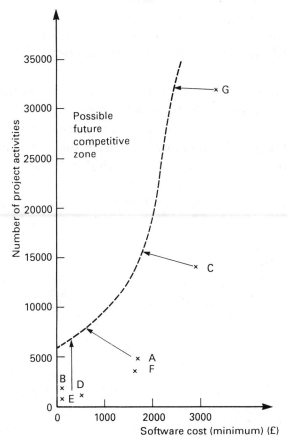

Note: For illustration it has been assumed that cost and 'number of project activities' supported by the package are the basis of buyers' decision-making. It is also assumed that all 'qualifying criteria' have been met.

Figure 7.2 Perceptual map: price and performance of project management software packages

Such maps should then be used creatively to explore strategic options and likely competitor responses. They provide an important input to the process of strategy formulation. The factors incorporated in the map are referred to in Hill (1985) as 'order-winning criteria' and along with the 'qualifying criteria' mentioned above are an important feature in determining manufacturing strategy as described in Chapter 8. A crucial observation to be made at this point is that the composition of the sets of both qualifying and order-winning criteria will change over time and in relation to the product life cycle (see below).

The Product Life Cycle and portfolio planning

A useful, if controversial, concept in helping us to visualize the dynamics of product lives is the Product Life Cycle (PLC). A typical form of the PLC is shown in Fig. 7.3, though it must be emphasized that real life cycle graphs are far more irregular than this idealized form. Variations exist in the descriptions attached to the various stages of the PLC but the ones used here (introduction, growth, maturity and decline) are widely understood. A Product Life Cycle model should

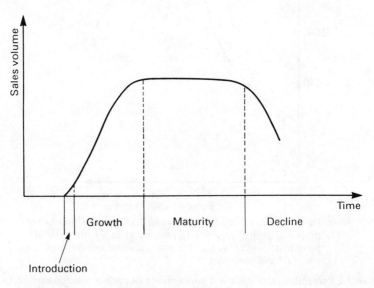

Figure 7.3 Product life cycle

only be considered for a well-defined product within a well-defined market segment, that is, it shows the relationship of the product to the segment over a period of time. Critics of the use of this model refer to problems in defining 'product' and in particular agreeing when a product is really 'new' and its PLC is beginning. However, for our purposes the PLC serves as a useful tool for discussion and a valuable reminder that innovation is important.

Product Life Cycles should be seen in the context of the stages of maturity of the markets they refer to. One may also wish to consider Market Life Cycles (MLC), provided once again one is secure in one's understanding of how a particular market is defined.

The stages of the PLC model can be linked with a number of aspects of product management. In Fig. 7.4 we link typical cash flows and profits to PLC stages, while in Fig. 7.5 a number of organizational functions and actions are seen in a PLC context. As we mentioned earlier, qualifying and order winning criteria (to use Hill's terms) are likely to vary with the stage of the product cycle. Thus, in the early stages of growth, prompt delivery may win orders, whereas in the mature stage low prices may win orders, while quality and delivery may be qualifying criteria. These are only examples, however, because the whole point of product positioning analysis is to find the criteria which actually hold in a given situation and base one's competitive strategy for marketing and manufacturing on the insights which this brings.

Traditional PLC theory tends to suggest that a company invests during the introduction and growth stages of the PLC in order to gain a long-term advantage through high market share which will yield considerable profits for many years to come. More recently, in some markets (a quoted example being Casio products in the calculator market) life cycles have become dramatically shortened and such situations are only profitable if development and manufacturing set-up costs can be recovered very quickly during the growth phase.

The PLC model refers to a single product and it is obviously important that a company considers also the totality of its products, i.e. its product portfolio. This is of particular utility from a financial point of view, as product cash flows vary considerably at different stages of the PLC, i.e. it would present considerable financial problems

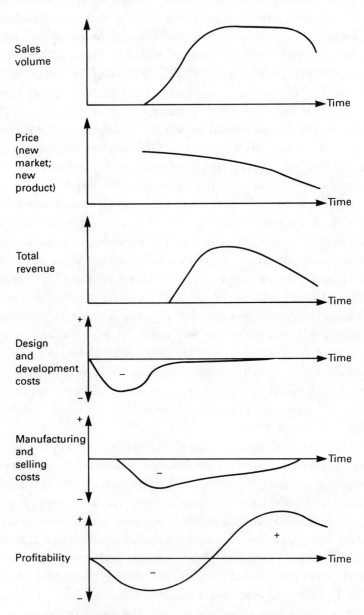

Figure 7.4 Product life cycle: cost, revenue and profit

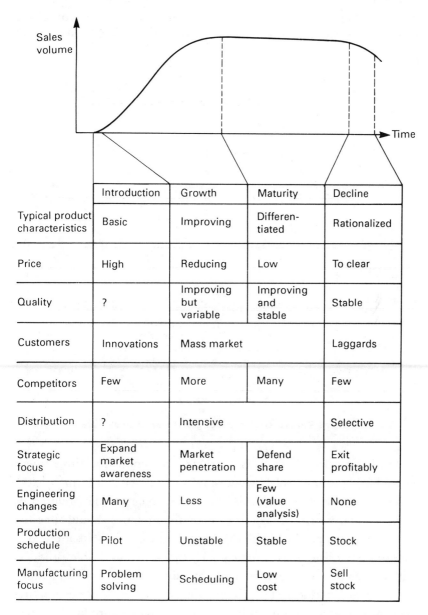

	Introduction	Growth	Maturity	Decline
Typical product characteristics	Basic	Improving	Differen-tiated	Rationalized
Price	High	Reducing	Low	To clear
Quality	?	Improving but variable	Improving and stable	Stable
Customers	Innovations	Mass market		Laggards
Competitors	Few	More	Many	Few
Distribution	?	Intensive		Selective
Strategic focus	Expand market awareness	Market penetration	Defend share	Exit profitably
Engineering changes	Many	Less	Few (value analysis)	None
Production schedule	Pilot	Unstable	Stable	Stock
Manufacturing focus	Problem solving	Scheduling	Low cost	Sell stock

Figure 7.5 Product life cycle: management implications

to a company if all its products were at the introduction or growth
stages. In Fig. 7.6 we show a variation of the BCG (Boston Consulting
Group) portfolio model which links the BCG approach to the PLC
model.

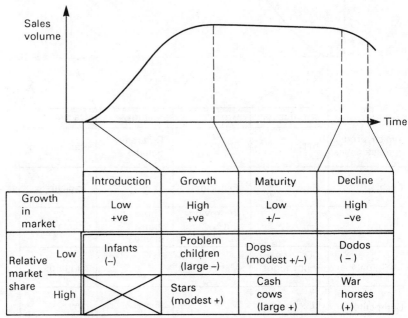

Cash flow assessment in brackets

Figure 7.6 Product life cycle: growth and market share

Market portfolio models draw their inspiration from investment
portfolio planning models where investments with differing yields,
growth and risk factors are mixed in ways which suit the preferences
of individual investors. The idea is that companies should time the
development of products with differing characteristics so that the total
picture is consistent with their goals, that is, some stable products
with proven markets and moderate profitability are mixed with a range
of promising products which should yield a proportion of outstanding
successes. This approach has led to a proliferation of product portfolio
models, some specific to particular large companies, which are
described in texts on corporate strategy. The operationalization of
this concept is quite difficult and requires considerable amounts of

market and competitor research, but at the very least it provides a rational basis for the formation and co-ordination of company strategy.

The BCG approach is based on the assumption, supported by considerable empirical evidence, that unit costs are inversely related to production volumes (the experience curve effect) and hence that the rate at which cash is earned is associated with relative market shares. In contrast, growth in a market requires the use of cash and it is this balance between relative share (cash inflow) and growth (cash outflow) which is reflected in the BCG matrices. A matrix might show a portfolio of a company's products to indicate relative cash inflows and outflows (i.e. how one product may support another at a less profitable stage of its life cycle), or it might be used in comparison with similar charts of other companies to show relative competitive position and gain some insight into the strategic choices available to competitors.

Another valuable strategic analysis tool which overlaps to some extent with the BCG approach, but also relates to a range of manufacturing and financial issues, is the PIMS (Profit Impact of Market Strategy) approach (see for example Chandler (1987)).

However, in the context of the PLC and BCG approaches it must also be said that a number of writers are highly critical of such methods. The PLC model has been subjected to vigorous criticism, for example, that it is based on a possibly inappropriate biological analogy, its stages are hard to define, and perhaps of most importance, that it gives an impression of inevitability, while in fact, product, or rather brand, lives are actively managed (see contributions in Baker (1987), in particular pp 242-3 on critiques of the PLC and on the relationship between PLC models and Porter's evolutionary stages of industry development, and also the popular James (1984)). Many quoted examples of PLCs may indeed be idealized reconstructions of reality long after the real, competitive events have taken place.

Possibly the best view to take is that such models are 'tools for thought', to use a phrase of the biologist C.H.Waddington (1977). They represent conceptual models for structuring complex events and facilitating communication between a wide range of concerned managers.

Relationship between the marketing and design functions

While in this book we have been concerned with AMT, and integration in manufacturing has provided a focus for discussion, an alternative approach might have been a consideration of integrated product development (see Andreasen and Hein (1987)). A vast literature exists on the management of product innovation and development and on the relationship between design and manufacturing. We have sought merely to emphasize the role of CADCAM systems in facilitating product development.

Many companies derive their competitive edge from the relationship between their design and marketing functions, often with manufacturing being sub-contracted out of the organization entirely. We have briefly explored this relationship in Chapter 5 in the context of the management of quality and would point to the increasing use of Taguchi-style methodologies as providing manufacturable design specifications.

Recent literature on design integration points to the need to develop systems which best complement human and machine attributes. At least we have as yet been spared workerless design studios and 'lights out offices'! Many of the ideas on project management found in Chapters 13 and 14 have their origin in product design projects. One positive point we should make, therefore, is the value to be gained from the regular movement of technical and managerial staff between design and manufacturing, always allowing for the very specialist skills and knowledge needed in each area. This advice might be extended to movements into and out of the marketing function.

Concluding example

We finally illustrate the ideas presented in this chapter with a historic example of an entrepreneur who successfully combined a knowledge of market needs, design inventiveness and manufacturing innovation.

Josiah Wedgwood — an example of the entrepreneur in action

Josiah Wedgwood was born in 1730 in the area now called the Staffordshire Potteries. In 1759 he set up his own production facilities and by his death in 1795 had played a very prominent part in transforming the area and the local industry from a primitive and isolated collection of pot-makers to an internationally respected centre for the manufacture of high quality tableware and ornamental pottery. The company he founded has continued as a leading member of the industry to this day with new designs existing side by side with many from the company's past.

Wedgwood's influence spread from technical developments in the constituents of his product, through production innovations, a highly entrepreneurial approach to the market place, and a leading role in promoting the Potteries as a centre of manufacturing. The latter was most obvious through the development of the transportation infrastructure, in particular through canal building.

His understanding of the market and production implications of the product life cycle (if such jargon is not too anachronistic) is shown in his development of Queensware. The origin was an order, received in 1765 from Queen Charlotte, to make a tea service. This successfully completed order opened the door to a series of aristocratic fashion leaders whose adoption of Wedgwood products facilitated their sale to a wider market. Wedgwood, however, was careful to maintain his prices at a high level and thus maintain the association of his name with high quality and innovative products.

A wide range of products was designed for specific market niches. The depression of the early 1770s was survived, partly through a refusal to drop price and quality levels. Problems in this period included a cash flow crisis, with excessive showroom stocks, and industrial disputes. Despite the obvious craft basis of the industry, Wedgwood developed mass production techniques based on standard moulds so that much of the less elaborate ware could be produced by semi-skilled labour. He similarly increased mechanization and produced families of similar items in large batch sizes to reduce set-up times and losses. This is possible in an industry where much product variety, in tableware at least, is based only on the later decorating stages of production.

Production changes allowed Wedgwood to vastly increase production while maintaining quality. Thus a wider, middle-class and international market could be exploited, based on the prestige created by his Royal commissions. The latter included the publicity coup of a 952 item table and dessert service ordered by Catherine the Great of Russia. The items made were decorated with 1,244 views of land and property whose owners flocked to an exhibition of the completed ware. The original commission made little profit on its £2,700 price but its publicity value both directly to property owners and indirectly to the general population was obvious.

Wedgwood achieved a balanced development on three fronts. First of all, his products included new designs and materials and he made innovations in manufacturing processes, including being elected a Fellow of the Royal Society in 1783 for his invention of a pyrometer. His organization of production adapted to changing trading conditions, though he seems to have had difficulties in controlling the logistics of distribution and sales. Finally he had an excellent understanding of why people might buy his products – the order winning criteria, and managed to move his products through a life cycle which started with Royal patronage and moved on to large batch production without losing his competitive edge. (The life of Josiah Wedgwood and the development of the pottery industry have been extensively chronicled; see Tames (1984) for a simple introduction.)

8 Manufacturing strategy

Introduction

The previous two Chapters have laid the foundations for a consideration of manufacturing strategy by dealing with the strategy of the organization as a whole and with the way the organization approaches the market place. Having decided where the organization intends to go we must consider the management processes concerned with how it gets there.

This involves the formulation and implementation of a manufacturing strategy which in turn has implications for design, information, service and human resource strategies. The manufacturing strategy also cannot be seen in isolation from the financial strategies of the organization. The next two Chapters deal with the financial appraisal of alternative manufacturing and associated choices, a process which must be consistent with the organization's financial strategy.

A useful characterization of types of strategy is used in Wheelwright (1987). This defines three levels of strategy as follows:

(i) Corporate strategy: concerned with fundamental questions such as 'what business are you in?' and with the acquiring and allocating of resources. This may include a corporate view of the development of technological resources.

(ii) Business strategy: the level addressed by, for example, Porter's ideas of competitive strategy, i.e. how does a company actually compete in a chosen segment of a market.

(iii) Functional strategy: deals with how separate functions (e.g. manufacturing, design) support the business in meeting its objectives.

It is important to avoid any simplistic linear interpretation of the process of strategy formulation at any of the above levels. It is easy to think that a corporate strategy gives rise to a market strategy which in turn gives a manufacturing strategy and hence on to human resourcing, and so on. In practice the process is one of going back and forth between strategic levels and functions until a coherent balance has been achieved. In particular, some strategic decisions involve very long timescales in their development and use of resources. Examples of these might be:

(i) investment in new sites and major items of plant and equipment;
(ii) investment in the development of people, in particular technical and managerial skills;
(iii) the whole process of arriving at well established products and the development of market reputation for quality or responsiveness to client needs;
(iv) the acquisition of data and information reflecting the long-term design, engineering and commercial activities of the organization;
(v) the development of systems and procedures (for example quality assurance, production management).

It may well be that problems of market research and forecasting entail the market strategy of a company having a shorter lead-time than manufacturing and human resource development. The logical implication of this situation is either to reduce the time it takes to develop manufacturing systems and their infrastructure, or to develop systems which are flexible in terms of range of options and response time. Though easy to state this is particularly hard to do and is at the core of the problem many companies have with practical implementation of manufacturing strategy.

However, it would be unwise to assume that all companies even attempt to take an enlightened long-term view of all manufacturing-related investment decisions. Hayes and Wheelwright (1985) have suggested that a range of generic roles exists for the manufacturing function within an organization. While qualifying this list as key stages along a development continuum, the roles provide a useful reference point and a series of managerial postures which are readily identifiable. In their latter work (Hayes, Wheelwright and Clark (1988)) the authors expand on their theme by providing prescriptions for moving from a Stage 2 to a Stage 4 company.

The stages in the development of manufacturing's strategic role are listed below and summarized in Fig. 8.1.

	Internal	External
Neutral	Stage 1 (low grade technical operation)	Stage 2 (parity with similar organizations)
Supportive	Stage 3 (manufacturing strategy)	Stage 4 (compete through manufacturing excellence)

Figure 8.1 Development of the strategic role of manufacturing

Stage 1
The 'internally neutral' stage when manufacturing is seen as a low-grade technical operation whose potential for causing problems should be minimized. Outside consultants will be used when major decisions are necessary and internal control systems monitor efficiency.

Stage 2
The 'externally neutral' stage when parity with similar outside organizations is sought, usually through capital investment in plant and equipment.

Stage 3
The 'internally supportive' stage when a genuine manufacturing strategy is formulated to be consistent with the strategy of the business, i.e. long-term manufacturing goals are recognized and pursued imaginatively.

Stage 4
The 'externally supportive' stage when the organization's competitive strategy is at least partly dependent on the manufacturing strategy. In this case new technologies are anticipated and seen as a real source

of competitive advantage. Process and product technological developments proceed together and are mutually supportive learning activities.

A further set of characteristics of Stage 4 companies are given in Wheelwright (1987) as their five capabilities:

  (i) they develop the skills of their workers until they are the best in the industry;
 (ii) they see long-term worker involvement in the business as essential;
(iii) they continually make incremental improvements in their technological capability;
(iv) they improve their process technologies through manufacturing engineering until actual machines and systems perform better than any in comparable firms;
 (v) they compete through superior product and service quality.

This list will hold no surprises for those familiar with the 'excellence' stream of literature discussed in Chapter 3, particularly Peters (1987). However, it would be a mistake to assume that a given company consistently fits into one of the above categories. Different sites or different product lines may exhibit the characteristics of different stages or perhaps an inconsistent mixture of attributes. The stages may best be seen as a vehicle for debate, rather than unique classification.

Though this Chapter will concentrate on manufacturing decisions, largely due to the very useful ideas which have been put forward to aid strategy formulation in this area, we should remember that the customer receives a package of benefits from a manufacturing company and we will later consider the strategic development of such an integrated package.

Formulation of a manufacturing strategy

In recent years a very real contribution has been made by researchers to the idea that manufacturing strategy is a coherent discipline with its own body of knowledge and techniques. These are mainly concerned with the choice of appropriate process forms and with the development of a supporting infrastructure. In this section we will concentrate initially on the set of ideas presented in Hill (1985) and amplified in the diagram shown in Fig. 8.2.

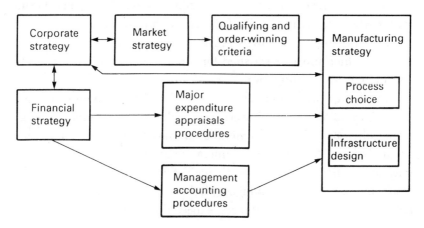

Figure 8.2 Manufacturing strategy

It should be remembered that a strategy makes explicit a set of choices, each of which involves trade-offs between alternative costs and benefits. It is often simplistically stated that manufacturing's role is to provide the customer with 'the right product at the required quality at the right time and the right price'. Whilst obviously these are necessary conditions for success (depending on what is meant by 'right') they are not sufficient conditions – the organization must also be profitable in a competitive set of markets. Thus a series of decisions must be made which have repercussions over differing time horizons. Typically, one must decide whether to make or buy at each stage of the product. If manufacturing is chosen, decisions about capacity (amount, form, etc.) must be made. Decisions about the form of wage payment system and the practical organization of the shop floor are not easy to make or implement in a stable market environment. Inflexibility in such areas may be very damaging in a dynamic and evolving market. Any prescription for strategy formulation, such as that given below, must be seen in the context of the positive support it gives to the decision-making processes of real managers in a complex world.

Hill begins with a consideration of corporate and market strategies but is then concerned with finding appropriate links between these and manufacturing choices. One way this can be done has been outlined in Chapter 7 above, that is, through the stages of product life cycles and the main criteria the customer is likely to use at differing stages when deciding which of the competing products to buy.

In any buying decision there are likely to be a number of 'qualifying criteria' which must be satisfied for a particular product to even be considered as a potential purchase. A number of products may satisfy the qualifying criteria and then the choice between them must be made on the basis of 'order-winning criteria'. If this two-stage process sounds rather obvious it must be remembered that these two sets of criteria are not static. What is at one time a winning property of a product may at another time become a widely offered qualifying property. Thus, the sets of criteria change with the stage of the product life cycle and they also change as customers' expectations adjust to actual market conditions.

So, in principle it is not possible to state what are unchanging qualifying and winning criteria, but the following list expresses some of the main possibilities.

  (i) *Price* (including all extra costs and benefits such as financing arrangements).
 (ii) *Product features* – quality as represented by the specification of the properties of the product and service.
(iii) *Quality* as demonstrated by the reliability with which actual products conform to specifications and requirements, indeed are fit for use.
 (iv) *Design flexibility* – tailoring of the product to meet specific customer requirements.
  (v) *Delivery lead-time* – delivery dates quoted.
 (vi) *Delivery performance* – the reliability with which quoted delivery dates are met.
(vii) *Volume flexibility* – the ability to supply the product in the volumes required by customers without compromising delivery lead-times or performance.
(viii) *Quotation performance* – speed with which quotations are produced, in fact the general effectiveness with which a supplier

reacts from the first moment of an approach by a customer.

(ix) *Service* – professionalism of the delivery of the total service package, with particular emphasis on consultancy and customer training components.

(x) *After-sales support* – servicing effectiveness.

(xi) *Stability* of the supplier to be able to continue providing support and develop new, compatible products (particularly important for suppliers of computing hardware and software).

The length of this list shows the range of dimensions along which companies may compete in attracting and keeping customers. It also shows the complexity and necessary integration of the operational strategies needed to maintain competitiveness. Manufacturing process and infrastructure decisions are crucial and AMT provides potential sources of competitive advantage relevant to most of the above criteria.

It should be remembered that items in the above list may be viewed in more than one way. Though included in the list as potential competitive capabilities, they may also reflect actual tactical decisions. Thus 'quotation performance' refers to the development of the ability to provide speedy quotations if required. The same phrase might indicate a company's actual performance on a given occasion.

If we examine this more closely we see three ways of looking at the criteria.

(i) From the customer's point of view:
 – qualifying criteria give threshold values;
 – winning criteria are the basis for choice;
 but both require extensive information regarding what is on offer from competing firms.

(ii) From the supplier's tactical point of view:
 – the technological and capacity characteristics of the company give a set of feasible criteria (allowing for trade-offs between them; for example, a given level of customization of the product may require an extension of the quoted delivery lead-time though this may be critically effected by the CAD/CAM links in existence);
 – the current order book and existing priorities further reduce the set of available options;

>   – management must now compete within these constraints
>   in an attempt to satisfy customer needs profitably (see Chapter
>   6 on the objectives of an AMT-based system).
> (iii) From the supplier's strategic point of view:
>   – the supplier must decide on the set of criteria he/she wishes
>   to be feasible in the future;
>   – capital investment and training must take place to produce
>   the required characteristics;
>   – management processes must be in place which enable
>   managers to compete profitably in meeting customer needs
>   through the use of the capabilities available.

We have not explored which functional sub-systems should be charged
with developing the criteria listed or with their effective delivery. This
is a particularly demanding challenge for organizational designers.
We have also not provided a detailed indication of the potential role
of AMT. However, it should be noted that such sub-systems are
inextricably linked to each other and to other systems in providing
market support. Companies at each of the Hayes and Wheelwright
stages of development will have differing views of the role of
manufacturing in providing the above. We will assume an organization
at the later stages, seeking a decisive contribution from manufacturing,
and therefore expecting manufacturing to be flexible in its response
and to learn from experience.

Assuming that an analysis of qualifying and order-winning criteria
for all products has been performed and related to product strategies,
Hill is next concerned with relating this to process choice. One
prerequisite is that decisions have been made on the extent to which
parts are bought in or manufactured, and another is that engineering
alternatives have been outlined on how things might be made. Process
choice relates to the alternative manufacturing approaches or modes
of operation and not, as might be thought, to the actual equipment.
This choice is strongly related to sales volumes expected and to the
qualifying and order-winning criteria listed above.

Hill lists five 'classic' types of process, though much of his argument
concentrates on the three types most common in general
manufacturing, i.e. jobbing, batch and line. These, however, should

be taken as archetypes, as much of modern manufacturing is aimed at combining the advantages of each into more integrated systems.

Jobbing or job-shop production involves the manufacture of unique items to meet the requirements of specific customers. Such production usually requires highly skilled employees rather than high levels of capital investment. The volume of items produced is low, but the value added to each item is considerable.

Batch production covers a wide range of manufacturing situations where more than one of a specific item is required either now or in the future. Traditionally a number of items might move together between production facilities until work on them is completed. The production system control methodologies described in Chapter 4 are mainly concerned with this type of process, which is difficult to manage due to the continual need to arrive at trade-offs between cost control and scheduling to meet due dates.

Line manufacture involves substantial capital investment in providing dedicated facilities for the cost-effective production of large numbers of similar items.

However, when one describes the classic process types, exceptions immediately spring to mind, for example, unlike the original Ford Model T production line, a modern car plant will produce a wide variety of products. However, the important principle here is that this variety is pre-planned and controlled whereas the variety in a job shop is inherent and involves day-by-day reaction to customer needs.

Figure 8.3 shows a graph which illustrates the relationship between process forms, while Fig. 8.4 illustrates how typical modern technologies facilitate specific processes. A particularly valuable device for exploring theoretical or actual differences between process forms is process profiling which is developed in considerable detail in Hill (1985). This form of analysis is valuable because it firmly links business and technical choices and implications in a simple framework. It also allows one to see quite clearly the intentions behind more modern ideas such as Group Technology and Flexible Manufacturing Systems in widening the options available to the manufacturing strategist.

This form of analysis also supports an idea developed some time ago often referred to as 'the focused factory'. An early paper by

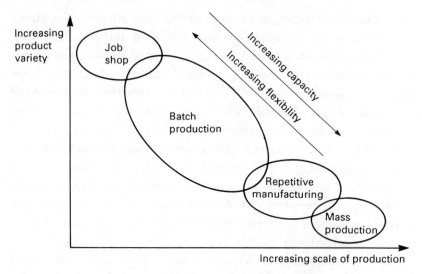

Figure 8.3 Relationships between process forms

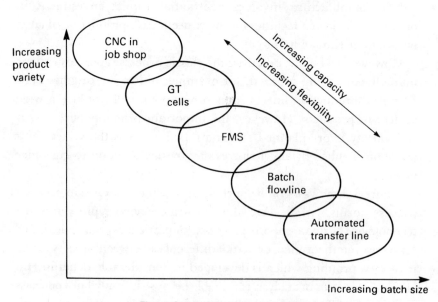

Figure 8.4 Process form and AMT

Wickham Skinner (1974) describes this very clearly by arguing that a production unit which focuses on a narrow and coherent range of activities will perform better than one which attempts to do everything at once. Skinner notes three basic concepts in support of this idea:

(i) 'There are many ways to compete besides by producing at low cost' – an idea consistent with the later work of Porter on competitive strategy. Focused factories and niche marketing go well together.

(ii) 'A factory cannot perform well on every yardstick' – once again an emphasis on explicitly trading-off one objective against another (e.g. low cost against flexibility). One wonders if the more recent 'excellence' movement provides contrary advice, a point to which we will return.

(iii) 'Simplicity and repetition breed competence' – the learning or experience curve effect described in greater detail in Hill (1985) and providing the basis of the BCG product portfolio planning matrix mentioned in the previous Chapter.

Skinner lists the main characteristics of the focused factory as: the use of mainly proven and mature technology; a matching of manufacturing objectives to specific customer demands (as described as qualifying and order winning criteria above); maintaining consistent volumes of flow (small exceptional orders are not mixed with mainstream large batch production); and consistent quality requirements. If a factory's product range has to be large and varied, the system should be split into smaller, more consistent, sub-systems which focus on the achievement of specific objectives in a concentrated manner. This set of ideas makes particular sense if one considers the management of the human resources required for production.

The diagram shown in Fig. 8.2 leads us now to a consideration of the manufacturing infrastructure, i.e. the systems which support manufacturing. These include an appropriate organizational structure, production control system, quality management system, costing and budget control system, and so forth. One must also look to the interface between manufacturing and other systems (such as design and order processing).

However, once again one must return to the problem of strategic timescales mentioned earlier. Can we really plan things so that the choice of process is always made before that of infrastructure? The answer must obviously be 'no' – the intention of our approach is to emphasize continual adjustment. One should note, for instance, that in the original Japanese version of JIT, human resource development is considered to be as much the main focus of attention as stock reduction. Thus, if one adopts a JIT philosophy, process and other choices all take place against a background of continual training and changes in the attitudes and skills of all employees.

Implementation of a manufacturing strategy

The practical steps which might be followed in formulating and implementing a manufacturing strategy are listed above. We commence with a set of analytical tools for the assessment of market position and then match the results against current manufacturing operations. This assessment is done through dividing manufacturing into a series of policy areas as briefly indicated below:

  (i) *Facilities* – number of sites, their location, focus and degree of integration.
 (ii) *Capacity* – level and flexibility.
(iii) *Span of process* – relationship with suppliers and degree of vertical integration.
 (iv) *Process technology*.
  (v) *Human resources* – organizational structure, skills available, training, security, payment systems and motivational level.
 (vi) *Quality* – techniques and procedures.
(vii) *Control policy* – use of MRP, JIT, etc; and pattern of information flows.
(viii) *New products* – ability to innovate.

The recommendation is that these policies are set against the previously listed market success criteria in a matrix reflecting current practice and its impact on market performance. This procedure shows strength and weaknesses, which should be built on or corrected in a systematic way, that is, any proposed changes should be seen in terms of their total effect. The set of policy areas may also be related to supportive sub-systems and AMT.

   If we place this in a real organizational context it will soon be evident that this complexity may lead to a planning paralysis, or at least to the situation where 'strategic planning' itself becomes too prominent a part of strategic implementation lead-time.

However, the opposite view of implementation as a purely technical activity of justifying, selecting and installing new machinery must be firmly resisted. Voss (1986) counters this by proposing three levels of objective setting and control in planning and implementing manufacturing technology. These are:

(i) *Technical* – the setting of objectives and controls based upon individual pieces of technology.
(ii) *Systems* – objectives and control based upon more general features such as product cost, quality, lead-time.
(iii) *Business* – relating to the company and its market. These objectives and controls are set prior to systems and technical design.

Voss discusses results from field studies which show that many companies in practice set only technical objectives, or even if systems objectives are set, only technical controls are used in practice. It was even found that technical control criteria were used which were in direct conflict with business objectives. This led Voss to assert that the integration of organizational procedures for setting objectives and for managerial control at all levels is an essential prerequisite for implementing AMT, which in turn derives much of its benefit from integration. The point, of course, is that this is very hard to achieve in practice, however elegant our analytical models may be.

It should also be noted that actual control of a system requires measurements of key factors. Much of the material presented above, in particular the competitive criteria, is an agenda of issues for our attention rather than well-defined features which may be controlled. We may think we know what we mean by 'delivery lead-time', but its actual measurement involves some sophistication to provide appropriate control statistics.

Boaden and Dale (1986) consider the practical planning of CIM systems and emphasize the importance of simple diagrammatic models in this process. Indeed the CIM maxim of 'simplify then integrate' applies not only to the technology but also to its planning and implementation.

An issue of considerable importance, but on which little reliable advice is available, is the order in which the implementation of various AMT components should be attempted. For example, Osola (1985) recommends that stock reduction be attempted before other improvements in order to provide a source of funds. This may turn out to be a very dangerous strategy as stock provides one form of systems buffering which may be essential to maintain the flow of products during AMT implementation. It should be remembered that JIT, which is most ambitious in attempting stock reduction, only does so after other substantial improvements have been implemented.

In the context of CIM and CIB one should note that the steps taken to develop a manufacturing strategy might, with modifications, be replicated in the development of an information strategy. Both involve the commitment of substantial financial resources to develop a long-term capability. Both involve a subtle relationship between machines and human resources and both may be the driving force in the development of genuine competitive strategies (see Marchand and Horton (1986)).

9 Introduction to financial appraisal

The need for financial appraisal

A major theme of this book is the need for AMT projects to be related to the overall strategy of the company. Previous chapters have emphasized the importance of market and manufacturing strategies in this respect. However, notwithstanding problems in measuring profitability and relating such measures to manufacturing decisions, AMT projects must be seen to make financial sense.

Most AMT investment projects will be analysed by using conventional capital appraisal methods, such as payback period and DCF. Large projects, involving major company changes, may well require special treatment, as shown in Chapter 10. This latter situation is discussed by Hayes, Wheelwright and Clark (1988) who note that major investments, supported by top executives, often short-circuit standard capital budgetary processes. It has been argued that management, faced with, say, the introduction of an MRPII system, may see little reason for formal evaluation using financial criteria because they see the investment as 'inevitable'.

Many observers have noted that financial appraisal in companies can degenerate into a game between accountants and engineers with the latter advancing ever more fanciful reasons for investing while the former place increasing hurdles in their path. How else can one interpret requirements and promises that radical systems changes will pay back their outlays in a matter of months! Hayes, Wheelwright and Clark (1988) give examples of this, commenting on the absurdities which may result from the misapplication of standard procedures. Typically, companies may apply discounting rates of 20 to 40 per cent while their own return on equity, to say nothing of prevailing market interest rates, are a fraction of such figures. An extreme case quoted is of a chief executive who on the one hand bemoaned the fact that Japanese companies have an unfair advantage through low interest rates (i.e. 10 per cent compared with 20 per cent in the USA at that time) while himself insisting on a six month payback period for some process investments.

There are a number of reasons why all investments should be financially assessed, however 'inevitable' they may seem. The first is that no decision really is inevitable. There are always some choices to be made even if some general direction has been chosen for 'strategic' reasons. Specific items of equipment must be selected and the financing of the investment must be considered.

There are two further considerations which must be taken seriously by managements who have grown impatient with the apparatus of financial appraisal. The first is that all projects must be controlled in terms of their resource usage and a key resource is cash (see Chapter 14). One feature of financial appraisal is that it requires the preparation of forecasts of cash flow which, if the project is accepted, may form the basis for cash flow planning and control. Secondly, though of no less importance, it is most damaging to staff morale if 'ordinary' though worthwhile projects put forward by middle management and engineering staff are rigorously appraised (and often delayed or rejected) while 'special' projects championed by senior management are seen to be readily accepted and proceed to use up a large part of available funds.

While emphasizing that financial appraisal should be rigorous and soundly based, strategic appraisal is an equally demanding discipline. Financial and strategic appraisal are inevitably inter-linked, the latter providing a context and information for the former. Together they should ensure that wealth is created for the shareholders of the company through the meeting of long-term objectives. Such objectives may include statements about market development, human resource development and the building up of all aspects of manufacturing process and infrastructure. Financial appraisal must not be seen as an alternative to the strategic appraisal of an investment. Both are important, complementary and must be carried out with as much care as circumstances and available information allow.

Writers on financial appraisal methodology will readily admit that their decision-making methods make up a normative rather than a descriptive theory, i.e. they outline how decisions should be made within the framework of a set of assumptions rather than describe how managers actually make investment decisions. Surveys of methods in use reveal that simple payback and accounting rate of return criteria are still popular despite their lack of consideration of the interaction of time and the value of cash flows. Such methods will not be used here, as AMT-related investments are in principle long-term decisions (though happily some may in practice recoup their outlay very quickly). Thus the Discounted Cash Flow (DCF) methods described below are more appropriate and perfectly easy to operate using spreadsheets and similar software. However, a warning is sounded in Lumby (1988) which includes a Chapter on financial decision-making in practice, pointing to a widespread lack of use, mis-use and misunderstanding of DCF methods. This is particularly evident in the way companies handle inflation and risk.

The fundamental objective of financial appraisal is that decisions are taken by management which as far as can be foreseen maximize the wealth of shareholders. The concern is therefore with providing a flow of cash to shareholders, ultimately through dividends, which provides them with an acceptable return on their investment in the light of the risks involved and alternative investments which may be available. One problem here is that it seems that each project undertaken by a company must be appraised in the light of its effect on shareholders and thus decisions about the value of projects are inevitably interwoven with decisions about how a company finances the project, e.g. whether debt or equity financing is used. For a very large project this joint consideration of technical and financial issues may well be inevitable and in such cases long-term projections of financial statements, which in turn involve a wide range of financial decisions, may be necessary. However, for smaller scale projects, in particular the many projects which will form part of a large-scale AMT development plan, it is desirable that appraisal methods are used which concentrate on the characteristics of the individual project.

The approach commonly recommended and described below involves considering the individual project as a human activity sub-system of the total company. This sub-system is financed by the company at some appropriate interest rate and generates differential cash flows on the basis of which its financial viability is assessed in absolute terms and also relative to alternative uses of the available finance.

Financial appraisal techniques based on Discounted Cash Flow

The remainder of this chapter is concerned with outlining the basic techniques of discounted cash flow (DCF) and drawing attention to assumptions which are made in its use. Chapter 10 uses these ideas in the development of models for the economic appraisal of AMT-related systems. So, while this Chapter is not explicitly concerned with AMT, it discusses methods particularly appropriate to AMT.

The basics of Discounted Cash Flow (DCF)

Despite its fearsome reputation, DCF is based simply on the mathematics of compound interest. Consider the following example:

    Initial amount to be invested = £100
    Interest rate = 12 per cent per annum
    Interest compounded annually
    Length of time for investment = 3 years

The defining feature of compound interest is that 'interest is earned on interest' and thus the length of the compounding interval, in this case a year, is relevant.

    Let r = interest rate (expressed as a proportion rather than a percentage, i.e. as 0.12 rather than 12 per cent). For the discrete form of DCF presented here, the interest rate is assumed to refer to the same length of time as the compounding period (typically one year in the above). Let:
    i = number of time periods
    PV = Present Value (initial amount of investment)

FV = Future Value (final amount of investment)

then $$FV = PV \times (1 + r)^i \qquad\qquad \mathbf{1}$$
$$\text{i.e. } FV = 100 (1 + 0.12)^3 = 140.49$$

This may now be inverted in order to answer a related question, i.e., with 3 years annual compounding at 12 per cent, what amount must initially be invested so that the final amount is £100? The answer may easily be calculated as $(100/140.49) \times 100 = £71.18$. If this is unconvincing consider the following:

Initial investment	£71.18
3 years interest on £71.18	£25.62
2 years interest on £8.54 (i.e.12 per cent of £71.18)	£2.05
1 years interest on £9.57 (i.e. £8.54 plus 12 per cent of £8.54)	£1.15
Total	£100.00

Now we may use equation **1** to find a present value which will grow to become some required future value:

$$PV = FV \times (1/(1 + r)^i) \qquad\qquad \mathbf{2}$$

Some representative values of the PV factors $(1/(1+r)^i)$ are tabulated in Fig. 9.1 for use with manual calculations but it is assumed that DCF calculations are done using software with appropriate facilities. A scientific calculator is, however, also quite adequate.

The real point of this equation is its re-interpretation as giving

The table gives the present value of a single payment of £1 received i years in the future and discounted at a rate of r per year. (i.e. formula is $1/(1 + r)^i$)

No. years	r values: 0.01	0.05	0.10	0.15	0.20	0.25	0.30	0.35	0.40
1	0.990	0.952	0.909	0.870	0.833	0.800	0.769	0.741	0.714
2	0.980	0.907	0.826	0.756	0.694	0.640	0.592	0.549	0.510
3	0.971	0.864	0.751	0.658	0.579	0.512	0.455	0.406	0.364
4	0.961	0.823	0.683	0.572	0.482	0.410	0.350	0.301	0.260
5	0.951	0.784	0.621	0.497	0.402	0.328	0.269	0.223	0.186
6	0.942	0.746	0.564	0.432	0.335	0.262	0.207	0.165	0.133
7	0.933	0.711	0.513	0.376	0.279	0.210	0.159	0.122	0.095
8	0.923	0.677	0.467	0.327	0.233	0.168	0.123	0.091	0.068
9	0.914	0.645	0.424	0.284	0.194	0.134	0.094	0.067	0.048
10	0.905	0.614	0.386	0.247	0.162	0.107	0.073	0.050	0.035

Figure 9.1 Present value factors

us a present valuation of the promise that we will receive some amount of cash at a future time. Thus, under the conditions of the calculation above, a promise that we will receive £100 in three years time is worth £71.18 now because £71.18 could be invested at 12 per cent annual compounding to give £100 in three years' time.

We now assume that we can forecast a series of cash flows to be associated with a project. A simplifying assumption often made at this point is that these cash flows occur either at the start of the project (time 0) or at the ends of each time period. Thus we have:

> $C(i)$ = Net Cash flow at time i, i.e. the aggregation of cash flows at that point in time. i is an integer and varies between 0 and n (the time horizon for the project). The components of $C(i)$ are negative for cash outflows and positive for inflows. In many cases the only net outflow will be $C(0)$. Thus the Net Present Value (NPV) for a project is the sum of all the terms $(C(i) \times (1/(1 + r)^i)$ from i = 0 to i = n.   **3**

The decision rule associated with this procedure applied to a single project with adequate available funds is to accept the project provided that the NPV is greater than or equal to zero.

An alternative procedure is to calculate the value of r such that NPV = 0. This value is termed the Internal Rate of Return (IRR) of the project and must be above some cut-off or hurdle rate for the project to be accepted. In simple situations these two decision rules are consistent but may well differ in their recommendations if used to choose between alternative projects, a situation well described in standard texts.

In Fig. 9.2 we show a worked example of this procedure using the NPV decision rule. The calculations in Fig. 9.2 follow a standard format we will adopt when cash flows are assumed to occur at the ends of periods. Also included in Fig. 9.3 is a bar chart based on Fig. 9.2 showing how Present Value accumulates over time for a variety of interest rates until the NPV is reached at the time horizon. There are a number of limitations to this procedure, in particular, how should we handle situations when cash flow occurs during the year? (i.e. it would excessively distort the picture if they were 'moved' to the end of a year). A simple and useful approximation in this case is to continue

```
Time horizon is pre-set to 10 years
All cash data in £000
```

	Interest rate =			0	0.05	0.15	0.25
Year	Cash out	Cash in	Net cash	Cumulative present value			
0	150		-150	-150.00	-150.00	-150.00	-150.00
1	30	40	10	-140.00	-140.48	-141.30	-142.00
2		60	60	-80.00	-86.05	-95.94	-103.60
3		70	70	-10.00	-25.59	-49.91	-67.76
4		70	70	60.00	32.00	-9.89	-39.09
5		70	70	130.00	86.85	24.92	-16.15
6		40	40	170.00	116.70	42.21	-5.66
7		20	20	190.00	130.91	49.73	-1.47
8		5	5	195.00	134.30	51.36	-0.63

Figure 9.2 Net present value calculations with end of period cash flows

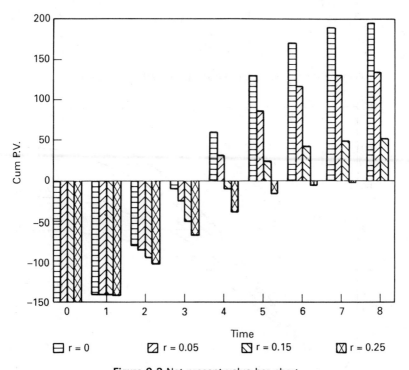

Figure 9.3 Net present value bar chart

to use the normal discounting formula, but with fractional values of the index, i. Similarly, if a cash flow, such as a maintenance cost or a production saving, is difficult to place in time, but we can reasonably assess a total annual value, we use this value but locate it at the mid-point of a period. These approximations are reliable and based on reasonable assumptions, provided interest rates are not too large.

In Fig. 9.4 we show a worked example using these approximations. We may also now review the graph associated with such an example, here shown as Fig. 9.5. The vertical axis represents NPV calculated

```
All cash data in £000
```

| | | | | | | Interest Rate = | 0 | 0.05 | 0.15 | 0.25 |

Flow start	Flow end	Mid point	Cash out	Cash in	Net cash	Cumulative present value			
0.0	0.0	0.0	150		-150	-150.00	-150.00	-150.00	-150.00
0.0	0.6	0.3	50		-50	-200.00	-199.27	-197.95	-196.76
0.6	1.0	0.8	10	60	50	-150.00	-151.19	-153.24	-154.94
1.0	2.0	1.5		80	80	-70.00	-76.83	-88.37	-97.69
2.0	3.0	2.5		80	80	10.00	-6.02	-31.96	-51.90
3.0	4.0	3.5		60	60	70.00	44.56	4.83	-24.42
4.0	5.0	4.5		40	40	110.00	76.68	26.16	-9.77
5.0	6.0	5.5		30	30	140.00	99.62	40.07	-0.98
6.0	7.0	6.5		5	5	145.00	103.26	42.08	0.20

Figure 9.4 Net present value calculations with varied cash flows

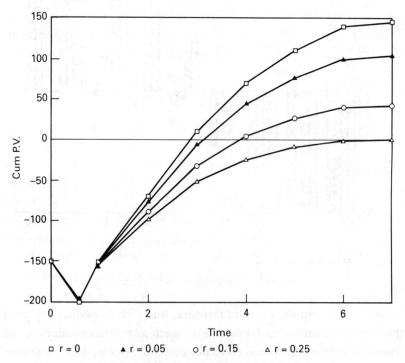

Figure 9.5 Net present value graph

to a series of time horizons as shown on the horizontal axis. This is a re-interpretation of the accumulation of Present Value used previously. The pre-set time horizon, n, is now merely the limit of the scale on the horizontal axis, i.e. the furthest limit of our cash flow forecasts. Vertical lines on this graph would represent point-based cash flows and the straight lines joining other points on the graph are approximations for cash flows assumed to be equal over a period of time. A range of interest rates is shown on the graph to illustrate the sensitivity of NPV to this parameter.

Several points of interest arise from this graph. First of all a line is shown with zero interest rate. The point where this cuts the horizontal axis (i.e. NPV is zero) shows the payback period in its traditional form. Other points where lines cut the horizontal axis show discounted payback periods. The interest line which just crosses the horizontal axis at the pre-set time horizon, n, gives the IRR. Thus the IRR seems to be based on a parameter which either reflects a dubious assumption (i.e. a time horizon pre-set for accounting convenience) or an equally dubious forecast. This is in addition to drawbacks evident when it is used to compare alternative projects and thus the IRR criterion will not be considered further.

Further issues in the use of the DCF method

There are a number of practical issues in the use of DCF techniques which are addressed at great length in accounting textbooks. Some of these issues are dealt with elsewhere in this book, while others are only mentioned in this section, not because they lack importance but because their resolution is not specific to the AMT-related issues which are the subject of this book.

A very considerable literature exists on the estimation of appropriate interest rates to be used in DCF calculations. Interest rates fulfil a number of functions which may be confused in everyday thinking. If an individual invests money in a bank or on a project he quite reasonably expects compensation (i.e. interest), in addition to the eventual repayment of the money, for a variety of reasons:

(a) the money invested is his property and he not unreasonably requires some 'rent' for being deprived of its use for a period of time. We refer to this as a 'real return';

(b) the buying power of money is likely to diminish over time (i.e. inflation takes place, often at differing rates for the different resources) and thus without sufficient interest to compensate the investor has actually lost buying power;

(c) the money may not be repaid in full (or at all) and hence the investor requires some return for his gamble, i.e. a risk premium.

The standard formula used to relate these factors is as follows:

K = rate of return, incorporating inflation and risk
P = real return
F = expected general rate of inflation
G = allowance for business risk
Then $(1 + K) = (1 + P) \times (1 + F) \times (1 + G)$ **4**

Thus the above factors accumulate and explain, for example, why shares (which are inherently risky investments) must in the long run provide higher returns than the much safer banks. However, even the latter should pay interest above the rate of inflation, otherwise investment will be unattractive (though macroeconomic theory shows that the relationships between interest, savings and consumption rates are not so easy to forecast).

A company accountant will analyse the financing of his/her business and arrive at an appropriate interest rate based possibly on the weighted average cost of capital for the company along with adjustments for the riskiness of specific categories of investment. However, care must be taken not to overload such interest rates. For example, one important rule is that an interest rate including an allowance for inflation should only be used if the cash flow estimates are similarly inflated, preferably with each cost inflated at a rate separately estimated for that particular category of resource (e.g. labour costs are likely to change at rates different from those for materials). Alternatively, if cash flows are quoted at current cost and price rates, the inflation component must be removed from the discount rates using equation **4**.

A very pertinent issue we shall not examine in detail is the effect of taxation on cash flows. The interested general reader might consult Hirst (1988) or Lumby (1988) for simple expositions of the UK tax system as it affects capital investment and for some worked examples. The laws affecting the amounts and the timing of the taxes a company must pay provide a useful means for the government of any country to encourage particular forms of company behaviour, e.g. the purchase of new equipment. How this is done in practice varies between countries and over time and is a very particular field of expertise for accountants and lawyers. In this book we assume that the effects of taxation have been calculated as adjustments in cash flows. Such calculations may, however, have a decisive effect on the attractiveness of an investment project. It might also be remembered that if tax allowances are used on one project, the financial viability of other projects may suffer. Thus a number of projects must be viewed in the context of a coherent strategy.

Techniques such as life cycle costing and problems which occur with inter-dependent or alternative projects where funding is limited are considered briefly in Chapter 10. An extensive literature exists on financial models relating to such situations though such modelling may be difficult to perform in practice due to uncertainties in data estimates. For this reason we will concentrate on a broad strategy framework and on models which uncover major success factors rather than financial details.

Risk and sensitivity analysis in DCF

In this section we introduce methods which attempt to allow for risk in investment decisions. A related question is the sensitivity of decisions to estimation errors in cash flow. This is a controversial area with no generally accepted method of approach. The impact of uncertainty and inaccuracy can be very considerable, as shown in the example given in Fig. 9.6. This illustrates the effects on NPV of changes in the amount and in the timing of a benefit in the context of the simple example on which Fig. 9.4 and 9.5 were based.

Risk and uncertainty are often handled in ad hoc ways by

Based on the example in Figure 9.4.
Cash inflow at original time 0.8 and original amount first benefit
of £60,000 with discount rate of 0.15.

(i)   Effect of varying amount of first benefit only (timing at
        0.8 years)

Cash inflow £(000)	NPV £(000)	% change in NPV
40	24.2	-42
50	33.14	-20
60	42.08	0
70	51.02	21
80	59.97	42

(ii)   Effect of varying the timing of the first benefit only.
        (Amount is £60,000)

Timing (mid-point)	NPV £(000)	% change in NPV
0.6	43.35	3
0.8	42.08	0
1.0	40.85	-3
1.2	39.65	-6
1.4	38.48	-9

(iii)   Effect of varying timings of all benefits by delay in start
        of first benefit (e.g. illustrates delay in commissioning
        of system) and similar delay for all subsequent benefits.

Timing of first benefit (mid-point)	NPV £(000)	% change in NPV
0.8	42.08	0
1.0	35.46	-16
1.2	29.03	-31
1.4	22.77	-46
1.6	16.69	-60
1.8	10.77	-74

The range of the above NPV% changes clearly illustrates the need
to explore carefully the effects of specific changes in amounts
and timings to discover those which critically affect the economic
value of the project.

Figure 9.6 Illustration of effects of variations in timing and amounts of cashflows

companies, for example stringent payback periods may be enforced
or short time horizons insisted upon. In the surveys quoted by Lumby
companies varied between complete rejection of even the idea that
systematic risk analysis could be performed, to enthusiasm for the
discipline of formal risk analysis as a means of showing the variety

of outcomes which might occur. The arbitrary methods used to avoid formal risk analysis should be avoided at all costs in AMT appraisal. If uncertainty is ignored, estimates of costs and benefits will either be based on averages of forecasts, which entails considerable danger, or on conservative assumptions (inflated costs and deflated savings) which will inhibit investment. The most important benefit to be gained from a thorough risk analysis is the discipline of performing the analysis rather than the simple answer to the decision problem. A good analysis should uncover possibilities for which contingencies may be planned. It has even been argued that senior management, when presented with an investment proposal, is really only interested (assuming the proposal is financially and strategically sound) in answering the questions 'what can go wrong?', 'how badly can things go wrong?' and 'what can we do about it?'. For this reason some form of risk or sensitivity analysis is obligatory.

Many companies avoid formal risk analysis by alternatively using sensitivity analysis. This is usually performed by developing a spreadsheet model of an investment decision and then adjusting each individual estimate (of cost, benefit, time horizon and discounting rate) until the NPV is zero (referred to as the breakeven values of the estimates). These give an indication of the extent to which a given estimate is critical and should be investigated further. An example of this approach is given in Fig. 9.7. In a book published by the

Based on example in Figure 9.4

Item to be analysed	Current estimate	Break-even	% change to break-even
Cash outflow at time 0 (r = 0.15)	150	192	28
Cash inflow at time 1	60	13	78
Discount rate	0.15	0.25	67

The '% change to break-even' column shows the percentage amount by which a factor might change before the project becomes only marginally worthwhile (NPV = 0), other factors remaining unchanged.

Figure 9.7 Illustration of sensitivity analysis

Institution of Production Engineers and the Chartered Institute of Management Accountants, *Justifying Investment in AMT* (1987), this method is strongly recommended even to the extent of quantifying the 'intangible benefits' which are required to bring a negative NPV up to a zero value.

The literature identifies two main ways of performing risk analysis. One is by the use of Decision Analysis involving the assessment of probabilities for events which affect an investment proposal. Typically, key environmental variables, such as those related to market growth and share, are assumed to follow a probability distribution whose parameters (e.g. mean, variability and so forth) are estimated on the basis of past data and judgement (the latter being associated with the Bayesian or subjective approach to probability). The assignment of probabilities may be extended to any factor whose value is not known with certainty – and this, of course, could well mean all factors. The danger of this approach if used incautiously is its passivity. Management as a process is about taking action and positively affecting markets, prices of materials and so forth. A balance needs to be struck in model building and analysis between what can be achieved by vigorous action and what risks must be accepted as inevitable results of a planned course of action.

The other major approach to including risk in DCF calculations is by means of Risk Adjusted Discount Rates (RADR). These have already been mentioned in the section on the basics of DCF and in equation **4** as the interest rates seen in the real world and including differing allowances for risk. Such rates may be arrived at arbitrarily, for example, a company may use a discount rate of 15 per cent for projects which are perceived to have normal risk profiles and 20 per cent for high risk projects, often including ones based on high technology. Alternatively a company may systematically analyse the risks inherent in various industrial sectors and projects (using, say, the CAPM approach (see Hirst (1988) and Lumby (1988))) to arrive at a RADR appropriate for a given investment proposal.

Two points must be made here to avoid mistakes and confusion. First of all one should not use both RADR and probability methods applied to the same source of risk at the same time. One may use a discount rate which is adjusted for some general categories of risk and then apply probabilities to assess the impact of other sources of risk, but care is necessary. For example, does a RADR which allows for a company being in the engineering sector also take account of the risks involved in implementing an MRPII system? Such a question must ultimately be answered on the basis of evidence in a specific case and must incorporate judgements made by the managers concerned. In particular the risks involved in implementing an MRPII system are, to put it bluntly, related to the experience, attitudes and competence of staff in the company.

The second trap to be avoided in the use of RADRs is to assume that the same RADR applies to all stages of a project's life cycle. Indeed, it is not right to use a constant RADR for all time periods unless one is willing to accept that its effect, relative to a non-RADR, increases geometrically over time. This effect is shown in Fig. 9.8. The use of variable RADRs is explored in Bodily (1985) who argues that the need to use them unfortunately detracts from the principle argument in favour of RADR based models, i.e. simplicity. Burke and Ward (1988) show how projects may be divided into differing 'risk phases' each with appropriate RADRs. Their excellent, if complex, analysis leads towards an 'options pricing model' of project analysis. In this approach managers have not simply a one-off, accept–reject decision to be made for a project, but a variety of decisions regarding timing, expansion and even abortion of a project. As events

```
Time horizon is pre-set to 10 years
All cash data in £000
'% effect' column is % reduction in Present Value through
using increased rate
```

	Interest rate =			0.1	0.1	0.2	0.2	
Year	Cash out	Cash in	Net cash	PV	CUM PV	PV	CUM PV	%effect
0	150		-150	-150.00	-150.00	-150.00	-150.00	0.00%
1	30	40	10	9.09	-140.91	8.33	-141.67	8.33%
2		60	60	49.59	-91.32	41.67	-100.00	15.97%
3		70	70	52.59	-38.73	40.51	-59.49	22.97%
4		70	70	47.81	9.08	33.76	-25.73	29.39%
5		70	70	43.46	52.55	28.13	2.40	35.28%
6		40	40	22.58	75.12	13.40	15.79	40.67%
7		20	20	10.26	85.39	5.58	21.38	45.61%
8		5	5	2.33	87.72	1.16	22.54	50.15%

Figure 9.8 Net present value calculations with end of period cash flows: comparison of risk-free rate and risk-adjusted rate

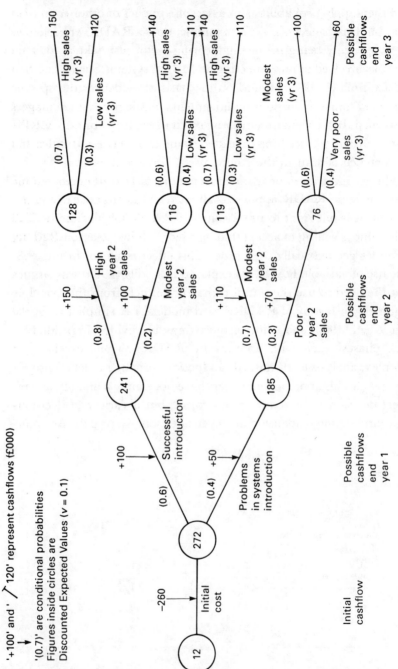

'+100' and ' ⁄120' represent cashflows (£000)
'(0.7)' are conditional probabilities
Figures inside circles are
Discounted Expected Values (v = 0.1)

Figure 9.9 Decision tree

unfold, risks and RADRs may be re-assessed. Indeed if things go well, the risks involved in the latter stages of a project could be so low as to necessitate the use of an RADR below that used for normal low-risk investments in a company.

The complexity of these methods takes us back to the formal use of decision analysis, if model building beyond basic sensitivity analysis is required. Decision analysis requires a textbook in itself for the explanation of technique to a level appropriate to making a real impact on AMT decision-making. In Fig. 9.9 we show a decision tree which illustrates the analysis of a greatly simplified investment decision. One very important point should be noted here with respect to the use of such methods in practice. Though the example given in Fig. 9.9 only involves a three-year time horizon and simple probability branching, it includes no less than 22 inter-related forecasts of costs, benefits and probabilities. Such model building methodologies require considerable effort in data collection and forecasting. Indeed if they are not approached with a great deal of professional care they will merely provide another example of 'Garbage in, garbage out'!

10 The management process of AMT appraisal

In Chapter 9 we were concerned with setting out the theoretical background to the financial appraisal of AMT investment proposals. In this chapter we are concerned with the management process surrounding such financial appraisal. This chapter also includes three case studies which are intended as vehicles for exploring these issues in realistic contexts.

The scale of AMT change

The first and most obvious point for consideration is that AMT investments differ very greatly in scale, that is, in the amount of resources committed, the time taken for implementation and the extent of the expected benefits. We have used a classification of systems' change contrasting small and large scale changes which may be evolutionary or revolutionary in nature. The simplest form refers to small and independent changes justified by their direct and obvious benefits, usually cost savings or productivity improvements.

Typical of such an investment would be the replacement of a machine by a similar but updated equivalent. Such replacement decisions are extensively analysed in the engineering literature. An example of a relevant approach is the MAPI method developed in the early 1950s in the USA. This seeks to answer the key question of the timing of machine equipment replacement by a trade-off of the operating inferiority of the existing equipment against the advantages of the new. The method may be extended to handle completely new situations. This type of approach is well known to engineers and is an example of life cycle approaches to decision-making at a technical level. Some specific problems in using such an approach for larger systems are the following:

- the need to be integrative in considering the impact of a local change on the wider system, particularly when a new investment has a potentially radical effect on material flows and quality
- an inability to predict the capability of a new technology
- a lack of sophistication in considering the impact of new technology on market competitiveness, and a similar lack of consideration of the implications for competitiveness of not investing (see below on the 'disinvestment spiral')
- issues in the measurability of costs and benefits (see below on 'intangible benefits').

The other categories of change referred to involve explicit planning and ultimately changes to all aspects of a business. In these instances, a case by case approach is necessary, involving the appropriate use of the techniques described in Chapter 9 in the context of an appraisal process.

Managerial procedures for AMT investment appraisal

As we discussed in the last chapter, much of the literature on investment appraisal is normative, that is, it seeks to instruct on what should be done rather than describe what is actually done in practice. A number of studies have described the patchy nature of the take-up of such techniques as DCF. A smaller number of studies describe (as in Bower (1985)) *Capital Budgeting as a General Management Problem*. Bower emphasizes the role of operations level managers in initiating investment proposals and submitting them to higher levels of management for approval. This general approach is well known but few have really examined its implications and political dimension. Bower, however, does this to great effect, as do a group of researchers at the London Business School. The latter have concentrated on three examples of Strategic Investment Decisions (SIDs) and documented their progress in great detail (see Marsh, Barwise, Thomas and Wensley (1988)).

Two of the SIDs investigated were manufacturing based and thus this line of research is of particular interest in an AMT context, though it might be argued that state-of-the-art AMT decisions would be even more problematic than those described. SIDs are decisions which have a significant impact on the long-term performance of a company as a whole. The study described in Marsh, Barwise, Thomas and Wensley (1988) looks at them from four perspectives:

- the process of learning and innovation as the investment project evolves through time and its implications become more clear
- the forms of financial, strategic and operational analysis used
- the political, negotiation processes which take place inside the company and with outsiders
- the effect of different formal systems and the actions of senior management.

In particular, the companies under consideration were large and diversified and frequent reference is made to actions which took place at group level as opposed to those in the division where the investment was intended to take place. Both financial and strategic theories of investment appraisal come under close scrutiny. In particular the value of the formal strategic approaches discussed above in Chapters 7 and 8 are questioned. Investment ideas do not seem to flow from strategic plans in quite the way one might envisage. They often seem to originate from far down an organization as the result of an acutely felt need to improve. They soon become identified with a group of proposers who develop a strong commitment to them and attempt to sell them to higher management.

An example is a project on which a divisional board director spent the equivalent of eight months on one proposal prior to approval, his project team members spending two man-years. One might ask how executives at group level could judge the results of such efforts. In another reported project, 2000 pages of documentary evidence was reduced to a financial proposal of 60 pages for group financial staff and then further reduced to two pages for the group board. Such a reduction in the variety of detail submitted is considered good practice. Indeed, if a proposal cannot be succinctly described it is doubtful if it has been thoroughly thought out by its proposers. Yet it is questionable if any sensible decision on an individual proposal can be made in the face of such 'information asymmetry'.

This brings into focus the role of top management in this process. If we take the mechanistic view that the decision on each case is that of the group board, this process is simply an ineffective ritual. Marsh and his colleagues argue that in practice the role of a good senior manager is far more comprehensive than rubber-stamping proposals. One extreme quoted example is when a chief executive felt that a proposal, though seemingly highly profitable, had considered too few options, and so forced a complete reassessment, as a learning exercise for the project team as much as to demonstrate his superior knowledge. Subsequently an equally profitable alternative was discovered which involved far less initial expenditure and hence, presumably, less risk.

It is argued that top management affects SIDs through early direct intervention, the questioning of assumptions, setting deadlines and imposing criteria specific to a given project. The whole process may be seen by senior management as a test of the commitment of the proposers rather than as an objective appraisal of the merits of a proposal. Top management can also influence a project through the appointment of staff and through their control of the organizational structure of a company.

The role of top management in controlling organizational structure is obvious. If the AMT proposals under consideration involve substantial integration between differing operating units and divisions then top management must be directly involved in determining the structure of the organization as it evolves, that is, the responsibilities of individual managers and the processes of decision-making and control which must be in place to ensure that business is carried out in an effective way. A computer-based formal information system within an organization is a key component in facilitating integration, and strategic decisions regarding such a system must not be left to computing specialists or CIM enthusiasts alone.

Top management also affect the investment process through the system of performance measurement and rewards. Champions of systems' change will naturally feel more committed to their proposals if their future careers and rewards are equitably related to valid measurements of the performance of their new systems when these have been implemented. Of the types of performance measure mentioned in Chapter 6, efficiency, effectiveness and responsiveness have obvious validity in the context of AMT investment appraisal. We can also now see how equity towards employees is not only relevant, but ensuring it is a key role of senior managers. The investment appraisal process may be regarded as 'political', but if it is also seen as unfair, a variety of ill-effects are likely to occur against which attempts at 'objective financial appraisal' will be ineffective. This once again comes back to the culture of the organization and the role of senior management in setting the climate for good ideas to come to fruition. As we discuss in Chapter 11, poor senior management has in the past proved a barrier to rather than a facilitator of new technology.

A final point to consider in the context of the managerial process of appraisal, whether technical, financial or strategic, is the cost of the resources used in this process. This will consist mainly of the opportunity cost of the time spent by professional staff in examining both projects which are eventually approved and those which are not. The cost is very considerable, but is offset to an extent by the benefits of the learning which takes place and which has more general application. The process of appraisal should uncover a number of facts of importance, typically data on current technical developments and market trends. The appraisal process should also involve extensive communication both within and between organizations. Finally staff involved should learn something about the actual process of appraisal and about their competence, or lack of it, in being involved in this process. In this context it should be remembered that learning is facilitated by feedback and criticism from others and once again we have described a senior management role of which an example has been given above.

The dynamics of AMT investment appraisal

Our discussion so far has avoided one of the major problems of appraisal by taking, as is so often done, a static view of the setting in which the investment takes place. This issue is explored in Hayes and Garvin (1985) which is concerned with the way in which standard financial investment appraisal techniques seem to be biased against investment in new technology. They put forward an argument termed the 'disinvestment spiral' which shows how a company which fails to invest may soon be forced to withdraw from a market.

Consider two companies, A and B, with identical but competing products, the same cost structure and the same opportunity for investment in new manufacturing technology. Let us assume that they carry out identical analyses of the projected investment except that company A discounts at a higher rate and arrives at a negative NPV while company B uses a lower rate and finds the investment marginally attractive. Thus, company B invests and we assume is successful, both technically and commercially. Company B is able to increase output and reduce prices (assumed to be the order-winning criterion in this case) and thus increase its market share. A couple of years later both companies are again considering an investment to improve manufacturing capacity and efficiency. Now, however, company A will be faced with tighter margins than before as it had to reduce prices to compete with company B while its costs were static. It is likely to have less profit-generated funds available for investment. Once again company B is more likely to be able to justify investment. Success does appear to breed success.

If one imagines companies involved in a series of such investments, a key competitive edge, assuming one decides to take regular risks and invest more frequently than the industry average, may be a company's ability to handle failure, that is, to avoid the more damaging effects of the inevitable non-effective investments. The existence of highly successful companies which avoid investing in new technology might be seen as a counter-argument to the proposal that companies should imitate company B. Alternatively it might show that companies which do invest regularly often do so inappropriately and fail to handle the inevitable set-backs.

An alternative view of the dynamics of this process is given in Fig. 10.1. The positive circle shows how success may lead to further success, while the negative circle shows why it may be very difficult to escape from the effects of non-investment. It should always be remembered, however, that such negative circles may be broken out of by

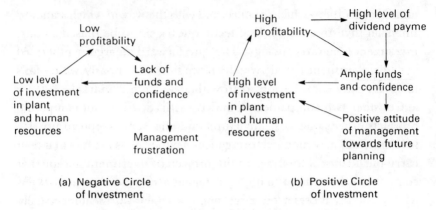

(a) Negative Circle
of Investment

(b) Positive Circle
of Investment

Figure 10.1 Negative and positive circles of investment

determined managerial action. Unfortunately the culture of a company
and the attitudes of managers at all levels may simply exclude this
possibility. If one looks at any company with out-moded plant, systems
and products one should remember that this situation has probably
arisen through the rejection over the years of all arguments to invest.
Presumably, responsible people with a good knowledge of their own
company and market have repeatedly found non-investment to be
the most rational course of action. In many cases they were probably
right but were unable to see when and how they should have broken
out of the disinvestment spiral.

Costs and benefits of AMT

The benefits and costs usually associated with the standard categories
of AMT are described in Chapter 2 and elsewhere as appropriate.
Two general points should be made, however, which warn of the
dangers of a facile acceptance of these information inputs to the
appraisal process.

The first point is that such inputs are based on an accounting system
which is likely to be built on a framework of assumptions suitable
(hopefully) for supporting on-going operations. Thus stated costs are
likely to include all manner of allocated overheads and it may be very

difficult to disentangle the basic data relevant to a projected new situation.

The second point refers to the frequent use of the term 'intangible benefits'. This curious notion presumably indicates advantages likely to come from an investment which are thought too difficult to measure and forecast directly. In Chapter 9 we described how one influential publication suggests the use of sensitivity analysis to place a minimum value on the amount of non-quantifiable benefit needed for a given investment to be attractive. While seemingly logical and reasonable this could easily be abused by managers who see the 'minimum necessary intangible benefit' as providing a guide for their imagination. The other extreme position is to deny that intangible benefits exist. If a benefit is real, it is measurable! Any statement that a real benefit is intangible is taken as a sign of laziness or incompetence. There is much to be said for this approach in that any benefit worth including will presumably come down eventually to an incremental cash flow. This is a point that should be continually borne in mind when examining investment proposals.

However, the idea that we can trace a direct 'cause and effect' line from a given investment to every one of its benefits cannot really be taken seriously except perhaps when the investment applies to a bounded and stable system whose action is well understood. In particular, as discussed in Chapter 6, many investments provide a potential for improvement which must in turn be successfully managed before a benefit can be realized.

A further problem relates to the difficulties which will be experienced in attempting long-term forecasts in dynamic situations. In the physical sciences, the limits to the prediction of future events are currently being explored through the mathematics of non-linear dynamical systems, often referred to as the 'mathematics of chaos' (see Gleick (1987)). If, as seems likely, such arguments may be applied to the social sciences, it may in principle be impossible to provide certain types of forecasts. Such arguments also apply to 'managed' systems because managerial control also depends on models which evolve over time.

It is interesting to speculate whether it could be proved that, for a given range of situations, DCF-style analysis is inappropriate in principle. It might also be remembered that such a proof would also undermine strategic analysis and all other approaches based on a traditional notion of rationality. Perhaps planners in the future will have to be more imaginative in taking radically new views of how organizations might judge the appropriateness of new technology investments (see Morgan (1986)). It is often stated that CIM, for example, will radically change the way a company is run. Should we therefore appraise investments in CIM sub-systems using conventional methods firmly anchored in present operations and organizational culture?

In fact, a number of publications seek to do exactly that for AMT. The NEDO AMT Report (Osola (1985)) and its accompanying computer models attempt to show precisely how the impact of different AMT sub-systems on the organization may be assessed, taking into account the size of the organization and its market situation. Similarly software has been developed (for example the IVAN package) which facilitates the analysis of AMT proposals. Most similar aids emphasize the need to see financial analysis in a strategic context but often fail to really say what this means and totally ignore the complex organizational context explored above and in the subsequent cases.

The view put forward in this chapter should not be seen as opposed to the use of financial and strategic methods of analysis. These provide a language and structure for a coherent debate within an organization on the merits of an individual AMT proposal and also for expressing the evolving body of knowledge in an organization referring to the totality of investment plans.

The cases which follow are intended as a vehicle for exploring the above issues and are based on observed industrial situations. The points for discussion are intended for group working and it is particularly important that major assumptions underlying the actions described in the cases are uncovered, critically analysed and alternatives suggested.

Case 1. The heat treatment units

Extract from the minutes of the Factory C Planning Group meeting of 1 February 1989:

> Consideration was given to the deteriorating state of the HT69 heat treatment units. There are four of these in Factory C, bought twenty years ago, and now require extensive maintenance. It was decided that a feasibility study be carried out by Mr Jones into the purchase of the updated HT89 units as replacements. A preliminary estimate of the cost of four new machines was £0.25M.

Extract from the minutes of the Factory C Planning Group meeting of 19 April 1989:

> Mr Jones reported, as development engineer, on his study regarding the replacement of the HT69 units. It was obvious that the HT89 units provided a substantial technical advance and he suggested that a capital paper recommending their purchase be drawn up.
>
> Mr Walker, as quality manager, apologized for his absence from the previous meeting due to a commitment abroad. He expressed surprise that an alternative to the HT89s had not been explored, particularly when most firms in the industry were now thinking about installing VT89s, based on a combination of heat and vacuum. He suggested that only one VT89 would be needed. Mr Jones replied that he couldn't see how Mr Walker knew what their competitors were thinking and that no one had actually installed a VT89. The VT89 was unproven in their industry and he considered it inappropriate that such a critical process be based on only one machine. Mr Walker replied that earlier forms of the VT89 had been installed in many factories making similar products and the machines were far more reliable than the old-fashioned HT units.
>
> Mr Stanhope, as works manager and chairman of the meeting, said that the feeling of the meeting was for HT89s and asked Mr Jones to draw up the appropriate documents.

Extract from the minutes of the Factory C Planning Group meeting of 14 June 1989:

> Mr Jones presented his capital paper for the purchase of HT89 units. This forecast that the new units would pay back their investment in 1.63 years, well within the time required by finance.
>
> Mr Walker argued that insufficient consideration had been given to VT89 units and attempted to table a paper showing their advantages. After some discussion this was allowed but it was noted that the VT89 required a longer payback period. Mr Walker argued that the two papers were not comparable and that his showed a discounted payback period. The chairman was happy to see Mr Walker's paper in the report of the meeting and thanked him for his efforts which demonstrated that a thorough exploration of alternatives had been undertaken before deciding to recommend the HT89 units. It was decided that Mr Jones's capital paper be forwarded to finance for approval and that the planning of the installation of the machines begin.

Extract from the minutes of the meeting of the Capital Approvals Sub-Committee of the Group Finance Committee on 25 July 1989:

> Consideration was given to the paper, reference CA/231/C/89, submitted by the Factory C Planning Committee and recommending the purchase of four HT89 units. A decision on this proposal was deferred until the next meeting of this sub-committee and it was requested that the Factory C Planning Committee give further consideration to alternatives to the HT89 units and prepare an expanded paper following, as a guide, the FMS paper submitted by Factory A.

Extract from the conversation at the above meeting:

> GMO: 'What on earth do we do with this proposal from Stanhope? Is he really suggesting we replace antique technology with reproduction antique?'
> NML: 'Yes, he probably is! And if it were a sound proposal then why not? Unfortunately the style of this paper is as old as the machines. Do Factory C really not know we're phasing out half

the stuff they make now and introducing the CVN range? I really don't know if you can make CVNs on HT89s.'

REK: 'They have been informed about the new range. In fact all works managers are members of the Group Product Planning Committee and besides the CVNs are common knowledge.'

GMO: 'How you make them isn't common knowledge! VT89s would be OK but why don't they look at VT95s? I gather George Walker tried to suggest VT technology but got nowhere. He sent me a copy of his paper recommending a VT89.'

REK: 'If he has a good argument for a VT89 then why is it not included in papers sent to us? This is a shambles. I suggest we reject and get on to the next proposal.'

NML: 'They have to do something about the HT69s. It might be more encouraging if we defer the decision and have a chat with them to sort out a reasonable paper.'

Extract from the minutes of the meeting of the Capital Approvals Sub-Committee of the Group Finance Committee on 17 October 1989:

A revised capital approval paper, CA/264/C/89, was received regarding replacements for the HT69 units. This proposed the following:

(a) the immediate purchase of two second-hand HT79 units currently available on the market;

(b) when the HT79s are commissioned, the removal of two HT69 units;

(c) the purchase in early 1990 of a VT98 and installation in the space now made available by the removal of HT69 units;

(d) when the performance of the VT98 reaches a series of defined benchmarks, the removal of the two remaining HT69 units.

The proposal was approved and forwarded to Group Headquarters.

Extract from the minutes of the meeting of the Capital Approvals Sub-Committee of the Group Finance Committee on 11 January 1990:

It was noted that the paper CA/264/C/89 had been referred back by the Board for clarification. In particular it was noted that the cost information and sales forecasts it contained must be updated in the light of current Group Plans and Budgets. It was decided that the paper be referred to the newly formed Joint Factories Productivity Improvements Committee (JFPIC) for action.

Extract from the minutes of the meeting of the JFPIC on 1 Febuary 1990:

> The return of capital paper CA/264/C/89 was noted. Mr Walker commented that the second-hand HT79 units were no longer on the market and, as the condition of the HT69 units had deteriorated still further to become a major bottleneck on production volumes, urgent attention be given to the purchase of a VT97 integrated flexible system.

Points for discussion

(1) Are there specific places within the above where significant mistakes are made or is the delay experienced the result of the bureaucratic decision-making process?
(2) Suggest actions for the key actors which might have facilitated the reaching of a more timely decision.
(3) Assume that in Febuary 1989, Mr Stanhope had had the authority to purchase replacement HT units and had simply gone ahead and purchased four HT89s. Would this have been a satisfactory decision-making process? What would have been gained and what would have been lost?
(4) Suggest an AMT investment appraisal process which might have been more successful in this instance. Is your suggested process of general application?

Case 2. Computer-Aided Design at UMC

UMC is a small company specializing in the design and manufacture of a range of materials handling equipment for erection within food manufacturing plants. Each installation is based on standard units and parts but is tailored to the needs of a specific customer.

UMC employs around 50 people and had a turnover of £4.6M in 1989. It was taken over by the Linton Group in 1985 though it functions as an autonomous unit. The exception is the purchase of capital equipment which must be sanctioned by the Group.

Each installation contract is handled as a separate project and may be worth anywhere between £50,000 and £1.0M. A typical project consists of between 30 to 50 sub-projects, each involving a specific unit made at UMC's factory. The units are transported to the customer's site and assembled there. An engineer from UMC will stay on site during the commissioning phase and ensure not only that UMC equipment works but that it is compatible with other manufacturing equipment.

UMC is based on a single site which contains administration and design offices and a workshop. The latter is involved mainly with the fabrication of units from bought-in components, including electronic parts. The company is well-known for the reliability and flexibility of its equipment which is as advanced as anything on the market at the current time.

The design office currently uses traditional drawing procedures. The intention is to introduce CAD in the form of 2-D drafting based on networked micro-computers. The justification for this expenditure is a projected increase of throughput through the design office, currently a bottleneck with the company having to turn away customers or suggest unacceptably long delivery times. In fact the company is currently overloaded in the sense that any change of specification or unforseen problem during a project that requires more work in the design office than originally planned can lead to considerable problems and delays for other contracts.

Company management have no prior experience with CAD and are looking to buy a standard system which hopefully needs little adaptation. To this end they have employed a consultant (supported by a DTI feasibility study scheme) to write a specification of their requirements. This includes all hardware, software, training and implementation planning. The result, a set of cost estimates, is shown below.

	Estimated cost (£)
Initial expenditure	
Two CAD Workstations	38,000
Plotter	12,000
Design Support System	6,500
Consultant support during implementation	11,000
Training (6 courses at £1,500)	9,000
Installation costs due to disruption	15,000
Total initial expenditure	91,500
Annual recurring expenditure	
Maintenance cost	5,000
Consumables (extra to existing)	1,000
Total annual recurring expenditure	6,000

The financial assessment of the benefit likely to come from this investment is that turnover might be increased by at least 10 per cent and possibly by as much as 20 per cent. It is not easy to forecast when this is likely to occur but it is hoped that the system is fully operational after one year. Roughly speaking, fixed costs (which for these purposes include staff costs) amount to around £2.8M per annum and variable costs (mainly materials and consumables) amount to 25 per cent of turnover, a low figure reflecting the high value added by the company through its design and project management expertise. It is not anticipated that manpower requirements will change in the near future.

Exercises

(1) Write a paper assessing the financial validity of the introduction of CAD at UMC, based on the above data supplemented by stated assumptions. The required rate of return is 23 per cent per annum and general cost inflation is around 8 per cent. What further data would be required to improve the validity of this analysis?

(2) Write a report to UMC senior management exploring the problems which are likely to arise during implementation of a CAD system and suggesting possible strategies to facilitate a successful outcome.

Case 3. MRP II in a traditional company

The Rockwood Manufacturing Company make a range of standard items of industrial machinery and offer an extensive maintenance service. Its operations are stable if somewhat traditional. Computer-based accounting and sales information systems exist along with an experienced data-processing department. The company plans the eventual development of CAD/CAM systems. Current number of employees is 826 and last year's sales amounted to £28M.

On advice from an internationally known group of consultants, who are currently examining a range of internal controls and procedures (for a fee of around £350,000), it has been decided that an MRP II (Manufacturing Resources Planning) system should be purchased. The company has no prior experience of operating in an MRP-style environment, current materials control procedures being manual and supplemented by computer-based records of doubtful validity. The MRP II system is intended to provide the basis for total control of materials related operations and in particular to enable considerable reductions to be made in stock levels.

The following includes a summary of a cost-benefit justification for this system. This does not include the consultancy fee. The estimates included in the cost-benefit analysis are based on the consultant's extensive experience gained over fifteen years of worldwide operations and they have been agreed with all relevant department heads. The estimates for computer hardware only include new equipment to be purchased. Considerable spare capacity exists on current systems and this will be utilized in the MRP II developments. On the basis of these estimates it is argued that the new system will pay back its initial costs in less than one year and that future annual savings will far exceed any extra costs incurred. The company requires a two-year maximum payback period on such investments and its average cost of capital is around 25 per cent. A time horizon of five years is normal for investment appraisal in this company.

Rockwood Manufacturing Company
MRP II system cost-benefit analysis (£000)

Implementation and on-going costs:

	Year 1	Year 2 onwards
Computing:		
Hardware and peripherals	400	50
Software	320	30
Enhancement to existing systems	100	0
Staff	40	40
Maintenance	20	40
Data Preparation:		
Bill of Materials restructuring	150	0
Database developments	100	0
People:		
Project team and support	173	38
Education – videos and facilities	8	0
– training	150	25
Outside consultancy	51	3
Miscellaneous	60	25
Total costs	1572	251

Annual savings:

	Year 1 onwards
Inventory related:	
Reduce inventory and work-in-progress	300
Reduce stocktaking	30
Reduce obsolescence	100
Reduce shortage costs (spares)	200
Labour related:	
Productivity improvements	110
Reduce overtime	460

Purchasing related:

Improve negotiation and vendor relationships	300
Reduce premium freight costs	25

Marketing related:

Reduce contribution loss due to shortages	200
Improve market planning	50
Total annual saving	1775

Exercises and points for discussion

(1) Carry out a preliminary financial analysis on the data given assuming an inflation adjusted discount rate of 17 per cent. What further data would be essential for a valid financial assessment to be made? Are the results of your analysis credible?

(2) Critically assess the basis of the cost/benefit analysis given and suggest alternative costs and benefits which should be taken into account.

(3) What problems are likely to arise if the implementation of MRP II is undertaken in this case without other organizational changes? Assuming MRP II is appropriate, what actions might be taken to facilitate its implementation?

11 Barriers, failure and dubious advice - management development for AMT implementation

Introduction

In the mid 1980s, the Manpower Services Commission (now the Training Agency) funded a number of reports on various aspects of the management of technical change. One of the earliest of these was written by Brian Twiss (Twiss (1985)) and included as a central feature the conclusions of a survey of the views of researchers and other concerned individuals of the barriers that exist to effective technical change in the UK.

Whilst it should be remembered that this information referred only to the UK at that specific time and was based on expert opinion rather than measurements taken for a controlled sample of respondents, the results were a thought-provoking input to a number of pieces of research, including that specifically on the management of AMT (Harrison (1987)).

This chapter commences with a summary and discussion of the barriers which are thought to exist to technical change before going on to further illustrate and explore such barriers. Prior to reading the next section you might like to make out a list of the managerial factors which you would expect to provide a barrier to technical change in an organization.

Barriers to technical change

The Twiss survey concentrated on opinions as to the major shortcomings of management in the UK with respect to technical change. Certain other potential barriers were briefly explored and dismissed as being of less importance. These included:

- the level of Research and Development expenditure in the UK (effective technical change often flows from appropriate rather than large expenditure)
- the level of industrial investment (more important is the way it is managed)
- Trade Union opposition (with certain well-publicized exceptions, workers are less resistant to change than managers)
- access to technical information (ample information exists if effort is made to explore it).

The general views of academics and managers in the reports mentioned above were that the following represented substantial managerial barriers to technical change in general and AMT-related change in particular.

Attitudes of senior management to future planning

There appeared to be what Twiss referred to as a 'lack of a future orientation' amongst senior UK managers at the time. This was thought to be the case, at least with reference to technical change, in most small to medium sized companies and even in many large companies.

This lack of a future view could well apply to technical, commercial or managerial issues. In the first instance it might reflect the attitude that technical change is unpredictable and that the best management can do is to seize opportunities which present themselves. The lack of a commercial long-term view would similarly refer to the uncertain nature of markets. A short-term view on management development might be caused by the assumption that the mobility of managers will rob a company of the value of its investment in training and education or more simply by the view that management development is not caused by planned educational actions but just happens through exposure to managerial life.

The potential consequences of such technical and business myopia are obvious. The strangest part of this situation is its reported pervasiveness in the larger companies and in small entrepreneurial companies. One problem with this reported barrier is that it does not differentiate between different reasons for myopia. It is one thing for the management of a company merely to be complacent about the future and another for management to be concerned but feel themselves helpless in the face of a turbulent environment.

Many managers take refuge in a pride in their ability to 'muddle through' rather than plan for the future. This, amongst other things, reflects a limited view of what constitutes a plan. Many managers sincerely feel that the environment and competition place a real barrier to long-term planning. If a 'plan' is, say, a detailed projection of product sales for the next five years, such planning is unrealistic unless the company totally dominates a stable market. However, a plan for such a period is more likely to refer to product development intentions, building up its manufacturing and management capability and promoting its image in the market place. Technological lead-times are such that long-term planning, with all its uncertainties, is essential.

If one discusses such issues with managers, one is often faced with anecdotes of bad past experiences, in particular of technology which either didn't work or was outdated when finally implemented. This may well colour the thinking of key individuals (either senior managers or respected opinion leaders) in a company as to the wisdom or otherwise of taking any risks where technology is involved. In hindsight, failure could always have been avoided. It might be argued that technical change is not the problem here. Rather that a lack of honesty in learning from the past, possibly fuelled by the desire to score politically over rivals, promotes a cautious approach whereby each individual avoids risking personal failure, resulting in a substantial risk of corporate failure.

Absence of a formal technical change strategy

Most organizations seemed to lack a clear strategy for technical change, a problem compounded by the feeling of many senior technical staff that they had little influence on decisions made at board level. This is similar to the problem of the poor self-image of manufacturing managers (see Hill (1985)).

The importance of a technical change strategy is not only its content, which should help decision-making at many levels, but the involvement of staff in the process of its formulation. One wonders, quite bluntly, if such involvement is not desired by many top managers, particularly in an area where their knowledge may be seen to be incomplete.

A comprehensive technical change strategy in a manufacturing company will relate research and development, product change, process change and the company-wide use of information technology. There can be little doubt of the practical value of such a strategy but there are also the political problems and inter-departmental rivalries which will be uncovered in formulating such a plan.

It might be thought that the content of a technical change strategy is itself entirely technical and specialized. In fact this is not the case. There are several things which should be made clear by such a plan in addition to technical intentions. These include the need to foster a corporate culture which supports and encourages technical change and the balance which must be struck between incremental and revolutionary change, an issue which is central to our model of the management of change.

Poor managerial integration

A common theme in organization theory is the need to strike a balance between the specialization which occurs as staff become more expert in performing particular roles, and the need to draw together all the separate activities of an organization to achieve common goals. The former is called differentiation and may refer to function (for example, being a good production planner) or to some other feature such as managing the problems associated with a particular product. The bringing together of these separate parts is called integration and is concerned with more than the flow of data associated with integrated computer systems.

Integration may be promoted by procedures and data flows. It may also be encouraged by training and the development of an appropriate set of managerial attitudes, a simple example being the willingness of senior management to be visible and approachable and to encourage their staff to do likewise. The sharing of views on the direction and future of the company is important in ensuring integration. An integrative feature common in large Japanese as well as some Western companies is the mobility of executives between functions and departments. This runs directly counter to the view that, say, an accountant must only work within the finance function. It also includes the possibility that the same accountant might hold a senior position in a technical area. Naturally some jobs specifically require professional training. A company should consider the trade-off between the short-term disadvantage of a manager having to learn how to manage a new specialism (and even in the short-term this may be outweighed by a fresh and enthusiastic approach) and the long-term benefits of the development of a corps of senior managers with experience in a range of functions.

Poor in-company educational processes

The Twiss report had much to say about the technical illiteracy of general management and the dismal levels of management and business knowledge and skills exhibited by many technologists.

An understanding of technology by managers from other disciplines is often not seen as important. This attitude may be rationalized as efficiency ('why bother to hire experts and then learn it all yourself?') but may mask a fear of being seen as inadequate. Yet how can a financial manager be supposed to understand a technical proposal without at least comprehending the basic language of the proposal and its inherent risks and opportunities?

The answer, unfortunately, is that he can only by insisting that the proposal is couched entirely in his own language, that is, in financial terms. This may even be thought desirable on the grounds that it brings technologists back to a consideration of the commercial realities of the business. In view of our discussion in Chapters 9 and 10 we might wonder if traditional financial appraisal methods really are so effective in reflecting commercial reality.

An obvious source of learning about technology in general and AMT implementation in particular is practice and experience. Contrary to the popular saying, practice does not make perfect – carried out in a critical vacuum it may simply reinforce bad habits and unhelpful attitudes. However, to have had extensive experience of all stages of the development of AMT, to have reflected constructively on those experiences, to have derived lessons for future action and to have interacted with others with similar experience is potentially of great value. Indeed, many forms of management training are based on such experiences and use them as a vehicle for learning.

There are strong indications that the professional training of engineers is taking on board the necessity for the acquisition of some business knowledge and personal skills (see Chapter 3). It is in the interest of companies to continue this process through in-company training provision. A major problem for companies using leading edge technology is the necessity for the updating of technologists on purely technical matters. This may involve substantial attendance at courses and may tempt managers to view management education for technologists as a further drain on their productive time. This may not be so if a modern approach to management training through work-based assignments and the development of competencies is pursued in association with well targeted open learning materials.

Poor attitudes to managerial work

A further set of barriers centres on attitudes of individuals which are not helpful to technical change. These include low commitment to the organization, a lack of real interest and determination to succeed, an unwillingness to collaborate with fellow employees and a general unwillingness to take risks. This set of attitudes might be present in technologists and in managers from other functions. They may be reinforced by a managerial reward system whereby a non-entrepreneurial approach is encouraged and occassional failures remembered. Much recent managerial literature addresses precisely this problem but many organizations and individuals will have to undergo a painful process of transformation if such attitudes are to be changed.

Failure in technological projects

An obvious barrier to technical change is failure, both actual and anticipated. Staff may fear failure and find excuses for not proceeding. In many organizations such fear is quite justified! On other occasions technical projects may simply fail to achieve their objectives. This has implications for current and future projects. It is useful therefore at this stage to review reasons for project failure. A classification based on the project management literature and responses of managers in a small survey is included below:

Reasons related to objectives, resources and control

- User requirements imperfectly understood
- User requirements incorrectly specified
- Project goals incorrectly stated
- Project goals overambitious
- Project too big
- Environment changes
- Organization changes
- Lack of suitable resources in the organization
- Conflict in resource allocation in the organization
- Poor planning and control of a project (time and cost)
- Poor planning and control of the portfolio of projects in the organization (time and cost)
- Necessary activities not performed
- Unnecessary activities performed

Reasons related to technology

- Poor use of available design technologies
- Poor use of available project management technologies
- Imported technology not available as expected (i.e. failure in 'intercepting' new technology)

- Imported technology does not work
- Internally developed technology does not work
- Internally developed product technology obsolete

Reasons related to people and communication

- Organization structure not appropriate for project management
- Project team structure not appropriate
- Poor 'people management' within the project team
- Clash of personalities within the team
- Clash of interests within the team
- Clash of personalities with outside individuals
- Clash of interests with outside individuals
- Lack of client contact by team members or leader
- Lack of end user contact by team members or leader

Whilst realizing that failure in a project is often due to an accumulation of problems, three fundamental failure modes are listed above. The first relates to problems in the setting of objectives, the allocation of resources and the control of the project. The 'user' whose requirements govern the project goals may be internal or external to the organization. For AMT related projects the user is most likely to be internal but this should not lead us to making over-ambitious assumptions about our knowledge of his or her needs and requirements.

The second area of concern is technology itself. An important issue when implementing state-of-the-art technology is the idea of intercepting new technologies. Thus our highly innovative CIM development project, say, may include the assumption that a software supplier will make available in a year's time certain products currently being designed. It is obviously prudent to make contingency plans in case the software fails to arrive on time or to specification. Such alternative plans may be difficult to make and thus at the very least regular and close contact with the software supplier is necessary to provide early warnings of problems.

The third area of concern relates to people and inter-personal communication. It includes a fine distinction between a client and an end user. The former may be more senior and approve payment for the project, but failure to meet the needs of the latter may ultimately lead to failure. One wonders how many machines have been installed in factories to the satisfaction of managers and engineers but with no genuine improvements in effective production due to mistaken assumptions about how they would actually be used. Many managers have themselves grown weary of 'information systems' imposed from the outside which were supposed to revolutionize their jobs. The result has been do-it-yourself, micro-based systems which have genuinely met the needs of their users, though often at considerable cost due to incompatibility with other systems.

How to discourage AMT developments – a guide for the top executive.

Inspired by Kanter's 'rules for stifling innovation' (Kanter (1983)), we suggest the following as a guide for top managers who wish to discourage AMT developments. It will be noted that most of the rules may actually sound good advice, indeed may even be good advice in other circumstances. The assiduous reader should in each case think very clearly why the rule given is of dubious value.

(1) Keep your mind on the job. The future can wait. We have to pay this week's wage bill first. Besides, the future never happens as you planned it. You need to be adaptive and fast on your feet to survive.

(2) There are enough inescapable risks in business. Don't add to them by attempting to use unproven technology. Let your competitors take that risk.

(3) When a complex proposal is put forward, insist that a number of managers are formally involved, must write reports on the proposal's validity and must sign their approval before it gets to you. Insist that they must examine the proposal critically while you preserve your independence. If the proposal survives and you sanction it, keep all the reports and documents as evidence.

(4) Protect the bottom line. Evaluate everything rigorously in financial terms. Every proposal must stand on its own merits.

When you hear the phrase 'intangible benefits' applied to something new be even more critical - someone is trying to sell you a dud.

(5) Don't involve your staff in your decisions unless you already know all the answers. If the decision is controversial and involves technology, delegate. But don't delegate or seek involvement in reorganization decisions. Remember that reorganizing a department and reallocating responsibilities carries with it the implication of past failure on the part of those being reorganized without requiring you to define precisely what failure occurred.

(6) Request information regularly and occasionally randomly, but don't give it out. Information is power. Remain in tight control.

(7) Planning meetings are just a substitute for work – and so is training.

(8) Don't employ experts and then do it all yourself. Maintain your personal competitive edge. You got where you are by being better than the pack. Keep it that way. Don't reward experts with praise. Like you they are only doing their job.

(9) Don't spend money training managers, technologists and workers just so they can take their skills to rival companies.

(10) Fear of failure is the best motivator.

AMT and management development

The line of logic we have been pursuing throughout this book is that AMT is a competitive opportunity for the company as a whole but that for AMT to be effective the company as a whole must change. This means that the management of a company must develop in order to take advantage of such opportunities.

By the management of a company we are not referring to a select few but, in the sense developed in Chapter 3, to everyone who as a professional worker takes a responsible approach to his or her role in the company. We assume that managers are concerned with the management of the enterprise as a whole and that AMT, if itself well managed, can contribute strongly to organizational success.

We may illustrate this by considering a company which has

developed its CAPM system and manufacturing responsiveness to the point where customer demands can be met, however small the batch or unusual the design (hopefully within reasonable limits). This has profound implications for the way in which non-manufacturing staff do their jobs. Consider a sales executive working at some distance from the factory and faced with a customer eager to place an order. Using modern communications technology such an executive could presumably obtain information on current designs, the time needed for design adjustments, available stocks of raw materials, availability of manufacturing resources and of competing orders. Hopefully a product price quotation system would be available. Should the sales executive thus be able to agree there and then the price, specification and delivery time for the product?

In this situation the use of the phrase 'sales executive' is justified – the individual has considerable authority to take action on behalf of the company as a whole. If one baulks at such an arrangement and requires the salesman to go through a process to gain approval, the customer might prefer to do business with the representative of the rival company who is patiently waiting outside.

The sales executive described above, like his colleagues in finance, personnel and administration, will require a considerable knowledge of the workings and limitations of AMT systems in order to make sound decisions. They will also have to be willing to take greater responsibility for their decisions as these will be translated into company-wide action with alarming speed.

A further implication of this diffusion of responsibility to the interface between the organization and its environment is the effect it has on the roles of production manager and production planner. Both will be increasingly charged with managing systems' improvements rather than routinely using systems. Their actions must be better integrated with those of other functions as stock buffers disappear and customers become more informed and demanding. Thus the ability of staff to manage change, particularly technological and systems change, is of prime importance and is explored below.

AMT design and implementation must be accompanied by substantial investment in human assets. Financially-orientated managers may be unhappy about investing in mobile assets but there is little alternative. It is, however, reasonable that such investments, whether through recruitment or training, should be appraised and monitored with the same thoroughness as applied to hardware and software.

The dynamics of management learning

The outward manifestation of learning is changes in behaviour leading to an improvement in meeting objectives. This may refer to people, systems (including expert systems) and organizations. It results from experience in one form or another through a process involving some variation on the following stages:

- data gathered as a result of action
- reflection on such data and communication with others
- a generalization of available data resulting in an adaptation of models of the relationship between cause and effect
- further action and a continuation of this process.

Such a description, being incomplete and based on induction, would not satisfy the philosopher of learning science but it draws attention to the continuing nature of learning processes and their need for some repeatability of experience in order for generalization to be made. Fortunately we do not, indeed could not, rely entirely on our own experience. The results of management learning are public and we can learn from the experiences and generalizations of others.

Thus the major sources of management learning are:

- our own experiences, provided they are used constructively
- diffusion of learning from within the organization
- diffusion of learning from outside the organization.

Intra-firm diffusion may come from reporting of experiences between colleagues, sharing of experiences (particularly within an explicitly supportive framework such as Action Learning), assignments, job mobility within an organization and through the rules and procedures used in the organization.

Inter-firm diffusion comes from inter-firm mobility and through the forms of professional development which use outside agencies. Potential sources of learning in the environment include educational institutions, consultants, researchers, employer associations, trade unions, equipment and materials suppliers, competitors and customers.

Outside agencies may provide knowledge and facts. Equally, they may provide ideas and alternative views. These might come in the form of traditional class-based teaching, open learning packages or opportunities to interact with individuals with different perspectives. Certainly the relationship between the organization and outside learning providers must be carefully managed, a considerable challenge for personnel and training specialists and management development gurus.

This outline discussion has so far concentrated on the 'who, what and how?' of learning. Of considerable importance in an AMT context is the 'when?'. In Fig. 11.1 we have a diagram illustrating the stages of learning relating to a new technology. Almost any branch of AMT would provide a suitable illustration of the ideas presented (see also Harrison (1987)).

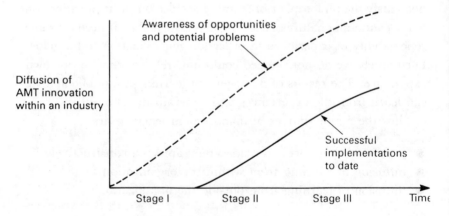

Figure 11.1 Diffusion of AMT innovation

With reference to each of the stages shown in the figure, here are several questions asked and answered ('company' refers to the user of AMT):

(i) What inputs are required into the learning process?

Stage I – Bright ideas to inspire the more adventurous companies and individuals.

Stage II – Information on what pitfalls have been discovered by the innovators and mature advice on possibilities.

Stage III – Effective communication of established ideas and case studies on successful practice.

(ii) What are the major sources of such inputs?

Stage I – Research findings and inventions.

Stage II – Consultants and systems suppliers.

Stage III – Providers of standard qualification courses.

(iii) Who is learning?

Stage I – Everyone actively involved.

Stage II – Specialist company staff.

Stage III – A wide audience of actual and potential company employees.

(iv) What is the cost of learning?

Stage I – High for all concerned.

Stage II – High for the company receiving the training and a substantial source of revenue for the training provider.

Stage III – Moderate.

This shows once again the need for careful planning and thought on the timing of AMT-related training. Such activity may be easier and cheaper in Stage III but by that time much of its competitive edge may have been lost. One should also remember that Fig. 11.1 may not only refer to each component technology but a specific technology, for example robotics, may go through several waves of development.

It is important that a company avoid the vicious circle illustrated in Fig. 11.2. If such a situation appears to exist, typical remedies which may be attempted are the use of consultants (to aid planning), the use of total system suppliers of proven technology (to ease implementation) and the use of outside training providers. It is worth care and investment to produce the positive circle shown in Fig. 11.3.

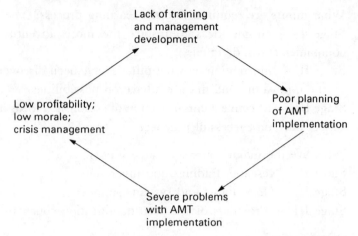

Figure 11.2 Vicious circle due to lack of management development

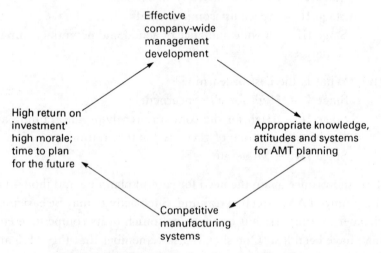

Figure 11.3 Positive circle of management development

Management development in practice

The literature on management development presents this activity as a systematic and continuing process of analysing present resources, estimating future needs and operating policies of recruitment, training, promotion and transfer to meet those needs. It is one of the duties of top management to ensure that this process is carried out. This may be done in an autocratic fashion or in a consultative manner.

The latter seems more appropriate in a situation of AMT development as it allows the knowledge held by a wide range of professional staff to contribute to the process.

Management development refers to the management team as a whole, perhaps to all employees. Manager development refers to individuals, and the issues present in this activity are the focus of considerable attention at the present time. Above all one should remember that manager development refers to adults who probably already possess considerable experience and knowledge of the world and its inhabitants. Adults often prefer to learn from their peers and from experience. The process of learning for managers is often about putting well-known ideas into practice and about challenging firmly held beliefs.

A popular idea is that managers should be entrepreneurial in their outlook. They should be champions for their product or process. Some characteristics of the entrepreneur were discussed in Chapter 3 and Kanter (1983) and Peters (1987) (to mention but two) are much concerned with their development. If only knowledge and logic were needed for AMT implementation, champions might not be necessary. In most organizations the introduction of something new also requires zeal, energy, political ability and the skills of argument and communication. Above all courage and a willingness to take risks are essential.

The emphasis here has been on the personal characteristics of the champion and it is no easy matter to develop those characteristics, quite apart from the fact that the champion may require large rewards to deter movement to the employ of a competitor. An alternative approach is to create an organizational culture and structure which encourages a wide range of individuals to act in an entrepreneurial fashion. Some 'dubious advice' on how to inhibit entrepreneurs was presented above. It is a far from easy task to encourage entrepreneurs whilst keeping the organization as a whole in control of its corporate direction. There is room here for imagination and innovative design. Possibly the factory of the future will be a loose collection of franchised parts? The management team which most effectively solves this conundrum will gain a substantial competitive edge to complement its use of modern manufacturing technology.

The complexity of AMT implementation.

Though much of the above is common to a wide range of technology management contexts, there are special features in AMT management which provide a special challenge. These arise from three sources. The first is the need for the integration of a range of very advanced specialisms, particularly in engineering and computing, for AMT to be successfully implemented. The second comes from the need in many implementations (i.e. those which are not based on greenfield sites) to maintain a continuing and cost-effective throughput of products while fundamental changes are being made. The third, which is the subject of this section, is the complexity due to inter-relationships between the sub-systems which are being changed. Yet it is this third source which also provides a rich training ground for real change agents.

We may view manufacturing as a simple input/output system surrounded by an infrastructure. The latter will include all the functional specialisms necessary to support the manufacturing process, in particular the production planning and control, quality assurance and human resource development systems.

Such a view is strategically static and should include in addition systems for changing products, processes and the infrastructure. These may be collectively referred to as the design systems, using the word design in the very general sense of being applicable to any socio-technical artefact. The design systems also require support from the organization, i.e. their own infrastructure.

We must, however, take this process of systems description at least one stage further. What is the mechanism of change for the design systems? For example, a traditional drawing office will not by itself transmogrify into CAD, let alone forge links with manufacturing to form a CAD/CAM system. In Fig. 3.1 we showed a fuller representation of this situation, which might itself be expanded endlessly.

The driving force for change is here referred to as the management of technological change, a part of technology management in the broadest sense. The key point is that changes to all the systems mentioned are likely to be progression at the same time if at differing pace. Combating the sheer complexity and potential for chaos of this situation requires determined action and a number of possibilities exist.

The first is a standard piece of advice given to designers of CIM systems – 'simplify then integrate'. This advice must be approached with some caution; indeed, it must seem strange to technological non-sophisticates to describe the components of AMT as simple! The point is that however complex the internal actions of a system might be (typical examples being our own bodies, computers, cars) we should be able to form models of the actions of such systems which, for a given purpose in a given environment, simply and effectively relate inputs to outputs.

It is argued that only when such simple representations are possible can the integration of the models into a more complex whole be contemplated. The CIM designer must fight a continual battle against being surprised by the non-intuitive action of the system under development.

An alternative approach is not to attempt to design such a system but to let it evolve, i.e. not to be too concerned with how things work but to see what they can do through experimentation. Such an approach is hardly new and is even becoming commonplace within such areas as mathematics, where exploring the behaviour of sets of equations relating to certain kinds of turbulent systems is accomplished through the use of computers (see Gleick (1987)).

Evolution, however, can be an expensive and time-consuming activity and must be attempted within a framework likely to lead to overall systems improvement. Typical is the JIT approach, though this involves a potentially slow process of improvement. One of the avowed aims of OPT is to speed up this process, but it is interesting to note that this in turn involves the acceptance of the use of a highly complex 'black-box' scheduling algorithm.

A third approach is to concentrate in top-down fashion on a development plan (often anachronistically called a 'blueprint') for AMT. The problems here are the feasibility of such planning in a rapidly changing market and technological environment and the barriers to AMT discussed above. However, there is little doubt that a corporate plan for the enterprise as a whole must exist and this must take account of technological opportunities.

The approach described in this chapter and complementary to those above is to concentrate on developing the human resource in an organization through the promotion of an enterprise culture and the encouraging of individuals to act as champions for process, product and infrastructure change. With this in mind the AMT-related changes affecting an organization provide a continuing source of action learning opportunities, providing it is remembered that learning is more than raw experience. It carries with it the connotation of continual personal improvement and demonstrated effectiveness.

12 Jobs, skills and training

Introduction

Although we have concentrated on the development of managers in earlier chapters, taking on board the idea that in the automated factory of the future everyone will be a knowledge worker, in practice much current attention is paid to the jobs and the training of operators, maintenance staff and technicians. In this chapter we explore some issues in this area.

It is important to remember that a vast body of social science literature exists dealing precisely with changes in the role of the worker in the face of new technology. We here introduce some ideas on the changes likely to take place in the job descriptions of factory personnel. We then move on to a discussion of how employees may be rewarded (wage payment systems) and the role of employee organizations (trade unions). Following this is an introduction to some aspects of safety in an automated environment and we end with illustrations of training approaches in the context of an example of an outline training proposal and a case study.

Jobs

While AMT has the potential to change all jobs in a company, the effect is most obvious on those within the production process. Accompanying job changes must be appropriate training and retraining and these issues are described in detail below.

Production operators

The most obvious effect of AMT implementation on operator jobs is de-manning. This is particularly evident as light, manual repetitive work is automated and the fewer remaining operators become machine minders. Working directly with the product is substituted by a watching brief on the machines, which can be exceedingly boring and de-motivating.

To counter this, the operator may be able, with appropriate training, to take on new roles. The first is in setting up machines, though a major objective of AMT is to reduce the required set-up times and job content to a minimum. An FMS would aim for automatic set-up. The second is statistical process control where the operator is expected, through measurement and charting, to monitor trends in key machine performance variables. Once again technology, through automatic testing, would aim to reduce such manual intervention. Indeed, one principle of the Japanese approach to manufacturing, confusingly called autonomation, is that machines should be self-monitoring to the extent that they will themselves signal the need for attention. In this way more advanced forms of automation aim to remove the need for continual operator attendance. In moving towards reliable, unmanned operations most plants still require operators though such jobs will change as the boredom of repetitive manual tasks is replaced by that of sentry duty. Care is therefore required in redesigning the content of jobs so that the operator can genuinely contribute and feel responsible for some aspects of production. A path to be avoided is the introduction of irrelevant tasks, such as taking readings of performance parameters already under automatic control, in order to maintain attentiveness. Such admissions of defeat in the design of socio-technical systems simply waste money and in the long term demoralize both the operator and the systems designer.

Skilled workers

Where automation has not currently replaced skills, the need for skills training remains as before, indeed is increased as quality requirements increase.

One view is that this situation is merely temporary as automation spreads, using expert systems and other artificial intelligence tools, to all production-related tasks. This is challenged in Rawlence and Cooley (1988) which reports on an Esprit Project concerned with the effective design of systems where decision-making is appropriately shared between people and machines. The argument is that while in medieval manufacturing the craftsman was the designer and the maker, a split between these functions occurred during the Renaissance when the designer/architect/manager role took over the key decisions of product and process design and the craftsman's contribution became limited to hand skills (with a number of supervisory and technician roles, such as quality inspection and scheduling, developing also). Automation threatens not only the limited craftsperson's role but also the technical and design roles. We should ask whether this is actually desirable and economic for all kinds of production. If we lose from the workplace all human experience, ingenuity and creativity, will the new automated systems actually be able to cope with changing demands? If they cannot, will the human skills remain to intervene and solve the problems which have arisen?

The crux of the argument here is less to do with the capabilities of traditional automation as it is honed to perfection in machining systems, and more to do with the capabilities of artificial intelligence-based systems in taking over the overall planning and control of production operations. A similar line of argument occurs in the automation of non-manufacturing tasks in office and managerial work. Such an extreme view of automation appears to simply miss the point that companies are human activity systems and all forms of computer-based automation should be aimed at complementing essentially human attributes. The problem of the precise line between human and machine action is particularly acute in manufacturing where the line appears to be steadily moving across what was previously thought to be human territory.

In the shorter term, an area where craftspeople are needed is in maintenance. Here the traditional mechanical and electrical skills are to some extent being replaced by the need for electronic skills and the ability to diagnose the causes of failure in complex, inter-connected systems. In particular a need for re-training is evident here, along with a need for training courses to be absolutely up to date not only in what skills are taught but also in removing traditional but marginal material from the curriculum.

Technicians and technologists

While some areas of technician responsibility in draughting, testing and planning may be lost to computer-based systems, other needs arise, principally in managing and implementing change. Many technical jobs now have far more management content, not simply in terms of communication, presentation and human resource management terms (though training courses for junior technical managers often give this impression) but also in the need to seek out new opportunities and act as champions for ideas within the managerial system of a company.

It is also now recognized that the scope of many technician jobs, in terms of the technologies they are able to apply, is now broadening and this is now a category of employees of great potential value to the company proceeding on a path towards AMT implementation. A further point to note is that a number of traditional management support roles, such as work study engineer, are changing as it becomes accepted that the techniques of, say, method study be more widely practised by staff (for example as part of the action of quality circles). Similarly the importance of value analysis and value engineering, along with the techniques of variety reduction, become more than occasional exercises carried out on the whim of a new manager. They are part of the new fundamental approach to work, as the philosophy of continual improvement becomes ingrained in all company staff.

Finally, as a result of the changes described above, the role of production supervisor will change, hopefully from a crude 'motivator' to a professional colleague with technical and managerial skills and able to fully represent the needs of his area within the managerial system.

Rewarding employees

Employees at all levels in an organization receive a package of benefits to compensate them for the time they spend at work. This may include a wide variety of things from status, training and the promise of future advancement, through perks of various kinds (subsidized pensions, health care, sports facilities and the like) to direct remuneration.

Wages, salaries and bonuses of various kinds make up the greater part of employment costs, which even in automated manufacturing plants are considerable if one includes all labour, management and professional staff. Of particular concern is the equity and motivational aspects of various payment systems and the variations in payments to staff which result from them. At one extreme a co-operative or group of professionals may decide that all employees should be paid the same regardless of length of service and perceived effectiveness. At the other extreme, door-to-door selling perhaps, all employees are paid only a commission calculated on some measure of actual individual performance. Just about every possibility between these two limits has been tried out in manufacturing industry at one time or another, so difficult is the problem of balancing motivation with productive effectiveness.

Some patterns of remuneration are commonplace. Much publicity has been given to the salaries of company chief executives which may well be an order of magnitude above average salaries. Similarly, in many companies senior and middle management are more highly rewarded than technical staff, though this may well cause problems in career paths and when shortages occur in the labour markets for particular areas of skill. However, in many plants the above are still regarded as salaried employees and their terms and conditions of service differ greatly from 'blue-collar' workers. The breaking down of this historic division is seen as a priority in many companies. The idea of a single status for all employees has a number of attractions, not least of which is the breaking down of what many have come to see as a class barrier.

Ironically, single status may not be welcome in some manufacturing plants where operators and technical support staff have become accustomed to large overtime payments and bonuses based on slack piece-work systems. In such cases it may be more in the interests of management to replace such payments with greater stability of employment and other benefits. This in turn may lead to constraints on the actions of management used to laying off staff in slack periods. It may also lead to dramatic reductions in productivity. Despite the glowing reports of harmony and productivity in foreign-owned plants in this country, no one approach to employee remuneration is perfect on all counts and many new approaches will require massive changes to the working culture in traditional industry.

Highly automated plants are the more obvious candidates for single status working in that employees are likely to be either highly skilled and of considerable market value to a company, or alternatively engaged in general tasks not directly related to output and therefore paid relative to attendance rather than measured output. The most urgent problems in the future are likely to be the motivation, career prospects and rewards of the design and technical staff whose work will have a crucial effect on the performance of a manufacturing unit.

The technicalities and implications of various wage payment systems are extensively documented in the operations and personnel management literature (see, for example, Child (1984)). The main choices are between the following:

- flat rate based on time worked
- incentive based on the output of an individual or group
- individual merit rating based on a supervisor's subjective assessment of performance
- measured day work based on meeting an agreed norm
- payment made for productivity, cost, quality or flexibility improvement
- profit-sharing.

Any mixture of the above entails trade-offs, broadly on the following dimensions:

- Simplicity (easier control) v. complexity (more options)
- Standardization (low cost of administration) v. differentiation (recognize individual situations and choices)
- Rigid (maintain control) v. flexible (avoid confrontation)

● Influence individual performance and motivation v. develop collective relationships

As will be readily apparent, such choices cannot be separated from decisions regarding other aspects of process and infrastructure. Many technological options, such as the choice of MRP II systems, place very definite demands on human resources (in this case discipline, for example) but are neutral as to how such demands are met. Other options, such as the use of JIT or TQM, almost automatically mean a movement to group responsibility, a widening of the scope of individual jobs and a greater identification with corporate aims and acceptance of culture. Such changes may be inhibited or even rendered impossible by inappropriate wage payment systems. The removal of such barriers must be handled sensitively and imaginatively, depending on the industrial relations history and current situation of the organization.

Employee organizations

The central focus of this book is the relationship between AMT, management and product markets. It could equally have been written from a completely different perspective, that of trade unions. It has been emphasized frequently that AMT is largely about control, either in the engineering sense of automatic control of equipment or in the managerial sense of controlling manufacturing operations. From the perspective of trade unions, AMT and new technology may be viewed as instruments of social control with considerable political implications at company, industry and national levels.

A much reported aspect of technological change concerns the newspaper publishing industry and the changes in industrial practice which have taken place in editing and printing papers. On a smaller scale, an individual working at a visual display terminal may find his or her work being extensively monitored for productivity, quality and variety and such information could be used as input to a range of decisions from payment, through appraisal and training to dismissal. Trade union officers see their organizations as a key safeguard against abuses which may arise within a company as technological change proceeds.

The traditional role of unions has been to leave company decision-making to management (unless redundancies are involved) and to negotiate on a range of issues including wages, conditions and safety. The more pro-active unions, in particular those representing workers whose jobs are concerned with information technology, have attempted to move ahead of companies in anticipating human relations and labour market problems which might arise as a result of technological change. They have then sought to participate in the process of change in a constructive partnership for the negotiated benefit of all concerned. Obviously this arrangement is easier to achieve in a prosperous and expanding sector than in one where labour is being substituted by technology. These issues are the subject of a large and specialist range of literature which places union actions in a theoretical and historical context (see, for example, McLoughlin and Clark (1988) and Preece (1988)).

Such literature is also valuable in contrasting various fundamental sociological approaches to the effects of technological change on work organization. The contingency approach, based on the work of Woodward, argued that the organization of production depends on specific factors such as product market, form of technology and company size, and was generally optimistic on the effects of new technology on the workforce. By contrast, Braverman's labour process theory emphasizes the conflict between labour on the one hand and capital, with its managerial representatives, on the other. More recently the complex strategic choice approaches emphasize the role of management in shaping the total socio-technical system. The latter is closest to the fundamental assumptions made in this book, though the detailed analysis is beyond our scope.

Safety

The safety of the automated environment is a subject of great concern. Some key issues of safety are explored in Fitzmaurice and Zairi (1988) which refers to risks inherent in the use of manufacturing equipment, such as robots, and risks present in office environments.

A great deal of experience has been gathered in the past about the isolation of the moving parts of otherwise fixed items of machinery such as CNC equipment. When in operation such equipment is isolated from operators while visibility of action is maintained so operators can observe any problems developing. However, much AMT is based on moving equipment such as robots, automatic guided vehicles (AGVs) and other materials handling equipment. Obviously problems are reduced if such equipment is part of, say, an FMS which itself is totally isolated when in operation. Problems may still occur for the operator and other personnel if equipment such as AGVs are required to move in unrestricted areas or if hardware and software problems in robots cause them to exceed their normal operational bounds.

Statistics show that the greatest dangers are for staff whose jobs include setting up, programming, repairing and maintaining material flow to such machines. Such individuals, by the nature of their jobs, may be close to equipment which is in motion and their protection may be based less on automatic controls than on training and an understanding and continual awareness of risks.

A range of problems associated with working at visual display terminals in offices are well documented and may spread to a wider range of staff as Computer Integrated Manufacture broadens its scope. Such problems may be physical (such as vision disorders, repetitive strain injury, etc.) or stress related, an unfortunate mirroring of earlier production line issues of boredom with machine paced work. Indeed many of the less fortunate characteristics of mass production seem to have been transferred from the factory floor to the office. The solution here lies partly with superior ergonomic design of facilities and working practices and also with the automation of data entry through sensing equipment and data capture at source. Certainly a modern manufacturing facility will use automatic testing, recording and communications technology as far as possible and where manual data entry is necessary ensure that duplication does not occur.

The role of safety practitioner as a specific area of professional expertise, and also the responsibility for ensuring safety which rests with all staff, still remains and is even growing and changing with the new challenges of automated working environments. The designers of AMT systems have a particular responsibility to think through ways in which accidents may occur in the use of their equipment or ways in which their products may be detrimental to the long-term working environment.

Skills training and general education

Though we deal extensively with project management in Chapters 13 and 14 and have discussed a number of general principles in the management of AMT change, we have not discussed the actual techniques of training and education which will support AMT developments. A large body of learning methods exists beyond the formal presentations and discussions which continue to be widely used. In particular, the role of external consultants and internal training staff should be carefully scrutinized to assess their real effectiveness. It is not unknown for departments introducing major new systems to adopt a 'do-it-yourself' approach regarding training on the assumption that direct relevance is far more important than presentational skills.

An exercise in designing a training programme

An important role for training staff is not in the actual delivery of programmes but in advising on their construction and facilitating learning in all forms. The following short paper describes a fictitious proposal for a training programme to accompany the implementation of an MRP II system at one factory of a major engineering company. The reader is invited to critically assess the advantages and disadvantages of the approach suggested.

The training and education proposal
There are two basic types of general staff training required when a production management system, such as MRP II, is implemented. One is concerned with the technicalities of actually using the system, how to enter data, what codes to use to get certain reports and so

forth. The other, which is very expensive in terms of time, is the education of the whole set of potential users in the aims and objectives of the system so its real value, and the need for discipline in its use, may be appreciated.

It is useful to divide the population of potential users, which includes all production related managers, technical staff and supervisors, into three groups. The first group, around 10 per cent of the population, consists of people who are so flexible and receptive to change that they would be willing to accept almost any new system. Another 10 per cent of the population are naturally rigid in their attitudes and suspicious of any change. These two groups include most of the potential opinion leaders. The remaining majority are the main target for general education showing the reasoning behind MRP II and its place in our plans.

People learn in a variety of ways, but of particular importance is reflection on past experience, relating experience to general concepts and ideas, and reinforcing the learning by communication to others and by continuing experience. When implementing a new, but proven, system the experience gained by other users and the resulting knowledge may be used as a starting point.

One possible education strategy is that we send all staff on an external course. This would be expensive, time consuming and possibly not well tailored to our needs. The proposal is that we adopt the cascade method by which a small number of our people are chosen, mainly those known to be receptive to change but including some known to be critical of MRP II, and bring in training consultants to not only thoroughly explain the system but also work with them in developing an appropriate in-company course and also improve their communication skills.

This initial course will include as a project the development of a full set of learning materials, including videos, specifically related to the introduction of MRP II at our factory. The course participants will be the first set of internal facilitators who will then themselves conduct short courses for another, wider, staff group. In doing this they will reinforce their own knowledge, show the company's commitment to the new system, but in particular they will be able to relate to the problems and objections of their audience. They will also act as long-term support for this second group who themselves will now be expected to explain the new system to other staff members and so on until all staff have received the basic required education.

The advantages of this approach in gaining commitment are obvious. The two major disadvantages are first of all that we may end up with misunderstandings being widely disseminated. This should be avoided by good, relevant learning materials being used. The second potential problem is a loss of impetus as the learning process continues. This will be countered by careful timetabling of learning events and also by the arrival and commissioning of the actual system. The learning networks which develop will continue to exist as experience is gained in actual systems' use.

Case 4.   Atlink – a case of mistaken identity

We had recently taken over Atlink, a highly regarded company which manufactures high precision components. It was an unusual move. We, that is the Linton Group, are well known for providing our shareholders with regular dividends and share price growth. Atlink have an international reputation for the highest levels of precision engineering. They do make a profit, occasionally, but even then it is minimal for a company of their size. Actually that is not quite true. If you look back into the archives you will see the odd gloriously profitable (and tax ineffective) year. I suspect that we bought them on the assumption that our management skills allied to their engineering skills and market reputation would provide a continual windfall. We shall see.

By a strange coincidence my name is the same as that of the Linton finance manager who tends to deal with requests for capital expenditure on machines and ancillary equipment. He's an ex-engineer who combines an ability to 'talk engineering' with a profound suspicion of the figures contained in capital request papers. Thus he ends up playing a game of 'move the goalposts' – as the individuals requesting funds manage to show a two-year payback he decides that one year is more appropriate. The whole process is a virility test rather than rational analysis. If you really want something you prove it by cheating imaginatively with the figures. My namesake is cunning, however, and indulges in post-implementation audits thus honing the skills of excuse-making in the recipients of the funds. The final result is that engineers, computing staff and others who have been in the Group for a while are either cautious or clever. Atlink's management has much to learn.

When I first arrived at Atlink's only factory, a sprawling ancient tip in a near derelict Victorian equivalent of the industrial estate, I was greeted with an enthusiasm never before bestowed on a management development specialist. A tour of the smarter parts of the plant was followed by a large lunch and a shopping list of the equipment thought necessary to revive Atlink's fortunes. I was very impressed by the way in which I would be touring one department with one manager and then accidently bump into another who would continue the tour in another direction. The set of tours miraculously ended at lunch-time near the board room. The team work seemed excellent until I realized that all the people I had met were from manufacturing or personnel. The finance and sales staff were as invisible as the managing director.

The failure to meet with finance and accounting staff was interesting in view of my presumed role. In particular I discovered that the finance department was the guardian of the computer. Around ten years ago the company had bought, with little discussion or justification, a mainframe to be used for accounts, sales invoicing and stock control. This machine was presently at the limits of its capacity in batch processing such data and provided little if any service to anyone else. Manufacturing had tried to get involved but to no avail, so they said. The only recent computing innovation, apart from a plethora of stand-alone CNC equipment, was the personnel director's purchase of a micro, ostensibly to keep personnel records but in fact to practise using database software. This had caused a furore as the data processing staff insisted they could have done the job, even if they quoted a six-month lead-time. It actually took just over a month to produce a fairly rough but usable personnel database. Of course it was incompatible with the mainframe and couldn't be linked with the wage payment system. In fact in operational terms I'm not quite sure what it did do beyond make a rebellious point. Strategically it encouraged manufacturing to think in terms of automation and Computer Aided Production Management.

Manufacturing is divided into a 'soft' and a 'hard' end. The former consists of routine operations (turning, milling etc.) carried out on soft metal. Atlink has CNC machining centres, limited robotic handling and some automatic inspection. Two shifts are worked with minimum manning but careful control of quality. This is not a Flexible Manufacturing System in the full sense but flexibility is essential.

The hard end consists of the high precision grinding of hard metal. This is the crucial area of the plant consuming 70 per cent of production lead time and 70 per cent of the cost. Past investment has been in simple but high quality machine tools, good operators and simple control systems. Changes in hard end equipment involves larger leaps in technology than in the soft end. If successfully implemented, new technology will reduce cycle times from weeks to hours. Last year Atlink bought a CNC grinding machine, more advanced than previous equipment but still limited in operation. It provided an excellent learning experience. Currently on order is a state-of-the-art grinding machine capable of unmanned operation and interfacing with other equipment.

This latest machine is being supplied by an overseas prime contractor. There are problems with delivery and with the software. Atlink manufacturing staff are at a loss as to what to do in this case. They planned everything with care but nothing seems to happen. It is quite possible that the supply contract was badly drawn up and the prime contractor is simply giving Atlink a low priority. The worrying thing is Atlink production management's inward-looking culture. They just don't seem to be able to handle relationships with the outside, including other functions in their own company.

One thing which they do show great perception in dealing with is the human relations and training aspects of manufacturing. At the grinding end in particular, operator skills are very high. New recruits are already good machine operators but their skills need to be enhanced by working with existing operators. In addition, a cocoon of support surrounds the operator and his machine.

Problems continually arise at this level. Excessive scrap, down-time and so forth will always be with us, not because the company is incompetent but because of the continuing attempt to improve. Manufacturing variation control teams have been set up to support the operator. Each team contains a range of engineering and management skills. The rule is this – an operator is in trouble if he doesn't report accurately and immediately that scrap levels, for example, are too high. He is not disciplined for the excessive scrap level but for the delay. Reduction of the scrap level is something for which he receives attention and support.

All this is very commendable. I'd christen it PQM – Partial Quality Management. Let me explain why. These support teams need a range of skills. In terms of engineering they need mechanical, electrical and electronic skills. Then they need to know about quality improvement, production planning. But in particular they have to be brilliant at diagnostics in terms of engineering and in terms of the broader systems within which the machines exist. There's no fundamental problem when they have to repair faults in a standard machine. Faced with a new Flexible Machining Cell with teething problems they manage reasonably well. Confronted with excessive stock, dilatory machine tool suppliers or an embryonic, computer-based materials planning system the excuse 'someone else's problem' is made. How you go from single discipline technicians, through multi-discipline technicians to problem solvers is an interesting challenge to a training specialist.

Atlink appears to want funds for a new mainframe computer, production management software, FMS and CADCAM. They need funds for training and management development. At the end of the day I still had no idea what their market plans were nor how the management team were going to set about the task of learning to talk to each other. The managers I spoke to insisted they hadn't confused me with my accountant colleague. They knew 'training and changing attitudes was the key to all this'. I went away promising to take positive and prompt action. I wonder if they realized the implications of what I had in mind?

Exercises

(1) Outline the strengths and weaknesses of Atlink for each functional area, as far as can be ascertained from this case. In addition, what

appear to be corporate strengths and weaknesses?
(2) What 'positive and prompt' action would you recommend (assuming a goal of profitability improvement in both the short and long term)?

13 Project management

Introduction

The implementation of AMT may involve relatively small changes, say the purchase and commissioning of a new machine. It may involve a major company-wide change, as with MRP introduction, or gradual evolution. These possibilities have been discussed earlier under a classification of systems' change. They all require the effective management of change and such changes are often referred to as projects.

We will define projects as change situations which have a beginning and an end. The beginning may involve a gradual build-up of activities through appraisal, design and implementation and we may think of the total change as several inter-linked sub-projects. The end may not occur when we wish it to occur, indeed the control of time is a key theme in this context. Strictly speaking we may argue that AMT implementation is a never ending progression of continual improvements. However, for the effective management of change we will find it useful to identify activities which, when finally completed, at the very least signify important milestones.

Projects have clients, who may be internal or external to the organization. Projects have goals, specified to be consistent with the requirements of their clients. Goals are not limited to clients' requirements in that they should include, in addition to such requirements, constraints on the use of resources and learning objectives for the project team. Lastly, projects are human activity systems. They need leadership, control, motivation and communication, and take place within a culture of work and an organizational structure which may or may not be supportive.

A particularly important process in project planning is the arriving at a statement of project objectives. A simple and widely used diagram reminding us of the types of project objective is included in Fig. 13.1. Project success means achieving quality objectives by a given time and within budget.

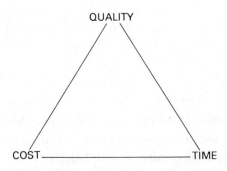

Figure 13.1 Project objectives

Quality is usually defined by a pre-set specification and nothing is achieved by exceeding that specification from the client's point of view, though the project team may learn from such over-achievement. This may be a dangerous temptation and many examples exist of the over-elaboration of projects under the guise of improving the result for the client. However, with very advanced AMT developments the quality specification can include both essential features which must be achieved and a series of highly desirable features which should, within a given set of priorities, be aimed for if cash and time resources allow. Such a specification obviously requires careful control. The monitoring of cost and time are dealt with in the next chapter. It should be emphasized that reporting on the cost time status of a project does not constitute project control. Control is exercised through decisions and actions which affect uncompleted activities and resources which are yet to be allocated.

In most organizational contexts, but particularly with AMT implementation, projects should not be seen in isolation from each other, though their effective control may well depend on clear project identification. The interlinking of sub-projects has been referred to earlier when we illustrated the range of changes likely to be entailed by CADCAM innovation. Other projects are also likely to be in progress, such as product launches, company mergers and so forth. The defining characteristic of modern management is thought by many to be the ability to cope with many simultaneous changes while continuing to earn revenue from normal operations. A useful analogy is the building of a new major road – a combination of sub-projects (e.g. bridge building, re-laying piped services, carriageway construction) while existing traffic flow is maintained. Most road users have experienced the effects of such projects and noted delays in project completion.

Without appearing unduly pessimistic, one should be aware of the likely causes of project failure. These were introduced in Chapter 11, though one should never imagine that such a list is complete. A similar exploration is attempted in Block (1983) who argues that causes can be divided into 'internal' and 'external' components. The latter relate the project to its environment and organizational context. The management of the external component is referred to as the politics of projects. Block argues that political skills are essential for the project leader in protecting the project from outside influences, a process familiar to experienced project managers and described in Kidder (1981) for a computer development situation.

As we argued in Chapters 9 and 10, the formal appraisal of costs and benefits for any systems' change is highly desirable though often resisted or thought unnecessary. Such appraisal, though primarily aimed at decision-making, is useful when one comes to setting goals and budgets for a project. Indeed, unless a time-phased assessment of likely costs and intended benefits is arrived at, project planning may become little more than listing the more obvious activities. If appraisal procedures are excessively combative with the proposers of change producing fanciful assessments of costs, timings and benefits in order to gain approval, effective control of implementation is doomed from the start. Theory recommends post-implementation audits as a cure for such events but few companies are rigorous in applying such procedures.

This is perhaps due to the fact that almost all projects deviate from plan in some way and project managers may be unnecessarily protective of their performance. Similarly, the organization and its environment change and benefits occur in ways different from those planned. Yet the auditing of projects seems to be one feedback or learning mechanism by which the organization may collectively learn from its mistakes. The alternative is that individual project leaders are honest when reflecting back on their own performance and will improve with successive projects as well as communicating their experiences in informal ways to their peers.

It is not easy to gather information on cost escalation and time over-run on projects within companies. Most cases involve public works, the most often quoted being Concorde, the Sydney Opera House and the Humber Bridge (see Bignell and Fortune (1984) on the latter). Such cases do illustrate spectacular problems but perhaps confuse inefficiency in appraisal with political motivation. Was the original estimate of the likely cost of Sydney Opera House realistic, or was it merely a publicly acceptable figure given by proposers who were convinced that the project should go ahead at any cost because of the prestige it would attach to the location?

Within companies, the proposers of capital expenditure might be similarly convinced that they are right and their technical expertise may make it difficult for other managers to challenge their estimates of cost, benefit and timing. An examination of the situation of Rolls-Royce in the early 1970s (see Bignell and Fortune (1984)) shows how this might happen. The ultimate result can be the collapse of a company, or an expensive public rescue, though Rolls-Royce management may argue that in the long term the technical advances they were making were worthwhile to the country. This type of situation might well occur in the context of major AMT change and is not easy to manage. An incremental or evolutionary solution, if possible, has much to recommend it and is exemplified by the JIT approach to systems' change.

Procedures for cost control of projects and an exploration of the effects of cost and time over-runs are included in Chapter 14. The remainder of this chapter is given over to an explanation of a typical project management technique, Critical Path Analysis, which has been found to be valuable in the control of small and large projects but is easy to learn and instructive in pointing to misconceptions in the logic of the management of inter-related activities. This and similar techniques are embodied in a number of commercially available software packages which usually include facilities for resource scheduling and report writing.

Critical Path Analysis

Critical Path Analysis (CPA) is the name given to several related techniques developed in the 1950s as aids to project planning. Extensions to them were discovered, the most prominent being PERT (Project Evaluation and Review Technique) which amongst other things allows for probabilistic activity time estimates. Modern specialist texts (for example Moder, Phillips and Davis (1983)) place these within a general framework of Network Analysis and include such complex variants as GERT (Graphical Evaluation and Review Technique).

The more advanced techniques may be of use to the specialist in planning large or unusual projects but have the disadvantage of inhibiting communication between interested parties rather than enabling communication, the strong point of the simpler project planning methods. However, it must also be said that AMT implementation often involves the management of a portfolio of inter-related projects and as such may pose complex co-ordination problems. At the very least, computer-based project planning methods may be necessary to allow for effective updating of plans. A wide variety of project management software is currently available.

One of the simplest and most widely known variant on CPA is the Activity-on-Arrow (AoA) method. This is presented in comprehensive detail in Lockyer (1984) in parallel with the Activity-on-Node (AoN) method and its variants. We will concentrate on the former though either are capable of use with modest amounts of training.

Activity-on-Arrow Networks

The basic concept of this method (and others) is that a project may be broken down into activities. These are logically related in that they may either occur in parallel or alternatively one activity must be completed before another begins (considerable variations of this simple logic are possible in the AoN formulation). The duration of each activity is estimated. Based on this information the set of activities which form the project is analysed and presented to show such key features as the critical path, i.e. the activities which if delayed or extended in their duration will delay the completion of the project. The activities in the main project might each themselves be sub-projects which can be similarly analysed, though complications occur if activities within differing sub-projects require co-ordination.

A simple example best illustrates this technique. Suppose a project consists of the following activities:

A   Prepare location for new machine
B   Deliver machine and set up
C   Train operators on similar existing machine
D   Train operators on actual new machine
E   Prepare special materials
F   Carry out test run

The next stage is to establish the inter-relationships between these activities by listing the direct pre-requisites for each. For example, let us assume that A must be completed before B is started because there is no room to temporarily store the machine. C depends on neither A nor B. D requires B and C to be complete (thus A is also an automatic pre-requisite for D). E may be done independently of A to D though F requires all the other activities to be completed. This latter stipulation only requires D and E to be listed as pre-requisites as the previous logic takes care of A to C. The logic may be summarised thus:

Activity		Pre-requisites
A	Prepare location for new machine	–
B	Deliver machine and set up	A
C	Train operators on similar existing machine	–
D	Train operators on actual new machine	B,C
E	Prepare special materials	–
F	Carry out test run	D,E

Different graphical representations of the above are possible. A common and useful one is shown in Fig. 13.2 though it should be noted that project planning software may use simpler bar charts. The

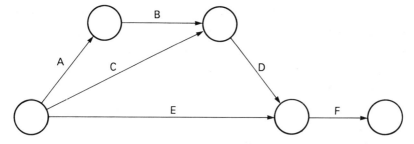

Figure 13.2 A simple activity-on-arrow network

circles in the diagram represent events, an event being the start or finish of an activity. A normal convention is that time flows from left to right on the diagram and that there are single start and end events. The events are numbered and activities (the arrows) may be identified by their tail and head events (these being unique and the former having a lower number).

One complication which exists for AoA networks is the often necessary use of dummy activities which have no duration but which exist to preserve the logic of the network or the unique activity numbering. We illustrate this by introducing two new activities into our project:

G   Prepare special tools
H   Write operator manual

If G has no pre-requisite but must be completed before F begins, and if H comes after C has been completed but before F begins, the new set of pre-requisites are:

Activity		Pre-requisites
A	Prepare location for new machine	–
B	Deliver machine and set up	A
C	Train operators on similar existing machine	–
D	Train operators on actual new machine	B,C
E	Prepare special materials	–
F	Carry out test run	D,E,G,H
G	Prepare special tools	–
H	Write operator manual	C

The network diagram is now as shown in Fig. 13.3. The dummy activity between events 3 and 4 is to preserve the logic of D following C without events 3 and 4 being the same, in which case we would have imposed the false pre-requisite of H following B. The dummy between events 5 and 6 preserves the unique head and tail event numbering for activities E and G. Dummy activities have no duration.

Network diagram

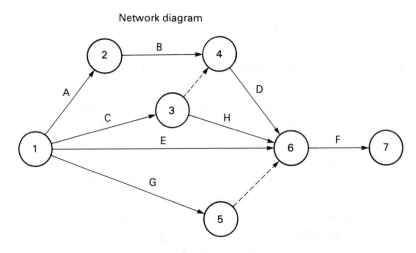

Figure 13.3 Network diagram

We now estimate durations for the activities. This may be a difficult task to perform and we may wish to attach probabilities to various activity duration estimates as described later. In this instance we assume that durations in days may be found as in the following list:

Activity	Pre-requisites	Duration (days)
A	–	3
B	A	7
C	–	20
D	B,C	15
E	–	20
F	D,E,G,H	15
G	–	11
H	C	9

The logical implications of this set of duration estimates can now be analysed directly on the network by finding earliest and latest event times. This is illustrated in Fig. 13.4. The calculation method is not described here but follows a similar line of logic to that described below. The alternative approach is to directly analyse the table of activities. We calculate the following for each activity:

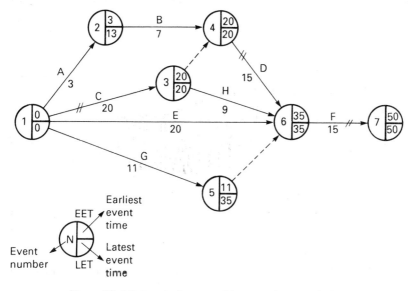

Figure 13.4 Network diagram with event times analysis

Earliest Start (ES) – assuming the project starts at time 0, activities with no pre-requisite are given an ES = 0. Other ESs are found by taking the highest Earliest Finishes for pre-requisite activities.

Earliest Finish (EF) – EF = ES + Duration. The highest EF value for any activity is the project duration.

Latest Finish (LF) – the final activity or activities are given LF = project duration. Latest Starts of activities are fed backwards to directly preceding activities to become their LFs using the rule that the lowest LS is taken when two or more activities feed back into a preceding one.

Latest Start (LS) – LS = LF – Duration

The ES and EF are calculated first for all activities in a forward pass through the network. The LF and the LS are then found by a backward pass. It is convenient to make a list of direct successors for activities to help with the backward pass. This is illustrated in Fig. 13.5. Though awkward at first, these calculations may soon be mastered with care and practice. The interpretation of the statistics

Activity	Pre-requisites	Direct successors	Duration D	Earliest start ES	Earliest finish EF	Latest start LS	Latest finish LF	Total float
A	–	B	3	0	3	10	13	10
B	A	D	7	3	10	13	20	10
C	–	D, H	20	0	20	0	20	0*
D	B, C	F	15	20	35	20	35	0*
E	–	F	20	0	20	15	35	15
F	D,E,G,H	–	15	35	50	35	50	0*
G	–	F	11	0	11	24	35	24
H	C	F	9	20	29	26	35	6

* Denotes critical path

Figure 13.5 Analysis of table of activities

is obvious from their names. The Total Float for each activity is EF – ES (which is identical to LF – LS). This gives the maximum delay permissible for an activity before further delay increases the length of the project. It should be emphasized that if one activity uses up some of its float, the floats of other activities may be affected. The set of activities with zero total float are the critical path(s) of the project. Any delay in any of these activities will delay the finish of the project as a whole. Total float may be further analysed into components (for example, free and independent float).

A situation which sometimes arises is that the time available for the project is less than the project duration as calculated above. This lesser figure may be introduced into the computations with the result that the critical path and possibly other paths will have negative float. This indicates savings which will have to be made to activity durations if project completion targets are to be achieved.

Activity time estimation

The estimation of activity times is obviously crucial to this methodology, but we may well ask what exactly do we mean by a time estimate? Some possibilities are as follows.

(i) A time estimate is simply a forecast of how long an activity will take for completion. Such an estimate is meaningless unless accompanied by a specification of the performance level required for the activity (i.e. a measure of quality) and a statement of the resources available for the activity to be completed.

(ii) A time estimate is an assertion of how much time an activity should take, i.e. it is a strong hint to the project leader of the performance level which is considered appropriate and of the resources which may be used. In this sense it is similar to a budget.

(iii) A time estimate is a motivational device, challenging the project team to raise their performance to an appropriate level.

It is obvious from the standard literature that many project planning methods automatically assume the first of the above is true, and furthermore assume simple and predictable relationships between time, quality and resources. This reflects an interesting view on the process of management, namely that the above relationships are unchanged by the quality of project management. It also leaves no room for learning during the progress of projects. Yet the management of technology takes place in a changing and evolving world where the ability to discover and learn can provide an essential competitive edge.

The use of more sophisticated methods of activity duration assessment, such as those embodied in PERT, does not radically change this mechanistic bias. It merely reflects uncertainty in our knowledge of the relationship between time, resource and performance by attempting to quantify that uncertainty using probability concepts and statistical estimation techniques.

There is no simple answer to this problem. A given set of activity duration estimates (whether fixed or following a probability distribution) provides input to a model which may then be used for project planning and control. The important thing is to understand in any given instance how those estimates were arrived at, what assumptions are embodied in them and what consequences are entailed. The strength of CPA is its attempt to answer questions of time-related consequence.

Resource allocation

Critical Path Analysis, as illustrated above, does not produce a plan for a project. It sets limits for possible plans consistent with the logic of the network and the durations of the activities. The production of a plan involves the timing of activities and this in turn involves considering when resources necessary for completing each activity might best be used, assuming some relationship between time, resource and performance. A number of approaches to this problem are possible, provided one is not obsessed with resource smoothing.

Resource smoothing is the method most often presented in textbooks and involves allocating resources to provide a smooth workload over a number of activities and projects in progress at the same time. Considerable mathematical sophistication is possible here as even the simplified approach in Lockyer (1984) demonstrates. While resource smoothing and the avoidance of peak overloads in resource usage is desirable, this consideration does not appear to be dominant in practical project management.

An examination of real projects shows a tendency to leave activities until the last possible moment. This may easily be dismissed as poor management but the following should be noted:

(a) There are considerable financial advantages in delaying payment for resources until the last possible moment.

(b) When faced with a range of competing uses for resources (staff time in particular) a manager may not feel a given project's activities have sufficient priority until the last possible moment – panic is an excellent motivator!

(c) Project specifications and client needs are often in a state of flux, as are information on available resources and even technological knowledge. There may be considerable advantages in leaving activities until the last possible moment so that when finally completed they meet current specifications using the latest available resources and techniques. This may be of particular importance in the design of leading edge technology-based products.

There may even be good reasons for completing activities as early as possible; for example, to publicize the existence of the project within an organization for political reasons, to pre-empt the use of scarce resources (which may be tempting for a project leader but disastrous for other projects and the organization as a whole), and in particular to leave a margin of error in case of delays and extensions of the durations of later activities.

The problems of resource allocation in a specific example – the completion of dissertations and projects as part of management and engineering courses of study – may be examined by inviting students to draw graphs based on their personal experience of project progress against time, as shown in Fig. 13.6. The horizontal axis in this graph is calendar time and the vertical axis shows project progress to date as measured by actual time spent on project-related tasks. The curves shown on the graph are typical of responses gathered on a number of occasions, particularly the curve leading to extensive work just prior to the deadline. Similar graphs may be attempted for organization-based projects, though the vertical axis is more likely to be resource usage in financial terms. This is extensively discussed in Chapter 14 which deals with project control.

An interesting observation on resource allocation is made in Brooks (1975), a short text dealing with the practical problems of software engineering management and therefore very relevant to some AMT

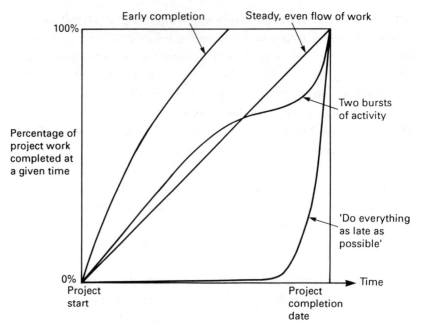

Figure 13.6 Styles of project time management

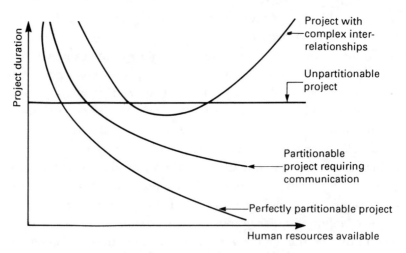

Figure 13.7 Possible complex inter-relationships of project duration and resources

applications. In discussing the reasons why such projects often fail to meet their deadlines, Brooks points to poor activity duration estimation techniques and inadequate control. He then notes that the response to a project being behind schedule is often simply to add manpower, which itself may further delay the project because the new team members require, for example, training by existing staff and briefing on project progress before they can make an effective contribution. The graph shown in Fig. 13.7 reflects these ideas and is a warning against simplistic approaches to team management and resource scheduling.

14 The control of AMT projects

Introduction

While in Chapter 13 we were concerned with outlining the basic ideas of project management, we now move on to considering how an effective project management information system can be set up for the control of AMT projects. By 'AMT projects' we mean either internal projects resulting in AMT implementation or projects with an outside client using AMT as part of the design and manufacturing system.

It is important once again to relate our ideas to the basic classification of AMT implementation used throughout this book. An extra dimension relevant to project management is prior experience in the management of similar projects. A number of opportunities and threats exist which are specific to project management situations and it should be readily apparent that opportunities and threats are often merely opposite sides of the same coin. Thus environmental turbulence may make project management very difficult while at the same time providing opportunities for capable staff to develop a competitive advantage. Similarly, a CAD system may be expensive and difficult to implement, but the experience gained may be invaluable in the future, provided the organization and its members are capable of learning from experience. These opportunities and threats may be placed alongside the modes of potential failure discussed in Chapter 11. Once again we emphasize that a recognized potential problem is a chance to demonstrate positive managerial ability.

An issue briefly alluded to in Chapter 13 was the handling of uncertainty in CPA/PERT. This normally arises when deterministic estimates of activity durations are replaced by probability distributions. Though this is an interesting technique it has the drawback of reducing the value of network analysis for inter-disciplinary communication. Also it might lull the project manager into thinking that fundamental problems have in some way vanished because a more sophisticated analytical tool had been used.

In fact the more basic problem in project planning lies in the structure of the project and its control. Are we certain at the start of the project that we actually know what activities are necessary? Do we know what resources will be available at appropriate times? How can we allow for the fact that as the project unfolds and experience is gained we might dramatically replan the whole thing? The answer to these questions is that we cannot pretend to know the future with certainty. Indeed management is notoriously easy with the aid of hindsight. The techniques mentioned earlier are ways of analysing a model of the future. After research and analysis, a project manager must move on to planning and the development of control systems, always knowing that experience and environmental changes might lead to a re-assessment of the project and its replanning or termination.

Two specific points should be noted at this stage before moving on to the techniques of project management. The first is that the time we take in planning a project is in a sense a part of the project, that is, it consumes time and resources in pursuit of the project's objectives. Thus, an overelaborate planning phase might well be detrimental to a project, particularly a small, low-budget one, unless the planning phase has considerable extra advantages such as the setting up of a management system which can be later used on other projects or for the development of project team skills.

The second point refers to large projects of long duration and considerable technological sophistication. Typically one might be designing a product or a manufacturing system which is required to be state-of-the-art. The problem comes in specifying components, say, which are required some time in the future and which have been promised by suppliers but not yet fully developed by them. Though seemingly very risky, this strategy of attempting to intercept technologies promised for the future may be inescapable in some situations. It does, however, bring into strong focus the need for careful control of projects and excellent communication at points of potential risk.

Project planning and control

In Chapter 13 we described the basic technique of CPA and introduced some of the ideas behind resource allocation. A CPA diagram is not a project plan. It describes the constraints within which a project plan must be formed. This is well illustrated, using the example developed in Chapter 13 (see in particular Fig. 13.4 and Fig. 13.5), by a bar chart, as in Fig. 14.1. This chart shows the Earliest Start and Latest

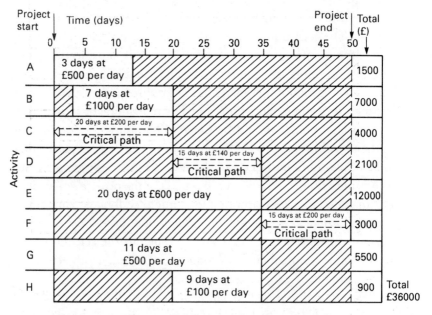

Figure 14.1 Bar chart of typical project

Finish for each activity along with some cost information we will be using below. This chart, read in conjuction with the CPA network diagram, will allow us to set Scheduled Starts and Scheduled Finishes for each activity which obey the precedence relationships and allow for a suitable pattern of resource allocation.

One resource we are likely to want to allocate with care is cash.

A useful exercise is first of all to set all activities at their earliest start times (see Fig. 14.2) and draw a graph of the resulting pattern of cash usage (see Fig. 14.4). Then we set all activities at their latest start times (see Fig. 14.3) and once again draw a graph of cash usage as illustrated in Fig. 14.4. This provides an envelope within which the cash usage of any activity schedule must lie, and thus enables us to judge the relative merits of different schedules with respect to this resource at least.

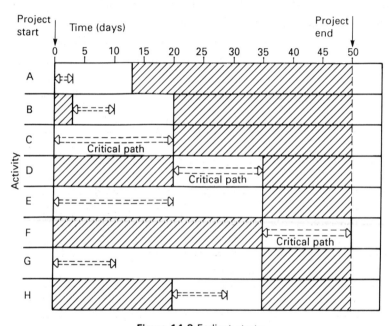

Figure 14.2 Earliest starts

A particularly valuable device in project control is the use of milestones. These are usually in the form of sets of actions which must be completed by specific times. However, there is a subtlety in the setting of milestones which is often ignored to the detriment of effective project control. If we remember that the objective of a control system is not merely to report on past failure, it is evident that there are two competing imperatives in specifying milestones:

(i) we need to check progress early enough for remedial action to be undertaken;

(ii) the most effective checks are on activities which are complete, otherwise one may be misled by assertions that activities are nearly complete when they have barely started (one author cynically notes that in his experience most activities are 99 per cent complete whenever progress is questioned!).

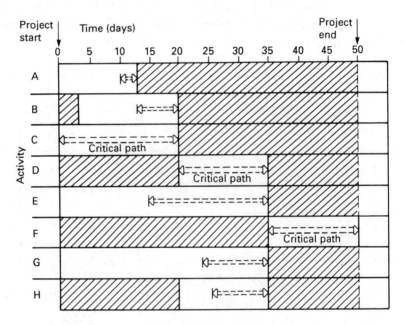

Figure 14.3 Latest starts

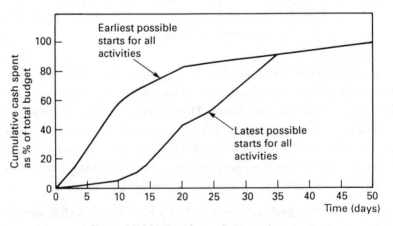

Figure 14.4 Limits of cumulative cash usage

We would recommend therefore that in order to satisfy the second of these imperatives a set of 'action milestones' is designed. These should be related to project objectives, involve review by senior management, and failure to meet them should trigger decisive action, such as a review of the capability of the project team, of available resource levels or even the termination of the project.

These action milestones are in turn supported by 'warning milestones' whose objective is to signal the possibility that an action milestone might not be reached. Warning milestones trigger action within the team, such as the activation of existing resources, re-scheduling of activities, communication or a renewal of motivation. They may be supplemented by more continuous reviews of progress but the important recommendation is that definite times exist when corrective action must be taken, rather than allowing a drift to take place fuelled by insincere promises and unrealistic intentions. Also control must be exerted through an escalation of action involving more senior management as problems become more intractable. The alternatives are that senior management are unaware of real problems or possibly unnecessarily concerned with routine review of satisfactory situations.

The modern trend is for the use of project management information systems which include not only classic CPA-style analysis but also support the control of an extensive portfolio of inter-related projects. The basic building block of such a system is the 'work package'. These are in effect small sub-projects in that they involve a discrete set of activities, have start and finish times and their completion results in some objectives being met. It is easily seen that projects may be viewed as a hierarchy of work packages usually termed the Work Breakdown Structure (WBS).

The WBS must be related to the organization as a whole in that responsibility for the completion of work packages must be firmly located. Similarly the control of direct costs fits easily with this approach though some means has to be found for fairly allocating overhead costs.

A further idea of particular value in this context is that of the 'rolling wave'. The idea is that a major project is divided into a small number of sub-projects taking place at differing times. Earlier sub-projects are further broken down until realistic work packages are agreed on and implemented. As time goes by later sub-projects are similarly analysed, thus removing the need, quite unrealistic in many long-term high technology situations, to plan the entirety of a project at the outset.

A further advantage of this hierarchical approach is that the final work packages may involve only a sufficiently small number of activities for day-to-day control to be devolved to middle, functional management. The obvious potential problem is one of control and communication which defines the task of the overall project manager who would usually need extensive computer-based information support.

Project cost control

From the earliest days of the use of PERT it has been obvious that the effective control of expenditure is as important as the control of time. This gave rise to a number of variants of PERT/COST which are extensively reviewed in the literature (see for example O'Brien (1971), Moder, Phillips and Davis (1983) or Harrison (1985) for the history of PERT/COST and extensive details of modern practice).

The basic tools of cost control may be applied to a whole project or to any other level in the hierarchy down to the work package. The basic terminology is given in Fig. 14.5. Care must be taken when interpreting the cost statistics to be sure what level is being reported on and whether the data is for a period or cumulative from the beginning of the project. Fig. 14.6 shows a graphical representation of the major statistics (here taken as cumulative).

One of the basic reporting tools used in this system is the representation of variances by the Cost Performance Index (CPI) and the Schedule Performance Index (SPI). It must be emphasized that both of these are important and should be viewed together. They should not be replaced by a single index, for example the ratio of BCWS and ACWP, which would confuse two quite separate potential sources of problems (overspending and work behind schedule). A useful graphical representation of CPI and SPI is shown in Fig. 14.7.

ACWP – actual cost ot work performed
BCWP – budgeted cost of work performed
BCWS – budgeted cost of work schedule

(above may be for a given period or cumulative;
they may be for a project or a work package)

Cost variance = BCWP – ACWP
Schedule variance = BCWP – BCWS

$$\% \text{ cost overrun} = \frac{\text{ACWP} - \text{BCWP}}{\text{BCWP}} \times 100\%$$

$$\text{Cost performance index, CPI} = \frac{\text{BCWP}}{\text{ACWP}}$$

$$\text{Schedule performance index, SPI} = \frac{\text{BCWP}}{\text{BCWS}}$$

For each index, I < 1 means poor performance
                I = 1 means par performance
                I > 1 means good performance

BAC (budget at completion) = cumulative BCWS
                             at end of project,
                             as budgeted

ETCP (estimated total cost for project)

$$= \frac{\text{BAC}}{\text{CPI}}$$

Figure 14.5 Basic terminology of project cost control

We may explore the use of these statistics by means of the example originally given in Chapter 13. In Fig. 14.8 we present a schedule for the project assuming that the day-rates given in Fig. 14.1 apply. Thus, for example, in days 1 to 5 we plan to spend £1000 on activity C (5 days' work at £200 per day) and £2500 on activity G (five days' work at £500 per day). This gives a Budgeted Cost of Work Scheduled

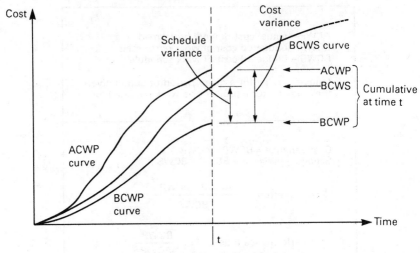

Figure 14.6 Project cost control graph

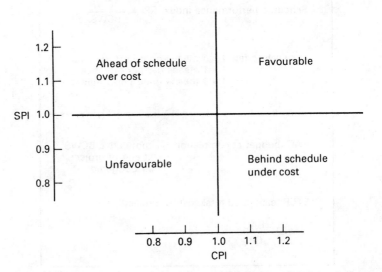

Figure 14.7 Relationship between cost and schedule performance indices

(BCWS) in days 1 to 5 of £3500. If we then examine the period data we find that the Budgeted Cost of Work Performed (BCWP) was £2500 (so we are behind schedule) and the Actual Cost of Work Performed (ACWP) was £3000 (and we are above cost relative to the amount of work actually done). Continuing performance is reflected in the CPI and SPI period data. Perhaps of more value is the cumulative

Budget for work as scheduled

Period: (days)	1-5	6-10	11-15	16-20	21-25	26-30	31-35	36-40	41-45	46-50
A		1000	500							
B			4000	3000						
C	1000	1000	1000	1000						
D					700	700	700			
E				3000	3000	3000	3000			
F								1000	1000	1000
G	2500	2500	500			400	500			
H										
Period BCWS	3500	4500	6000	7000	3700	4100	4200	1000	1000	1000

Period data

BCWS	3500	4500	6000	7000	3700	4100	4200	1000	1000	1000
BCWP	2500	3000	4000	6000	8000	5000	4000	1000	1500	1000
ACWP	3000	4000	4500	6500	8100	4500	5300	1100	1700	1400
CPI	0.83	0.75	0.89	0.92	0.99	1.11	1.14	0.91	0.88	0.71
SPI	0.71	0.67	0.67	0.86	2.16	1.22	0.95	1.00	1.50	1.00

Cumulative data

BCWS	3500	8000	14000	21000	24700	28800	33000	34000	35000	36000
BCWP	2500	5500	9500	15500	23500	28500	32500	33500	35000	36000
ACWP	3000	7000	11500	18000	26100	30600	34100	35200	36900	38300
CPI	0.83	0.79	0.83	0.86	0.90	0.93	0.95	0.95	0.95	0.94
SPI	0.71	0.69	0.68	0.74	0.95	0.99	0.98	0.99	1.00	1.00
BAC	36000	36000	36000	36000	36000	36000	36000	36000	36000	36000
ETCP	43200	45818	43578	41806	39982	38652	37772	37826	37954	38300

See Figure 14.5 for explantion of abbreviations

The BCWP and ACWP period data reflect actual work performed and cash spent on the project.

Figure 14.8 Project cost report

data which allows assessment, as the project proceeds, of whether cost and schedule targets will be met. We see by the final cumulative BCWP that we finished on time. However, the final cumulative ACWP shows we were above cost, as also reflected in the final cumulative CPI. This data may be better absorbed through a graphical presentation as illustrated in Figs.14.9 and 14.10.

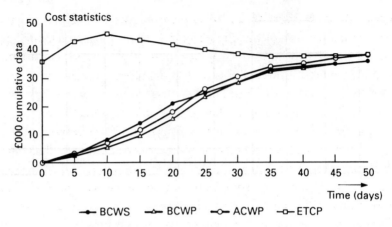

Figure 14.9 Project management − cost control

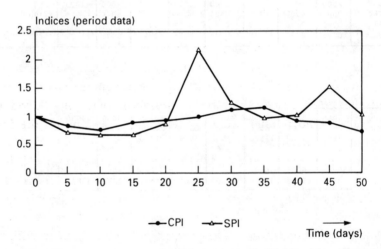

Figure 14.10 Project management − trends in the cost and schedule performance indices

Case 5. Computer-Aided Design at UMC (Case 2 continued)

(UMC finally managed to persuade the management of the Linton Group that a micro-based CAD system should be installed. The system physically arrived six months ago.)

'The system is fine. We really like it. It works!' I get worried when someone repeats the same message three times. Who are they trying to convince? Sitting next to an enthusiastic and obviously highly competent operator of an obviously functioning system made me wonder why I was here – a management development consultant being instructed in the delights of 2-D drafting. The challenge was to get Simon to talk about something other than the immediate task in hand, always assuming he had the remotest interest in anything else. My previous non-technical questions had met the response 'You had better speak to Dave about that'. My conversations with the design office manager, Dave Longstaff, had already been long, rambling and inconclusive – an interesting point for someone who professed to be so dramatically overloaded that he was averaging 60 hours a week.

I'd pieced together the following facts (or opinions?). The arrival of the system had coincided with changes in the type of contract being handled. UMC normally sold their materials handling equipment to food manufacturers but had now diversified to a range of new areas – a bottling plant, a small ceramic goods maker ... . This puzzled me because I had been told that the company could hardly satisfy its existing customers. Be that as it may, the designers were very busy and the CAD system had been introduced with no period of experiment and parallel working. The first job done on the first morning had been real.

Not surprisingly, the first job had taken rather a long time. Oddly enough this was not through incompetence, systems failure or suchlike. The six designers had received their basic training prior to system installation. Hardware and software has worked and proved robust in the face of any mis-use. The problem seemed to have nothing to do with CAD as such but with the management of computing systems in general. In the early months file-handling disciplines and systems procedures generally were not impressive. As an example, back-up copies of everything were taken on floppy discs but the UMC had no fire-proof safe in which to keep them. As a result Dave took them home each night, a situation which led to all sorts of confusion.

Another problem was that only two workstations had been purchased for six designers. This decision had been based on a work analysis of the time a designer actually spent at the 'drawing board'. It soon became obvious that three of the designers (two of them recent graduates and one in his fifties) could happily spend all day and night in front of a screen. UMC had three 'CAD hackers'. These characters had quickly gained a mastery of the features of the system way in advance of the training they had received and of the other designers. They could only really talk to each other and to Dave about what they were doing. Their productivity on the machines, and the quality of the results, were way ahead of that of the others and led to a difficult problem. It was obviously more efficient if they stayed working on the machines but in this case the other designers would never gain any real mastery of the system. The other problem nagging at the back of Dave's mind was this – was he merely training the two younger men on CAD so they could leave for better paid jobs elsewhere?

Talking to Simon I learnt a lot about the benefits and problems of the system they had purchased. In particular, the plotter had become an immediate bottleneck and a second one was on the way. Just as I was beginning to feel that no progress was being made he finished at the machine and gave me a conducted tour of the works. 'I don't see that we need more than one other workstation', he volunteered. 'What we do need are some PCs with other software such as Project Management and Estimating modules. Our relationship with the suppliers and consultants was all right as far as CAD but we're not in the business of producing electronic drawings. The designers are stuck in the office, the engineers go out to the customers and the managers think the technical side of the business is easy compared with selling and making a profit.'

I eventually got to see Dave just after lunch, not that he'd had any lunch. 'Well', he said in his usual polite but harrassed fashion, 'what can I do for you? Have you got the lads sorted out yet?!'

Exercises

(1) What do you see as the major current threats facing this company and the priorities for future action?
(2) What pattern of management and technical development do you recommend? In particular how might Dave be supported in his difficult role?

15   Case studies in AMT implementation

Case 6.   The storage carousels

My next call was back at divisional headquarters. Frank Hemmings was the materials manager. He was fairly new to the company having held this job for around a year and a half. As materials managers go he was an old hand. The company had had six in the last ten years. One had run for cover after only three days.

My appointment with Frank was timed for 9.30 am, giving him a couple of hours in the office to sort things out before seeing me. Obviously he'd made little progress. It was near the end of a quarter and he was surrounded by printouts giving a mixture of bad news (high stock levels) and very bad news (critical shortages). He was getting his act together for a meeting with his boss at 12.00, followed by the finance director at 5.00 pm. My mission, to promote management development, seemed of less than immediate relevance. In the face of adversity Frank was surprisingly cheerful. He seemed totally absorbed in the fine detail of the argument he would present later in the day. He was, of course, an expert in surviving these situations.

He spared me ten minutes of his time reviewing developments in materials storage technology, in which I had little if any interest, before suggesting I take a trip round the storage area with one of his graduate systems engineers, Sam Parker. Before Sam joined us Frank filled me in on some details of Sam's main project. Sam should have been managing several projects. He had been with the company for nine months and was seen as very capable and communicative. Unfortunately problems with the storage carousels in Area C accounted for most of his time.

I soon discovered that whatever else Sam had learnt from Frank, he had picked up his sense of humour. Our trip seemed to involve everywhere except Area C as Sam gleefully pointed out other people's problem areas, piles of raw materials awaiting allocation to stores and even bigger piles of scrap awaiting allocation to skips. The factory seemed in a state of controlled panic, another result of the approaching end of the quarter.

Finally we arrived at Area C and its new storage equipment. This consisted of two revolving carousels, purpose-built for the factory and each having 1,000 storage compartments adequate for batches of the small components used in Area C. Movement of the carousels was controlled by a micro-computer into which were fed details of stock inputs and outputs. Frank had told me that they'd been having a lot of trouble with the software but all seemed well with around ten operators busily checking components, re-batching them if necessary, and loading them into the jaws of the machine, perhaps never to be seen again.

I asked Sam what the problem was with this equipment, a question he attempted to evade, but with less skill than Frank would be demonstrating later in the day. Eventually I managed to piece together a picture of what was happening. Sam seemed to think that the worst thing in the factory when new technology was being introduced was the pressure put on engineers to work on several jobs at the same time. As a result they did nothing well and problems built up. This had been true of the carousels until Sam realized that a little strategic exaggeration about the time needed to solve the problems might be useful. So Sam had managed to arrange it so he spent all his time with this equipment, fine-tuning it and explaining its workings to the operators who had of course received minimal training.

Sam's decision appeared to have been justified and a couple of weeks later it was decided that the carousels had been successfully introduced and Sam was moved to his next project, in the design department. Frank was less lucky and the seventh materials manager was soon in post. The new man soon discovered that not only had he inherited too much stock in Area C but he couldn't actually find much of it. Somewhere in the carousels were critical components, wrongly classified and allocated. Finally things got so bad that the carousels had to be totally stock-checked and whole sections stripped of stock. A team was put in charge of re-classifying incoming parts and a bar-coding system was introduced with each batch tagged and automatically scanned on input and output.

A further innovation was that batches were now split between the two carousels so that any mechanical problem with one carousel would not mean that a particular type of component was unavailable. Software problems might still affect both carousels but there seemed to be a limit to the safety measures which could be built into the system.

A cynic might have noted that a lot of time, effort and expense was being devoted to stock when the company was proudly telling the world about its plans to be a JIT supplier.

Case 7. Problems in machine commissioning

I had been told that the situation required a management development input. When I arrived I was treated to a feast of engineering and accounting. The diagnosis had been right – management development was required.

The department was involved in electronic assembly, inserting components into printed circuit boards (pcbs). I was assured that this was just a temporary measure. Soon everything would be large-scale integration and surface mount technology but at the moment, in order to meet the needs of today's customers, some fairly tame automatic insertion equipment was needed. At least it should have been tame.

In the past, components had been inserted by hand (far too expensive for the needs of our present customers), by robot (flexible and slow) or by some standard equipment which was fast and inflexible, thus requiring a pcb to visit a number of machines.

The production manager, John Greentree, showed me a pile of technical specs and capital expenditure justification papers proving one inescapable fact – modern automatic component insertion (ACI) equipment was needed. This all assumed that we would remain as sub-contractors to the same customers doing similar work in the future, but as the papers showed an eleven-month payback period nobody had argued. In particular it was assumed that I wasn't going to argue.

My role, it appeared, was to be told how John and his men had done a magnificent, if unsuccessful, job in the face of adversity.

When planning the introduction of ACI equipment the technical requirements had been listed and it was found that only two companies in the world made machines which met these requirements. One of these, a Japanese giant, made excellent machines which, however, were judged to be less flexible than required and so the other manufacturer, the USA-based Galaxy corporation, were chosen. Our pcbs were run through other companies' Galaxy machines and the results seemed satisfactory, so we went ahead with our programming and maintenance staff being trained in the US.

The machines finally arrived in June of last year. They were quickly set up and would have been set to work except for two annoying problems. The first was a shortage of a particular type of special component needed for these machines. Most of the time normal components could be used but there is always an exception. John's production controller, Mary Wright, had ordered the correct parts and they had arrived in stock well in advance of the machines. Unfortunately they were also particularly appropriate for use elsewhere in the factory and had been 'stolen' with the usual justification of need to complete an express order for a valued customer. The shortage was rectified at a cost.

The next problem was a spectacular and totally predictable apathy on the part of the intended operators, who for some strange reason wanted to protect their piece-work earnings by staying with their normal equipment. The economics of this situation were also handled, at a cost, though the operators still had a reticence about using the new machines. This was eventually cured quite simply by the machines being there and being gradually accepted as part of the furniture. By September machines, materials and operators were all ready to work together.

Normal production was now attempted, but not for long. The new machines regularly broke down. Spares were soon in short supply and the wrong ones re-ordered. Some of the problems were traced to mis-use by the operators and to mis-direction during training. By December John had given Galaxy an ultimatum that, as their local engineers had been unable to correct the faults permanently, the machine designers must come out to the site and fix them. This happened with remarkable promptness. Two weeks before Christmas three engineers arrived from Galaxy and watched with horror the way their machines were being used in John's department. Several fast-moving parts had to be strengthened and the whole mode of operation changed, with a reduction in the range of components which the machines would be able to handle. Arguments with Galaxy over the supply contract and costs are continuing.

By March of this year the machines had achieved the specified level of performance, leaving John with three months in which to achieve his 'eleven months payback', quite apart from the increased costs of the delay.

The interesting thing is that all the above was told to me simply as background. The 'real problem' was an issue which arose last November when John's people were still trying to cope with the Galaxy machines. Gary Stanley, his senior engineering development manager, had spent all weekend working on the machines and through tiredness sustained an injury which, while causing no permanent damage, necessitated a short stay in hospital. An internal company inquiry was much concerned with the question, 'why was he working on a machine?' and had received no constructive response beyond an aggressive 'because it was broken down!'.

The point, of course, is that he was supposed to be a manager of engineers and technicians. His job description simply did not include actual maintenance work. I explored this with John. My first suggestion was that 'manager' was a courtesy title so we could pay him a reasonable salary – he was actually a practical engineer with limited supervisory duties. A glance at the list and importance of his managerial duties showed me that was not the case. My next suggestion was that by inclination he preferred practical hands-on engineering and left his more managerial duties to others, even to John. Evidently this was not so. Gary was most assiduous in carrying out his duties. He seemed to be rarely away from the site.

I finally drew up a list of plausible hypotheses to test out on John and Gary. Depending on their response a variety of actions will be necessary. The hypotheses are that Gary:

(a) didn't realise he shouldn't have been doing the job;
(b) considers management a 'non-job' compared with engineering;
(c) prefers engineering but is entitled to a manager's pay;
(d) has unique skills for the job he was doing;
(e) was the only person available to do the job;
(f) couldn't actually persuade anyone else to work that weekend;
(g) feels he must show leadership by being willing to handle difficult jobs himself;
(h) is so busy he hadn't the time to organize anyone else to do the job;
(i) doesn't trust anyone else to do the job as well as he can.

Exercise

What management development action do you recommend for Gary Stanley and for other managers in this case?

Case 8. Buying fine china

Mr and Mrs Highland wouldn't normally buy a customized fine china dinner service. They were very resistant to the sort of prestige advertising employed in this type of market, but their daughter's wedding was an obvious opportunity to visit Arkadia Pottery's Design Centre.

They had only expected to walk round the exhibition and see the videos but an appointment with a designer was available. Harry Watson had been with the company for around thirty years and was one of their most experienced designers, which made him one of their best paid employees. It was typical of Arkadia that people at the sharp end of the business, dealing with customers and suppliers or running production, were well rewarded but expected to perform to exacting professional standards.

After meeting the couple, Harry conducted them on a tour of the exhibits and showed them a short video of the manufacturing and design processes. The standard design appointment was one hour, but in this case Harry knew his diary would stretch to an extra half hour so why not spend more time with his new friends. Many recruits to this job were amused by its vocabulary. To refer to customers, the 'punters', as friends sounded just too much! Yet the nature of the job, and the culture of the company, meant that friends they had to be. As the sales trainers said, if they argued over the price and couldn't make up their minds they were more like family than friends.

The exhibition was stunning. Any doubts about the quality of the product were dispelled in a few minutes' browse through an area packed with colour, shape and design. These pieces weren't specials. In fact you could buy then there and then. All it would need were two simple electronic operations, one to change the security marking on the piece from the factory code to your code and the other to move money from your account to the Arkadia account. The company even insisted that the price you paid was less than you would expect. One effect of standing in this Alladin's cave was to alter the customer's perception of what constituted a reasonable price.

The video was intended not only to impart information but to give the customer a break from the subtle pressure of direct contact with sales staff and allow a little time for general interest to become an intention to buy. Then the Highlands, now converted, went into Harry's design studio.

The problem with the studio was that it was dominated by a large computer screen. At all times this contained images of plates, cups and saucers, serving dishes and so forth in a range of designs and colours. As the customer expressed preferences the range was reduced until the standard design closest to the customer's needs was shown. In addition the room contained yet more items from the Arkadia collection. One of the paradoxes of selling a prestige item is that its exclusivity could also be a barrier to purchase. This was overcome through visibility and proximity of the product. Customers could, if they wished, tour the factory and see most items made. Nothing they saw would reduce their impression of the value of the Arkadia product but it would become ever more attainable.

Over its long history the company had promoted a craft image. Even now, several operations in manufacture were literally done with great skill by hand. Everything else was done with equally great skill by computer-based design, manufacturing and planning systems.

Mr and Mrs Highland had little trouble talking to Harry and

arriving at an approximation to the dinner service they wanted as a present. Now Harry really started to earn his salary as he electronically manipulated images of plates, dishes, soup bowls and so forth, selectively changing colours and parts of the design motif to produce an individual style for his new friends. One thing he did not alter was the basic shapes. It was quite possible to customize shape but Harry guessed that the Highlands were not quite so insensitive to price.

Soon an acceptable design was on the screen, along with the delivery date. As the design could easily be put together from a combination of existing unglazed stock with limited hand painting, the major constraint was firing time in the kiln. The factory was fairly heavily loaded but Harry was able to keep to his original estimate, made in the exhibition room, of four days' delay before delivery. The price was moderately high but once again the Highlands had been made aware of what was involved. If the price had been a problem, the number of pieces in the set could have been modified, but in this case Mr Highland insisted it was increased.

After making an appointment to return to see Harry about a tea service for themselves – a standard design with a tiny monogram inserted to personalize it – the Highlands arranged for the delivery of the dinner service, paid and left. Harry confirmed the arrangements, completed all the necessary 'paperwork' for the transaction, made a series of notes about the Highlands' preferences and tastes in his personal files and moved on to the next appointment.

Before the day was over the unglazed items had been removed from stock and a print of the design applied. The following day they had a short wait until a painter with the right skills was available. The design necessitated some careful hand painting but this was eventually performed and the goods made their appointment with a kiln. A couple of days later they were polished, electronically tagged and packed. The design information was placed in the Highlands' file in case of further purchases.

A cost summary for this transaction revealed that normal margins had been made but suggested that, in future, items requiring similar hand-painting be subjected to a slight price increase. Labour in this area was beginning to form a constraint on production and recruitment and training would have to be increased, possibly involving a marginal wage rise.

The real constraint on the system was, of course, a shortage of skilled designers. For a number of years the company had been experimenting with the use of Expert Systems in CAD. These were already in place as supports to Harry and his design colleagues. The eventual aim was for relatively unskilled sales staff using a networked CAD system at a variety of design centres to be able to provide the same service. As it was, the customer had to travel to a very limited number of design studios and exhibitions.

There was another way of looking at this situation however. If one viewed buying Arkadia products not as a chore but as a day out, the siting of their design studios in shopping malls made sense. Could one take this a step further and make the Arkadia central design and manufacturing facility a theme park? The ultimate might be to arrive, view the exhibition, design your own product and tour the factory as it was being made. The discreet use of some very Advanced Manufacturing Technology could make this happen.

Case 9. MRP III at Zenon Manufacturing

Working at Eurman was like taking part in a baroque electronic in-tray exercise. A democratic and participative managerial style might be encouraged but thunderbolts still arrived on the screen, usually announced as 'Priority 1A' from Pietro. Anna self-mockingly sat to attention and ceremoniously entered the 'retrieve' option to reveal the message: 'Implement MRP III at Zenon Manufacturing by May 2000'.

The background was simple. The idea of using MRP III at the Zenon factory had been kicked around for months, usually from one executive to another in the hope it might go away. Unfortunately everyone assumed that Anna, as Integrated Business Systems Special Projects Manager, was taking the initiative in seeing it through. Pietro's memos on the subject had started as long rhapsodies on the benefits of MRP III but had, as usual, degenerated to one-line commands. This might seem autocratic on the part of the Group

Manufacturing Director but at least Anna knew that resources would be available, and the most recent memo provided the key to unlock them.

Zenon produced large items of industrial equipment tailored to meet individual customer needs. It was a job-shop, adapting products from a narrow range and assembling them from machined and bought-in components. It followed in the tradition of the medieval craftsman, always assuming you were willing to pay millions of new ECUs for your new toy.

Thus production planning at Zenon was in essence a series of inter-related projects with the key strategic priority being the balance between lead-time reduction and cost control. Hence MRP III (Materially Related Projects) was being seen as the appropriate planning and control paradigm. There were hundreds of project planning software packages, some dating from the 1960s. MRP III is an extension of PERT/COST, using AI to clear away most of the gruesome detail which had clogged up programs in the 1990s, and incorporating organizational learning characteristics, i.e. it continually pushes the manager towards incremental improvement. The other interesting feature of MRP III is its integration of CADCAM with project management. MRP III intends to do for the job-shop what MRP II eventually did for batch production.

The history of Zenon was interesting in terms of its information handling methodologies. It could be divided into a series of phases:

Phase I (1965 onwards)
The company, then independent, used traditional batch processing of accounting and stock information. Engineering applications were on a mainframe with slow response.
Phase II (early 1980s)
Zenon was now part of a UK Group. Interactive use of a Group mainframe was possible for technical work and some accounting. Stock control was through an on-line database.
Phase III (late 1980s)
In-house computing was developed based on networked minis supporting CAD, materials management and engineering design. An integrated Management Information System was rejected as a goal.

The systems design objective was to identify sub-populations of users with common interests and design appropriate information systems for each, always allowing for data exchange when necessary.

Phase IV (1990s)

Zenon's parent group became a founder member of Eurman. Information Systems paradigms continued to oscillate between centralized and de-centralized as the shock of genuine global communication took effect.

Eurman has a finance-based decision-making core. Throughout the Group, internal data capture of accounting information, times, quantities and locations is total. Customer and supplier environments are monitored with similar zeal. Operating units negotiate plans with the Corporate Core which then uses its information processing capability to support local decision-making and control.

The result could have been mechanistically bureaucratic but for the policy of the company to develop professional staff at all levels and locations to the extent that the Core provides mainly a public face for the organization and a clearing house for plans and intentions. The exception was when an intention was not being translated into action. The Core, in the form of Anna's boss, was now providing 'motivation' in its most literal and mechanical sense.

Thankfully the days were long gone when Anna's attention would now have had to be concentrated on hardware and software specifications, supplier negotiations, and so forth. MRP III was produced in-house and it would require little effort to make it available to Zenon with appropriate databases prepared. The task on hand was to find out how the staff at Zenon would be able to use it creatively.

She decided that the system could be introduced incrementally with staff gradually learning its capabilities, i.e. it could be placed in the background and features brought to the front as their utility was discovered. A review of current customer projects revealed three which would provide a reasonable initial basis for discovery learning. Each had problems without being so weird and awkward that lessons learnt would be non-transferable to other situations.

The first one chosen was a fairly standard item which had unaccountably suffered from delays and cost escalation. Customer specification changes and material delays were being blamed, as usual. Over a period of weeks Anna had a shadow information system developed for this project based on MRP III. She then took the key actors (all fairly junior and inexperienced) away from their normal activities for one day and used the shadow system as the basis for an Operational Game. The new system didn't work too well. Its behaviour seemed counter-intuitive at times, suggesting lines of action which were simply odd, but this would improve. Most important was the reaction of the players who went back to the old system and the real project with a new set of action priorities. In particular, they now realized the extent to which their relationship with the customer was ineffective and a radically new specification had to be drawn up. On the one hand this delayed the project further, but on the other hand working with the new system had shown them that they were heading for a real mess.

By May 2000 MRP III was being used creatively on several projects. Thus Anna could send off the message: 'MRP III implemented as requested'. It was a nonsense, of course, like the original message. What did the word 'implement' actually mean in this context? Partial use by six people on five projects with a projected return of 18 per cent on investment?! Implementation was continuous and never-ending. Pietro knew that and was simply saying 'raise the priority of this task' – a reasonable request which had been acted on.

Case 10. The new recruit

Anna mounted the showroom's demonstration platform and surveyed the audience of fresh managerial talent with the practised lecturer's mixture of slight apprehension and pleasure: 'Welcome to the factory of the past'. As an opening remark it usually got a laugh. Surrounded by a range of supposedly state-of-the-art technology most people expected the time-worn phrase 'factory of the future'. On one occasion she had used the latter phrase and then spent the first half hour of her introduction defending Eurman's record of research and development against an over-informed bunch of pure technology graduates. She continued the introduction with that story, on the basis that if it's just come into your head, it's probably a natural progression of ideas, and followed it with the standard comments on the history, geography and general organization of the company.

Whatever Anna's view of the intrinsic fascination of all matters concerning Eurman, Robert was bored – mainly by the lack of opportunity to exercise his own skills of oratory. A degree in general engineering, management and european languages, followed by postgraduate specialization in the application of artificial intelligence to manufacturing operations, had left him with an inflated view of his value to industry and in considerable debt. He was also adept at globe-trotting and working in restaurants to finance his studies and might have been offended to know that these had carried more weight at his interview. He would have needed tying down to his seat if he had realized what job was actually lined up for him.

Robert's boredom deepened when the speaker started on about the organizational structure of Eurman. He had not yet learnt to appreciate the subtleties of institutional life. 'You might be forgiven for thinking that you've all just started working for the same large, multinational corporation, if "working" describes sitting on your backsides listening to me!' (most of the audience thought it was very hard work). 'You haven't. You may have been employed through Eurman but you will work for different companies, most of them small, who supply goods and services for Eurman. If you're any good you will be running one of those companies in a couple of years at the most.'

That provoked a reaction, the usual mixture of anticipation and disbelief. Robert was interested. It sounded like an opportunity to solve all his problems in one go, though the time-scale sounded rather slow. Like most new graduates he rather fancied trying Eurman out for a few months and then moving on with his new found experience and inside knowledge. The idea of savagely segmenting a large organization wasn't new. He remembered doing case studies of the problems which arise when maintenance, sales, catering and even individual machining systems of a company were contracted out. The flip side of intrapreneurship is chaos. It was essential to retain a set of core activities and systems to provide direction, impetus and for security of data and the competitive edge of the business. Nevertheless, this sounded promising whether he was working in the central core or a satellite.

Anna was relieved to have progressed beyond the statistics of Eurman to the whole point of the morning. In front of her was a group of highly qualified, potentially valuable but immediately useless individuals. They would soon discover how little they knew about manufacturing technology, the commercial realities of general manufacturing and the organizational realities of survival. But most important of all was motivation. They had spent years in an individualistic, competitive culture. The trick was to move them over to a corporate, competitive culture without losing them (at least without losing the ones you wanted to keep).

The morning continued with a mixture of tours, group discussions, videos and meetings with Eurman's management. Any manager or technology professional at Eurman spent a third of their time on the continuing development of themselves and others. Another third was spent on managing change, and the final third on managing current operations. This triad of activities put great emphasis on the effective management of time and supporting systems. It was designed to counter the new version of Parkinson's Law which states that as operational support systems take over routine managerial tasks, other routine tasks expand to fill the time available.

Organizations like Eurman do not invest in comprehensive, integrated management decision support systems in order to leave more time for tea-drinking. At first it had been thought that the technology would lead to a decimation of middle management. Companies which tried this out discovered the hard way the true purpose of middle management. It was then thought that all the free time could be used in managing change and being entrepreneurial but it transpired that there was a natural limiting speed of change for most organizations and environments. The triad of activities, with local adjustments in unusual circumstances, seemed to work.

Robert spent the next few days learning about the company and its operations, mainly on a one-to-one basis from a variety of other staff. He was fascinated by the integrated commercial and engineering systems which allowed only hours between orders being placed and goods going out for most lines. Designs tailored to customer needs might take longer, possibly even days. He eventually discovered what niche had been planned for him. He was to be part of a team showing overseas (or 'through Chunnel') visitors around the plant.

If he had been told this when he had first arrived he would simply have walked out. Now he viewed his new role as a way of finding out about all aspects of the company, widening his language skills and paying off his debts in around half the expected time through the performance payments linked to the job. The future could be in marketing or even in direct overseas selling if he were good enough. It could also involve a move back into creative engineering if that took his fancy and if he were willing to spend around five years learning some real engineering applications. He could also, of course, move on or start his own enterprise because frankly he wasn't impressed by the total service package for overseas visitors. They were well catered for at the factory site but often at a loss for something to do in the cultural desert surrounding it. It would be quite easy to organize a comprehensive set of activities ... .

References

ACARD (1983) *New Opportunities in Manufacturing: The Management of Technology*, HMSO, London.

Andreasen,M.M. and Hein,L. (1987) *Integrated Product Development*, IFS (Publications), Bedford.

Baker,M.J. (1987) *The Marketing Book*, Heinemann, London.

Ballew,V.B. and Schlesinger,R.J. (1989) 'Modern factories and outdated cost systems do not mix', *Production and Inventory Management*, 30, 1, 19-23.

Beaton,D.D.M. (1987) *Justifying Investment in Advanced Manufacturing Technology*, Kogan Page, London.

Bessant,J. and Haywood,W. (1986) 'Experiences with FMS in the UK' in *Managing Advanced Manufacturing Technology* (ed.Voss,C.A.), IFS (Publications), Bedford.

Beuret,G. and Webb,A. (1983) *Goals of Engineering Education*, CNAA, London.

Bignell,V. and Fortune,J. (1984) *Understanding Systems Failure*, Manchester University Press, Manchester.

Block,R. (1983) *The Politics of Projects*, Yourdon Press, New York.

Boaden,R.J. and Dale,B.G. (1986) 'Development of a model for use in planning computer-integrated manufacturing' in *Managing Advanced Manufacturing Technology*, (ed.Voss,C.A.), IFS (Publications), Bedford.

Bodily,S.E. (1985) *Modern Decision Making*, McGraw-Hill, New York.

Bower,J.L. (1985) 'Capital budgeting as a general management problem' in *Implementing New Technologies* (eds Rhodes,E. and Wield,D.), Basil Blackwell, Oxford.

Bowman,D.J. and Bowman,A.C. (1987) *Understanding CAD/CAM*, Sams, Indianapolis.

Brooks,F.P. (1975) *The Mythical Man-Month: Essays on Software Engineering*, Addison-Wesley, Wokingham.

Browne,J., Harhen,J. and Shivnan,J. (1988) *Production Management Systems*, Addison-Wesley, Wokingham.

Buchanan,D.A. and Huczynski,A.A. (1985) *Organizational Behaviour*, Prentice Hall International, Englewood Cliffs.

Buffa,E.S. and Sarin,R.K. (1987) *Modern Production/Operations Management*, Wiley, Chichester.

Burke,C.M. and Ward,S.C. (1988) 'Project appraisal – finance approaches to risk' in *Developments in Operational Research* (eds Cook, N.B. and Johnson, A.M.), Pergamon Press, Oxford.

Caulkin,S. (1988) 'Britain's best factories', *Management Today*, September.

Chandler,J. (1987) *Practical Business Planning*, McGraw-Hill, London.

Checkland,P. (1981) *Systems Thinking, Systems Practice*, Wiley, Chichester.

Child,J. (1984) *Organization: A Guide to Problems and Practice*, Harper and Row, London.

Chisnall,P.M. (1985) *Strategic Industrial Marketing*, Prentice-Hall, Englewood Cliffs.

Clifton,P., Nguyen,H. and Nutt,S. (1985) *Marketing Analysis and Forecasting*, Heinemann, London.

Cox.T. (1989) 'Towards the measurement of manufacturing flexibility', *Production and Inventory Management*, 30, 1, 68-72.

Coyle,R.G. (1977) *Management System Dynamics*, Wiley, Chichester.

Crosby,P.B. (1979) *Quality is Free*, New American Library, New York.

Cullen,J. and Hollingum,J. (1987) *Implementing Total Quality*, IFS (Publications), Bedford.

Ebers,M. and Lieb,M. (1989) 'Computer integrated manufacturing as a two-edged sword', *International Journal of Operations and Production Management*, 9, 2, 69-92.

Ferdows,K., Miller,J.G., Nakane,J. and Vollmann,T.E. (1989) 'Evolving global manufacturing strategies: projections into the 1990s' in *Global Operations Perspectives* (eds Sheth,J.N. and Eshghi,G.S.), South-Western Publishing, Cincinnati.

Fitzmaurice,C.T. and Zairi,M. (1988) 'The automated environment: A challenge for the safety practitioner' in *Proceedings of the International Conference on Ergonomics, Occupational Safety and Health and the Environment*, Vol.1, Beijing, China.

Gleick,J. (1987) *Chaos: Making a New Science*, Heinemann, London

Goldratt,E.M. (1985) 'Devising a coherent production, finance and marketing strategy using the OPT rules', *BPICS Control*, April/May.

Goldratt,E.M. and Cox,J. (1986) *The Goal*, North River Press, New York.

Goldratt,E.M. and Fox,R.E. (1986) *The Race*, North River Press, New York.

Goodridge,M. and Twiss,B. (1986) *Management Development and Technological Innovation in Japan*, Manpower Services Commission, Sheffield.

Greenwood,N.R. (1988) *Implementing Flexible Manufacturing Systems*, Macmillan, London.

Groover,M.P. (1987) Automation, *Production Systems, and Computer Integrated Manufacturing*, Prentice-Hall, Englewood Cliffs.

Harrison,F.L. (1985) *Advanced Project Management*, Gower, London.

Harrison,M.R. (1986) 'Advanced manufacturing technology and management development', *International Journal of Operations and Production Management*, 6, 4, 61-73.

Harrison,M.R. (ed) (1987) *Advanced Manufacturing Technology: Implementation, Training and Management Development*, Manpower Services Commission, Sheffield.

Hawkes,B. (1988) *The CADCAM Process*, Pitman, London.

Hayes,R.H. and Garvin,D.A. (1985) 'Managing as if tomorrow mattered' in *Implementing New Technologies* (eds Rhodes,E. and Wield,D.), Basil Blackwell, Oxford.

Hayes,R.H., Wheelwright,S.C. and Clark,K.B. (1988) *Dynamic Manufacturing*, Free Press, New York.

Hill,T. (1985) *Manufacturing Strategy*, Macmillan, London.

Hirst,I.R.C. (1988) *Business Investment Decisions*, Philip Allan, Oxford.

Industrial Computing Sourcebook (1989), EMAP, London.

Institution of Production Engineers (1985) *Current and Future Trends of Manufacturing Management and Technology in the UK*, I.Prod.E., London.

James,B.G. (1984) *Business Wargames*, Penguin, London.

Johnson,H.T. and Kaplan,R.S. (1987) *Relevance Lost*, Harvard Business School Press, Boston.

Kanter,R.M. (1983) *The Change Masters*, Unwin, London.

Kidder,T. (1981) *The Soul of a New Machine*, Penguin, London.

Lockyer,K. (1984) *Critical Path Analysis*, Pitman, London.

Lumby,S. (1988) *Investment Appraisal and Financing Decisions*, VNR, Wokingham.

McLoughlin,I. and Clark,J. (1988) *Technological Change at Work*, Open University Press, Milton Keynes.

Mandelbaum,M. and Brill,P.H. 'Examples of measurement of flexibility and adaptivity in manufacturing systems', *Journal of the Operational Research Society*, 40, 6, 603-610.

Marchand,D.A. and Horton,F.W. (1986) *Infotrends: Profiting from your Information Resources*, Wiley, New York

Marsh,P., Barwise,P., Thomas,K. and Wensley,R. (1988) 'Managing strategic investment decisions' in *Competitiveness and the Management Process* (ed Pettigrew,A.M.), Basil Blackwell, Oxford.

Meyer,A. and Ferdows,K. (1989) 'Integration of Information Systems in Manufacturing' in *Global Operations Perspectives* (eds Sheth,J.N. and Eshghi,G.S.), South-Western Publishing, Cincinnati.

Moder,J.J., Phillips,C.R. and Davis,E.W. (1983) *Project Management with CPM, PERT and Precedence Diagramming*, Van Nostrand, New York.

Morgan,G. (1986) *Images of Organization*, Sage Publications, Beverly Hills.

New,C.C. and Myers,A. (1987) *Managing Manufacturing Operations in the UK: 1975–1985*, British Institute of Management, Corby.

O'Brien,J.J. (1971) *CPM in Construction Management*, McGraw-Hill, New York.

Osola,V.J. (1985) The Impact of New Technology on Engineering Batch Production, NEDO, London.

Parnaby,J. (1987) 'The need for fundamental changes in UK manufacturing systems engineering' in *Proceedings of the 4th European Conference on Automated Manufacturing*, IFS (Conferences), Bedford.

Pedler,M., Boydell,T. and Burgoyne,J. (1989) 'Towards the learning company', *Management Education and Development*, 20, 1, 1-8.

Peters,T. (1987) *Thriving on Chaos*, Macmillan, London.

Peters,T.J. and Waterman,R.H. (1982) *In Search of Excellence*, Harper and Row, New York.

Pettigrew,A.M. (ed) (1988) *Competitiveness and the Management Process*, Basil Blackwell, Oxford.

Popper,K.R. (1965) *Conjectures and Refutations*, Routledge and Kegan Paul, London.

Porter,M.E. (1985) *Competitive Advantage*, Free Press, New York.

Preece,D.A. (1989) *Managing the Adoption of New Technology*, Routledge, London.

Primrose,P.L., Creamer,G.D. and Leonard,R. (1985) 'Identifying and quantifying the company-wide benefits of CAD within the structure of a comprehensive investment programme' in *Implementing New Technologies* (eds Rhodes,E. and Wield,D.), Basil Blackwell, Oxford.

Rawlence,C. and Cooley,M. (1988) 'Look, no hands' in *Equinox, A Guide to the 1988 Series*, Channel 4 Television, London.

Rhodes,E. and Wield,D.(eds) (1985) *Implementing New Technologies*, Basil Blackwell, Oxford.

Rowe,A.J., Mason,R.O. and Dickel,K.E. (1986) *Strategic Management*, Addison-Wesley, Wokingham.

Saunders,D. (1989) 'What MAP means to the production manager', *International Journal of Operations and Production Management*, 9, 2, 58-68.

Schonberger,R.J. (1982) *Japanese Manufacturing Techniques*, Free Press, New York.

Schonberger,R.J. (1986) *World Class Manufacturing*, Free Press, New York.

Senker,P. (1985) 'Implications of CAD/CAM for management' in *Implementing New Technologies* (eds Rhodes,E. and Wield,D.), Basil Blackwell, Oxford.

Sheth,J.N. and Eshghi,G.S. (1989) *Global Operations Perspectives*, South-Western Publishing, Cincinnati.

Simon,H.A. (1981) *The Sciences of the Artificial*, MIT Press, Cambridge, Massachusetts.

Skinner,W. (1974) 'The focused factory', *Harvard Business Review*, 3, 38-46.

Slack,N. (1987) 'Flexibility and the Manufacturing Function - Ten Empirical Observations' in *Proceedings of the Operations Management Association UK Conference* (ed. Rhodes,D.), Nottingham.

Tames,R. (1984) *Josiah Wedgwood*, Shire Publications, Aylesbury.

Towill,D.R. (1985) 'A production engineering approach to robot selection' in *Implementing New Technologies* (eds Rhodes,E. and Wield,D.), Basil Blackwell, Oxford.

Twiss,B.C. (1985) *Non-MSC Research and Initiatives in the field of Management Development for Technical Change*, Manpower Services Commission, Sheffield.

Voss,C.A. (1986) 'Implementing manufacturing technology: A manufacturing strategy approach', *International Journal of Operations and Production Management*, 6, 4, 17-26.

Voss,C.A. (ed) (1987) *Just-in-Time Manufacture*, IFS (Publications), Bedford.

Waddington,C.H. (1977) *Tools for Thought*, Paladin, St.Albans.

Wang,M. and Smith,G.W. (1988) 'Modelling CIM systems: Part 1 methodologies', *Computer Integrated Manufacturing Systems*, 1, 1, 13-17.

Waterlow,J.G. and Clouder Richards,F.J. (1988) *Report of the CAPM Workshop and Tutorial (Sept.1988)*, ACME, Swindon.

Wheatley,M. (1989) 'Variable factor', *Management Today*, February.

Wheelwright,S.C. (1987) 'Building excellence in manufacturing' in *Quality, Productivity and Innovation* (eds Shetty,Y.K. and Buehler,V.M.), Elsevier, New York.

Wheelwright,S.C. (1989) 'Restoring the competitive edge in U.S. manufacturing' in *Global Operations Perspectives* (eds Sheth,J.N. and Eshghi,G.S.), South-Western Publishing, Cincinnati.

Wheelwright,S.C. and Hayes,R.H. (1985) 'Competing through manufacturing', *Harvard Business Review*, 1, 99-109.

Index